Civil Procedure in Belgium

Civil Procedure in Belgium

Piet Taelman
Claudia Van Severen

This book was originally published as a monograph in the International Encyclopaedia of Laws/Civil Procedure.

Founding Editor: Roger Blanpain
General Editor: Frank Hendrickx
Volume Editor: Piet Taelman

Wolters Kluwer

Published by:
Kluwer Law International B.V.
PO Box 316
2400 AH Alphen aan den Rijn
The Netherlands
E-mail: international-sales@wolterskluwer.com
Website: lrus.wolterskluwer.com

Sold and distributed in North, Central and South America by:
Wolters Kluwer Legal & Regulatory U.S.
7201 McKinney Circle
Frederick, MD 21704
United States of America
Email: customer.service@wolterskluwer.com

Sold and distributed in all other countries by:
Air Business Subscriptions
Rockwood House
Haywards Heath
West Sussex
RH16 3DH
United Kingdom
Email: international-customerservice@wolterskluwer.com

ISBN 978-90-411-9580-7

e-Book: ISBN 978-90-411-9581-4
web-PDF: ISBN 978-90-411-9583-8

The Authors

Piet Taelman is a Senior Full Professor at Ghent University Law School (Belgium) and Head of the Department of Interdisciplinary Study of Law, Private Law and Business Law. He teaches courses on Civil Procedure and has written on a wide variety of topics on civil procedural law in national and international journals and book chapters. Piet Taelman served as dean of the Ghent Law School from October 2008 till September 2014.
He has been appointed editor of the Civil Procedure Monographs, within the International Encyclopaedia of Laws in 1998.
He is a member of the High Council of Justice (2016–2020), a member of the Council of the International Association for Procedural Law (since 2007 onward) and of the Executive Committee of Cepani (Belgian Centre for Arbitration and Mediation).
He has been admitted to the Ghent Bar in 1982 and has practised as an attorney and arbitrator during almost the whole of his academic career.
E-mail: piet.taelman@ugent.be

The Authors

Claudia Van Severen obtained a Master of Law degree at Ghent University Law School in 2010. After having completed her three-year traineeship, she was admitted to the Ghent Bar in 2013. Currently, she works as a civil litigation attorney at Everest law firm. Since 2013, she also works as an academic assistant at the Ghent Law School, in the framework of which she teaches (practical) courses on civil procedure. She has written on a variety of topics regarding civil procedure in specialised Belgian law journals, and is a member of the editorial board of the Civil Procedure Monographs, within the International Encyclopaedia of Laws since August 2014. She is currently working on a doctoral thesis regarding the necessary joinder of parties in Belgian civil procedural law.
E-mail: claudia.vanseveren@ugent.be

Table of Contents

Table of Contents

General Introduction

§1. General Background

I. Geographical

1. Belgium is one of the smaller nations of Europe, located in the north western part of the continent and covering an area of 30.528 km^2. It extends about 139 km from north to south and about 240 km from east to west.

It is neighboured by the Netherlands on the north and the north-east, Germany and Luxembourg on the east, France on the south and south-west, and a 67 km long stretch of the North Sea on the north-west (with, across the channel, the United Kingdom).

2. The population counts about 11.3 million inhabitants.[1] The majority (57%) lives in Flanders; another 32% lives in Wallonia (including its small German-speaking districts); about 11% lives in the region of Brussels Capital. About 11.5% of the whole population are foreigners.[2]

3. Geographically, Belgium can be divided into three major regions. Upper Belgium, in the south, consists of the densely forested Ardennes highland that reaches its highest point at the Mt Botrange (694 m above sea level). Middle Belgium (60–175 m above sea level) comprises undulating loam soils. It is a fertile region, dissected by tributaries of the Scheldt River (*Escaut – Schelde*). Lower Belgium comprises the flat, low-lying (up to 100 m above sea level) plain of Flanders (*Flandre – Vlaanderen*) in the north-west and the Campine plateau (*Capine – Kempen*) in the north-east.

II. Historical

4. Celtic and Germanic tribes inhabited the area of Belgium at the time of the Roman conquest (first century BC). Roman rule lasted until the early fifth century AD and was followed by that of the Frankish Merovingians (mid-fifth to late seventh century) and the Carolinians (early eighth to mid-ninth century).

5. Secular and ecclesiastical principalities emerged between the early tenth and mid-fourteenth centuries. It was during this period that the count of Flanders became

---

1. *See* http://www.ibz.rrn.fgov.be/nl/bevolking/statistieken-van-bevolking/ (accessed September 2017).
2. *See* http://statbel.fgov.be/nl/statistieken/cijfers/bevolking/structuur/huidige_nationaliteit/belgisch_vreemd (accessed September 2017).

a vassal of the king of France. Philip of Burgundy gained control of Flanders in the late fourteenth century. The houses of Burgundy and Habsburg were united by marriage in the late fifteenth century, and what is actually Belgian territory came under Spanish Habsburg rule in 1504. In 1579 the southern Spanish provinces formed the union of Arras (Artois), pledging allegiance to the Spanish King and Roman Catholicism. The Protestant northern provinces formed the United Provinces of the Netherlands.

6. The Spanish Netherlands remained under Habsburg rule until 1700, when Philip V, grandson of Louis XIV of France, ascended the Spanish throne. In the war of the Spanish Succession (1701–1714) that followed, the Spanish Netherlands, including Belgium, were ceded to the Austrian Habsburgs.

7. After a short period of annexation by France, Belgium was reunited in 1815 with the northern provinces into one country, named the United Kingdom of the Netherlands, and ruled by the House of Orange.

8. Belgians revolted against Dutch sovereignty in 1830 and in 1831 the independent Kingdom of Belgium was established.

9. As far as the international field is concerned, Belgium is a member of the European Union and of the Economic Monetary Union.[3] Belgium belonged to the six original Member States that signed the Treaty establishing the European Economic Community in Rome on 25 March 1957. Further, it signed a treaty, together with Luxembourg and the Netherlands, on 3 February 1958, establishing an economic union between the three countries, called The Benelux Union (*Union Benelux – Benelux Unie*).

III. Legal System

10. The Belgian Constitution of 1831 established a constitutional monarchy with a parliamentary form of government. The King is the head of the state; however, he reigns but does not rule.[4]

Throughout major modifications of the Constitution in 1970, 1980, 1988, 1989, 1993 and 2014, the Belgian State has been transformed from a unitary state into a federal state.[5] Next to the central system of government, there exists a regional as well as a community system of government. It consists of three regions (Wallonia, Flanders and Brussels) and three communities (the French, Flemish and German communities). Each region, resp. community takes the place of the state for the definition of policies and the management of matters that fall within the scope of its respective responsibilities. The regions are responsible for national and regional development of the territory, urbanisation, environmental protection, transport, communication and economic activity, whereas education and culture are the communities' responsibility.[6]

3. The euro (€), the official currency of the Eurozone, was introduced on 1 January 2002.
4. The Constitution of 1831 established a hereditary and exclusively male monopoly, but since June 1991 the Crown goes to the firstborn in line, whatever its sex may be.
5. Since the 1993 reform, Article 1 of the Constitution explicitly states that 'Belgium is a federal state which is composed of communities and regions'.
6. F. Delpérée, 'Belgique', in *Dictionnaire Constitutionnel* 73 (O. Duhamel & Y. Meny eds, P.U.F. 1992).

11. The legislative power is divided between the federation and the federated entities according to a system in which each legislative body (i.e., the federal legislature, the legislature of the communities (community councils) and the legislature of the regions (regional councils)) has exclusive powers. The federal statutes (*loi* – wet) and the community and regional statutes (*décret – decreet*) have equal force of law throughout the territory over which the respective legislatures have jurisdiction, insofar as they are enacted within the allocation of powers provided under the Constitution. It is a special feature of the Belgian federal system that there is no hierarchy between national or federal statutes and the statutory instruments enacted by the federated entities. A special court, i.e., the Constitutional Court (formerly called the Court of Arbitration), ensures that the rules governing the distribution of legislative power are complied with. If necessary, the Constitutional Court can nullify any statutory instrument, whether federal or regional, promulgated in breach of the division of legislative power (*see also infra*, paragraphs 96–99).

12. As far as the organisation of public powers is concerned, the Belgian Constitution distinguishes three traditional powers within the federal state: the legislative power, the executive power and the judiciary.

The *legislative power* is exercised jointly by the King and both Chambers of Parliament, consisting of the Chamber of Representatives (*Chambre des Représentants – Kamer van Volksvertegenwoordigers*) and the Senate (*Sénat – Senaat*). The members of the Chamber of Representatives (150 in total) are elected directly by the people. The majority of the members of the Senate (50) are elected by and among the state parliaments. A small number of senators (10) continues to be elected by co-optation. Since 2014, with the latest state reform, the Senate is no longer a truly legislative chamber, but rather a chamber of reflection or a forum of political discussion.[7]

Draft statutory texts are submitted for advice to the Legislative Section of the Council of State (*see infra*, paragraph 101) before Parliament votes on them, in order to check on their wording and their compatibility with Belgian law and applicable international treaties.

The King's role is limited to the last stage of the legislative procedure, i.e., the rejection or approval of statutes that already passed Parliament. In practice, the King never withholds his consent.[8]

Eventually, after being promulgated by the King, statutes are published in the Belgian Official Gazette (*Moniteur belge – Belgisch Staatsblad*), always in both Dutch and French. The Home Affairs Federal Public Service (*Federale Overheidsdienst Binnenlandse Zaken – Service public fédéral Intérieur*) is responsible for the translation of the statutes in German, which translation is also published in the Belgian Official Gazette within a reasonable time after the publication in both Dutch and French.[9]

---

7. F. Delpérée, 'Constitutional Law', in *Introduction to Belgian Law* 58 (M. Kruithof & W. De Bondt eds, Kluwer Law International 2017).
8. Only once in history he has done so, namely in 1990, with a statute that legalised abortion under certain conditions. This caused a constitutional crisis which was solved by declaring the King unable to reign for a limited period of time, in which case the Constitution provides that the Chambers of Parliament can appoint a regent, carrying out, temporarily, the duties of the King.
9. Article 1 (as amended) of the Act of 31 May 1961, *Belgian Official Gazette*, 21 June 1961.

The *executive power* is also exerted by the King. In practice, however, it is the government, supported by the political parties that have the majority in Parliament, which issues decrees and regulations implementing the statutes voted by Parliament. Legislative acts are implemented by the executive by way of royal decrees (*arrêtés royals – koninklijke besluiten*) and for matters of secondary importance, ministerial decrees and decrees of the state secretaries (*arrêtés ministériels – ministeriële besluiten*) at the national level, and by regulations and orders of the regional governments at the level of the communities and regions.

The *judicial power* is exercised by the judiciary, i.e., the ordinary courts, to which a 'public prosecution office'[10] is attached. The ordinary courts have to apply both federal legislation and community or regional legislation, depending on the particularities of the case.

Beside the ordinary courts, there is also a Constitutional Court (*see infra*, paragraphs 96–99), and there are administrative courts, especially the Administrative Section of the Council of State (*see infra*, paragraph 102). These courts are not part of the judicial branch of government.

Among the three branches of government, the judiciary – which is also the most federal power, since it has no equivalent power within the federated entities – has an interest in appearing as the most 'distinct, the most autonomous and the most independent'.[11] Justice has to be done without undergoing any outside pressure or influence and without being accountable to the other branches of government.

§2. Delimitation of the Subject Matter

I. Definition of the Term 'Civil Procedure'

13. Procedural law is the area of law that deals with the organisation and administration of justice, i.e., the settling of disputes by a judicial body. Within the general area of procedural law, a distinction can be made between procedures dealing with so-called subjective rights, procedures of an objective nature, disciplinary procedures and criminal procedures.

The ordinary courts, i.e., the courts that are part of the judicial branch of government, have exclusive jurisdiction to settle all matters pertaining to 'civil rights', being the private rights recognised and organised by the Belgian Civil Code (*Code civil – Burgerlijk Wetboek*) and its complementary statutes.[12] They also have jurisdiction, albeit not exclusively, to settle disputes over 'political rights', being the rights that one possesses *vis-à-vis* a public authority acting with a significant degree of the state's

10. Which also holds some powers in civil matters (*see infra*, paras 85–89).
11. A. Alen, 'Séparation ou collaboration des pouvoirs', *Administration publique: revue du droit public et des sciences administratives* 1990, 223.
12. Article 144, para. 1, Constitution. However, pursuant to Article 144, para. 2, of the Constitution, the legislature may authorise administrative courts to decide upon the (private) civil law consequences of their decisions (*see also infra*, para. 102).

authority,[13] e.g., the right to pay taxes, the right to vote. To the extent that the adjudication of these disputes is not assigned to administrative courts created for that purpose by the legislature, the ordinary courts are competent.[14]

14. In disputes about civil and political rights, together forming the subjective rights, a legal subject's right to demand a specific attitude from another legal subject is central. Subjective rights are said to correspond with objective legal obligations which compel legal subjects to behave in a certain way against one another. The main characteristic is that the existence and the extent of such rights are based on legal rules, and not left to any appreciation of, for example, administrative authorities. This illustrates the difference with disputes of an objective nature, which are not concerned with the subjective rights of a legal subject, but instead concern the validity of acts emanating from an administrative authority.

15. In the light of the above, civil procedure can be defined as the procedural rules governing disputes over subjective rights before the ordinary civil courts belonging to the judiciary.

II. Distinction with Other Types of Procedure

16. Civil procedure must be distinguished from procedures of an objective nature, disciplinary procedures and criminal procedures.

It should be stressed, however, that the rules of civil procedure, i.e., the Judicial Code, are in principle applicable to these other types of procedure, without prejudice to any special rules or general principles of law which derogate from the general rules of the Belgian Judicial Code and of which the application would be irreconcilable with those rules.[15]

A. Procedures of an Objective Nature

17. Procedures of an objective nature concern the validity of acts emanating from the discretionary power of an administrative authority. They belong to the exclusive jurisdiction of the administrative courts, of which the most important one in Belgium is the Administrative Jurisdiction Section of the Council of State (*see* further *infra*, paragraph 102).

B. Disciplinary Procedures

18. Disciplinary procedures may be initiated to examine whether an individual's behaviour has violated the established rules of professional ethics. The disciplinary authority is in most cases exercised by non-judicial bodies.

Special disciplinary authorities have been set up for a number of liberal professions: doctors, pharmacists, veterinarians, architects, attorneys, etc., whereas the disciplinary

13. Constitutional Court No. 14/1997 of 18 March 1997, *Belgian Official Gazette,* 8 May 1997, 11.276.
14. Article 145 Constitution.
15. Article 2 Judicial Code.

jurisdiction over members of the ordinary courts is still largely entrusted to the judiciary itself (*see infra*, paragraph 116).

C. *Criminal Procedures*

19. The criminal procedure is mainly governed by the Belgian Code of Criminal Procedure (*Code pénal – Strafwetboek*), organising the prosecution of individuals and determining the competence and organisation of the bodies and institutions concerned with criminal matters. Nevertheless, the rules of civil procedure fulfil a complementary role in case there is no regulation with regard to a specific issue, provided that these rules are reconcilable with the general principles of criminal procedure.

Since the criminal courts are part of the system of ordinary courts, the Court of Cassation acts as the Supreme Court in these matters.

§3. Sources of Civil Procedural Law

I. A Brief Historical Overview

A. *The Belgian Judicial Code of 1967*

20. The Belgian civil justice system has its roots in the French Code of Civil Procedure (*Code de procédure civile*) of 1806[16]. Whereas the 1806 French Code lost its position as central point of reference in the international procedural debate by the end of the nineteenth century, the Code remained in force in Belgium for a long period of time.[17] It was not until 1967 that a fundamental judicial reform was realised, with the promulgation of the Judicial Code (*Code judiciaire – Gerechtelijk Wetboek*), which gradually came into force between 1967 and 1970. The objective of its founding fathers – Charles Van Reepinghen, Royal Commissioner for Judicial Reform, and his successor, Ernest Krings – was to make justice quicker, less expensive and less cumbersome.[18] In view of the ongoing problem of judicial backlog (*see also infra*, paragraphs 21 et seq.), it appears that this goal has not been achieved.[19] The most sweeping innovation of the Judicial Code was that, finally, the rules of civil procedure were described in

16. *See* also M. Storme, 'Honderdvijftig jaar Belgisch Procesrecht', in E. Spanoghe & R. Feenstra (eds), *Honderdvijftig jaar rechtsleven in België en Nederland*, Leiden, University Press, 1981, 131–160.
17. C.H. van Rhee, *Introduction*, in *European Traditions in Civil Procedure* 14 (C.H. van Rhee ed., Ius Commune Europaeum Series, Vol. 54, Intersentia 2005).
18. Report to the King preceding the Royal Decree of 17 October 1958 appointing a Royal Commission for Judicial Reform, cited in C. Van Reepinghen, *Report on the Judicial Reform* (*Rapport sur la Réforme Judiciaire – Verslag over de Gerechtelijke Hervorming*), *Belgian Official Gazette*, 1964, I, 3.
19. *See* for instance: B. Schoenaerts & M. Lamiroy, *De Belgische justitie – Een kafkaiaanse nachtmerrie – Analyse en remedie*, Ghent, Mys and Breesch, 1995.

one single code. Until then, those rules were scattered over hundreds of statutes.[20] Additionally, the Judicial Code introduced a common procedural model that is, in principle, applicable to all ordinary (civil) courts in each instance. Further on, the Judicial Code is undeniably a product of the liberal thinking at the time of its promulgation. It is exactly this liberal attitude that is currently recognised as one of the major flaws in the Belgian procedural model.[21] For example, the liberal regime as to the extension of the scope of the case on appeal, which does not preclude the introduction of new claims which have not been submitted in first instance, is said to have resulted in first instance proceedings not being taken seriously (*see infra*, paragraph 362). Also, the liberal attitude towards the timetable of the proceedings is considered as an important cause of the currently existing judicial backlog.

B. Numerous and Significant (Ongoing) Amendments

21. Since its entry into force some fifty years ago, the Judicial Code has been amended several times.

22. In an attempt to reduce the backlog of cases, the judicial procedure has undergone a great number of changes. Important reforms regarding the time management of cases were implemented by the Act of 3 August 1992[22] and the Act of 26 April 2007.[23] The latter act intended to create a more powerful, so-called active judge, who has (more) control over the timetable and progress of proceedings, thus embedding the idea that the judge has to see to the orderly evolution of the proceedings in order to ensure that a judgment is rendered within a reasonable delay.

23. The optimisation of the proper organisation and functioning of the judiciary is also an ongoing priority of the Belgian legislature. Several significant measures were taken in the wake of the case (and escape) of Dutroux in 1998.[24] The so-called Octopus Agreement of 24 May 1998[25] laid the basis for a comprehensive and far-reaching reform of the judiciary.

---

20. M. Storme, 'De parlementaire goedkeuring van het Gerechtelijk Wetboek of de modernisering van een drie eeuwen oude procedure', *Rechtskundig Weekblad* 1966–1967, 2083.
21. C.H. van Rhee, *Introduction*, in *European Traditions in Civil Procedure* 15 (C.H. van Rhee ed., Ius Commune Europaeum Series, Vol. 54, Intersentia 2005).
22. *Belgian Official Gazette*, 31 August 1992.
23. *Belgian Official Gazette*, 12 June 2007.
24. In the mid-1990s, six young Belgian girls were kidnapped, four of whom were murdered. The atrocities were committed by a man named Marc Dutroux. A number of shortcomings in the Dutroux case caused widespread discontent with the country's justice system and the functioning of its law enforcement agencies in Belgium. The reform of the justice system was catapulted up the political agenda in April 1998 when Dutroux, while being transferred to a court house without handcuffs, managed to escape (but was caught a few hours later).
25. The term 'octopus' refers to the fact that eight political parties (at the time all government and opposition parties except for the extreme right-wing party) concluded the agreement.

24. In November 1998, Article 151 of the Belgian Constitution was amended, with a view to anchor the principle of judicial independence constitutionally,[26] as well as to establish the High Council of Justice, an external body for controlling the proper functioning of the judiciary, which also has certain powers in relation to the nomination, evaluation and training of members of the judiciary (*see also infra*, paragraphs 94 and 104–108).[27]

25. During the term of the Di Rupo Government,[28] the structure of the judiciary was given a major make-over on three fronts.[29] First of all, the number of judicial districts was reduced from twenty-seven to twelve. Second, the mobility of the judges and court staff within districts was enhanced, which should make it possible to deploy them according to the districts' needs, taking into account the districts' workload and the judges' specialisation. These first two pillars were mainly aimed at reducing judicial backlog as well as achieving better service through specialisation. Third, the judiciary was given greater autonomy as to its management. A shift of responsibility regarding budgets and deployment of staff should allow to achieve better judicial management and more efficiency regarding the use of public means, as well as quick, modern and accessible justice. To this end, the legislature created two new managing bodies, which are responsible for the central management of the operating means allocated to the bench (Management Committee of the Courts and Tribunals) and the public prosecutor's office (Management Committee of the Public Prosecutor). In time, the respective committees and the Minister of Justice will conclude management contracts, establishing commitments and objectives for the judiciary and the resources made available for this. The committees will in turn distribute the allocated resources between the different entities of the judiciary. Different sources, however, criticise the legislature for having unrealistic expectations of the judiciary, which is now being burdened with the difficult

26. Up until then, the principle of judicial independence – a cornerstone of every democratic state – was an unwritten norm in Belgium. *See* for a recent and thorough analysis: B. Allemeersch, A. Alen & B. Dalle, *Judicial Independence in Belgium*, in *Judicial Independence in Transition. Strengthening the Rule of Law in the OSCE Region* 307–356 (A. Seibert-Fohr ed., Springer, 2011).

27. Act of 20 November 1998 (*Belgian Official Gazette*, 24 November 1998). *See* also the Act of 22 December 1998 (*Belgian Official Gazette*, 2 February 1999), which further specifies the powers and functions of the High Council of Justice. For further reference, *see* J. Laenens en M. Storme (eds.), *In de ban van octopus – Dans l'encre d'octopus*, Interuniversitair Centrum voor Gerechtelijk Recht – Centre interuniversitaire de Droit judiciaire, Brussel, Kluwer-Bruylant, 2000.

28. December 2011–October 2014.

29. Act of 1 December 2013 (*Belgian Official Gazette*, 10 December 2013) and Act of 18 February 2014 (*Belgian Official Gazette*, 4 March 2014), which both entered into force on 1 April 2014.

task to restore public trust in the justice system on the one hand,[30] while reducing the available budget on the other hand.[31]

26. In a new attempt to resolve the backlog of cases, the current Minister of Justice of the Michel Government[32] has committed himself to do everything in his power to ensure that all ordinary (civil) courts in each instance will render judgment within one year after the initiation of proceedings.[33] This is a very ambitious promise, taking into account the fact that the current average lead time for civil cases on appeal amounts to two and a half years.[34] In his plan for justice entitled 'More Efficiency for More Justice',[35] a series of measures is announced which aim to improve the proper administration and functioning of the judiciary, as well as the efficiency of the procedural rules, without making any concessions in terms of quality. In other words, the goal is to assure 'reasonable justice in a reasonable delay at a reasonable cost'. In particular, it is the Minister's ambition to reduce the number of cases on appeal and to stimulate the proper treatment of cases at the first instance level. With reference to the courts' heavy workload, the Minister also announced measures to stimulate out-of-court dispute resolution. One of these measures is the implementation of an extrajudicial order for payment procedure for the recovery of unchallenged claims (*see infra*, paragraph 325). Furthermore, the Minister is putting his efforts towards the digitalisation of the judiciary, in which area only very limited progress has been made in the past decades (*see also infra*, paragraphs 251, 269 and 448). Concrete steps towards implementing these objectives are being taken with the so-called Potpourri Acts.[36]

---

30. A survey carried out by the High Council of Justice in 2014 with a view to sound out public opinion on justice indicates that 61% of the Belgian citizens has confidence in the Belgian justice system. This is undoubtedly a step forward in comparison with the results of 2002 (41%), but there is still room for further improvement. *See* www.hrj.be/en/content/barometer (accessed September 2017).
31. Recent European research has demonstrated that the Belgian justice system faces a budgetary deficit: the budgetary effort for justice only represents a tiny 0.7% of Belgium's annual public expenditure, whereas the European average is 2.2%. *See* European Commission for the Efficiency of Justice (CEPEJ), Report on 'European judicial systems – Edition 2014 (2012 data): efficiency and quality of justice', 24, Figure 2.2, www.coe.int/t/dghl/cooperation/cepej/evaluation/2014/Rapport_2014_en.pdf (accessed September 2017).
32. Since October 2014.
33. Policy Statement of the Ministry of Justice, Parliamentary Acts 2014–2015, No. 54K0020/18, 6, www.dekamer.be/FLWB/PDF/54/0020/54K0020018.pdf (accessed September 2017).
34. Moreover, simulations for the implications of the attempted cutting on staff costs have indicated that the average lead time over the period 2015–2019 will increase with six months. *See* www.tribunaux-rechtbanken.be/sites/default/files/public/content/download/files/persbericht_college_van_hoven_en_rechtbanken_01-12-2014.pdf (accessed September 2017).
35. K. Geens, *Plan justice-Une plus grande efficience pour une meilleure justice – Justitieplan-Een efficiëntere justitie voor meer rechtvaardigheid*, 2015, https://cdn.nimbu.io/s/1jn2gqe/assets/Plan_Justice_18mars_FR.pdf (French) – http://justitie.belgium.be/sites/default/files/downloads/Plan%20justitie_18maart_NL.pdf (Dutch) (accessed September 2017).
36. So far, the most important acts with respect to civil justice were the first, third and fifth Potpourri Act respectively promulgated on 19 October 2015 (*Belgian Official Gazette*, 22 October 2015 (ed. 1)), 4 May 2016 (*Belgian Official Gazette*, 13 May 2016) and 6 July 2017 (*Belgian Official Gazette*, 24 July 2017 (ed. 1)).

II. Proliferation, Compartmentalisation and Internationalisation of Procedural Rules

27. The Constitution, being the pre-eminent source of law in the internal legal order,[37] and the Judicial Code of 1967 are the most important, albeit not the only, sources of national civil procedural law.

28. Despite the fact that the Judicial Code was intended to introduce simplified and unified judicial proceedings, some topics have become heavily crisscrossed with complex and deviating rules in specific separate statutes that are not incorporated in the Judicial Code. To name but one: Book XVII, entitled 'Specific Procedures', of the recently established Code of Economic Law, which stipulates, among others, the rules governing the Belgian consumer class action procedure – *see also infra*, paragraphs 327–332).

29. Another important statute dating from the period before the Judicial Code and which has not been incorporated therein is the Act of 15 June 1935 on the Use of Languages in Judicial Matters (*see infra*, paragraph 240).[38]

30. Apart from national legislation, international and European treaties, regulations, directives and recommendations play an important role in civil procedure as codifications of fundamental principles of due process, as well as regulatory instruments in international, cross-border and even in purely domestic (e.g., protection of consumers) judicial matters (*see also infra*, paragraphs 190–193, 471–472 and 555–558).

31. As far as case law is concerned, precedents have no legally binding force. There is a strong separation of powers between the legislative branch, the executive branch and the judicial branch. The courts do not have any legislative powers and are not allowed to decide the case by way of general rulings.[39] On the other hand, the courts may not refuse to render judgment for reasons of silence, obscureness or incompleteness of the law, as that would amount to a 'denial of justice'.[40] Notwithstanding the absence of legally binding precedents, court decisions, especially decisions of the Court of Cassation, have a strong authority, especially when confirmed repeatedly over the years.

32. Over the last few decades courts have accepted and recognised a new legally binding source of law, notably the unwritten general principles of law (*principes généraux du droit – algemene rechtsbeginselen*). Such general principles of law are mostly derived from existing elements of the legal system. As in many European countries, the general principle of good faith, for instance, has been derived from the

37. As far as civil procedure is concerned, the Constitution lays down: (i) the principal functions of, and the interaction between the legislative, the executive and the judicial branches of government; (ii) the basic principles for the adjudication of disputes over subjective rights; (iii) the principle that no court or any other entity capable of rendering judgment may be established other than by law, voted in Parliament; (iv) general rules regarding procedural guarantees offered by the courts and (v) the principle of judicial independence as well as some principles regarding the legal status of the members of the judiciary. Furthermore, the Constitution contains the foundations of the High Council of Justice, the Constitutional Court, the Council of State and the other administrative courts.

38. *Belgian Official Gazette*, 22 June 1935.

39. Article 6 Judicial Code.

40. Article 5 Judicial Code.

statutory rule that a contract must be performed in good faith.[41] In the field of (civil) procedural law, the general principles governing the proper administration of justice play an important role. Some of these principles are explicitly recognised by international treaties such as the European Convention for the Protection of Human Rights and Fundamental Freedoms (ECHR) and the International Covenant on Civil and Political Rights (CCPR) (*see infra*, paragraphs 48–60).

§4. General Features of the Administration of Justice in Civil Matters

I. Characteristics of the Procedure

A. Adversary Procedure

33. Belgian civil procedure is adversarial, meaning that it is solely within the discretion of the parties to decide if and when proceedings are initiated and ended.

B. Role of the Judge and of the Parties[42]

1. Party Disposition as the Guiding Principle

34. Belgian civil procedure is guided by the principle of party disposition (or party autonomy), which means that the parties set the limits of the dispute. They decide what the subject matter of the proceedings will be and who will be involved therein. This implies that the parties are responsible for specifying the relief sought (the so-called object or '*petitum*' of the claim) and that the court is bound by the claims, c.q. defences[43] of the parties. In other words, it is for the parties to define their judicial controversy, i.e., the disputed issues which the court is requested to adjudicate. The court should not identify issues that the parties have not brought to the table, even if these issues seem to the court to arise on the basis of the alleged facts. The Judicial Code explicitly stipulates that the court cannot ex officio change or modify the object of the claims, nor can it grant a claim that was not expressed ('*ultra petita*') or grant more than was claimed ('*extra petita*').[44] Furthermore, the court is prohibited from ordering ex officio that third parties be joined in the proceedings.[45]

41. Article 1134, para. 3, Civil Code.
42. *See* for a thorough analysis: B. Allemeersch, *Taakverdeling in het burgerlijk proces*, Antwerp, Intersentia, 2007.
43. The defendant can widen the limits of the dispute. He does not have to stick to a simple denial of the facts but can also invoke procedural exceptions (e.g., a plea of lack of jurisdiction of the court or inadmissibility of the claim), substantive means of defence and even submit a counterclaim.
44. Article 1138, 2° Judicial Code. Conversely, Article 1138, 3° of the Judicial Code requires the judge to render judgment on each of the claims presented by the parties.
45. Article 811 Judicial Code.

35. The parties' freedom to decide which claims and allegations they wish to make may be limited, however, in particular by rules of public policy (*ordre public – openbare orde*), which are to be considered ex officio by the court, provided that the facts of the case make it sufficiently clear that such rules apply.[46]

2. The Active Role of the Judge

36. The abovementioned principle of party disposition does not entail, as traditionally argued, that the judge is nothing more than a passive bystander, who just sits back and enjoys the show. On the contrary, the judge plays an active role on various fronts.

a. With Respect to the Conduct and Progress of the Proceedings

37. As far as the orderly conduct and progress of the proceedings is concerned, there is a clear shift in Belgium – as in most other countries of the EU – from the court being a 'mere passive observer' to the 'master of the proceedings'. The court has a case management responsibility, meaning that it must ensure that procedural rules are respected and that a judgment is rendered within a reasonable amount of time. The latter implies that the court has the power – and even the obligation – to direct and instruct the parties in order to ensure that the progress of the proceedings is maintained or even accelerated.

b. With Respect to the Settlement of the Dispute

i. Factual Allegations and Evidence

38. As stated above, the principle of party disposition implies that it is the responsibility of the parties to present the facts relied upon to substantiate the relief sought, as well as to bring forward appropriate evidence in support of the factual allegations. The court may not introduce new facts on its own motion or rely on facts that have not been (eventually) properly advanced by the parties. Nevertheless, the court has the power (or even duty) to adopt a certain 'inquisitorial' or 'investigative' role in relation to the facts and evidence.

39. The least far-reaching form of this investigative role of the court consists in the power to rely on information deduced from the facts or from evidence material presented by the parties, even though the parties did not mention this information explicitly in their briefs[47] or did not make the deduction themselves.[48]

40. A more far-reaching form of the court's inquisitorial role comprises of the power to ask appropriate questions to the parties at the hearing regarding the case and the presentation of the facts and relating evidence. Although the court's right to ask

46. Court of Cassation 9 May 2008, *Rechtskundig Weekblad* 2008–2009, 1765.
47. Court of Cassation 4 November 1994, *Arresten van het Hof van Cassatie* 1994, 931
48. Court of Cassation 4 December 1995, *Arresten van het Hof van Cassatie* 1995, 1069.

questions does not go so far as to confer a 'truth-finding' mission upon the court,[49] it may to a certain extent influence the substantive outcome of the case, as the information resulting from the court's questioning may induce the parties to alter their claims or introduce new claims (*see also infra*, paragraphs 202 et seq.). The court must, however, make sure that it does not make use of its right to ask questions in a way that would endanger the perception of its impartiality, and may never provide legal advice.[50] Moreover, the court must evidently stay within the limits of the claims and the main factual background of the case.

41. Most far-reaching is the active role of the court with respect to the production and means of evidence with which facts that are asserted and contested by the parties can be proven. If a party fails to produce (sufficient) evidence, allowing the court to grant or reject the claim, the court may order any additional investigation measure (e.g., (forced) submission of documents, witness depositions, personal appearance of the parties in court, the official visit to the scene of the facts, etc.), which may provide it with more certainty as to the substance of the claim (*see also infra*, paragraphs 452–470).

ii. Rules of Public Policy

42. As stated above, the judge must invoke *sua sponte* all rules of (substantive and procedural) law which are considered to be of public policy (*see supra*, paragraph 35).

iii. The Court's Obligation to Apply the Law on its Own Motion[51]

43. While it is up to the parties to decide on the claims and factual allegations they wish to make, it is for the court to render the judgment based on the relevant legal provisions. In line with the maxims of '*iura novit curia*' ('the court knows the law') and '*da mihi factum dabo tibi jus*' ('give me the facts and I shall give you the law'), the court has an obligation to independently, i.e., regardless of the legal arguments of the parties (if any), and ex officio consider which legal rules, whether national or foreign[52] (*see also infra*, paragraph 439), are relevant and applicable to the case. The standing of the applicable legal rules is deemed to be irrelevant in this respect; the duty to apply the law ex officio applies to all rules of law, whether of public policy or not. The standing of the legal rules is only relevant with respect to procedural agreements, i.e., agreements by which litigating parties limit the legal boundaries of their dispute.

49. As is the case in some Eastern European countries.
50. As such, the court may not suggest to invoke certain claims, facts or arguments and should refrain from raising issues that the parties have not mentioned at all.
51. *See* for a recent analysis: W. Van Eeckhoutte, 'Schuifelen op de rechterstoel – De taak van de rechter in het Belgisch privaatrechtelijk procesrecht: een kwestie van moeten of mogen', in VVSRBN (ed.), *Preadviezen 2015*, Den Haag, Boom Juridische Uitgevers, 2015, 251 et seq.
52. Court of Cassation 3 December 1990, *Arresten van het Hof van Cassatie* 1990–1991, 366.

Such agreements are binding upon the court, provided that the application of rules of public policy cannot be ruled out.[53]

44. In other words, the court is not bound by the parties' legal qualification of the dispute and must, where appropriate, complete and/or substitute the parties' legal argumentation, provided that the court must stay within the limits of the claim and the factual background of the case, as well as respect the rights of defence.[54] The latter means, *inter alia*, that the court must give both parties the opportunity to express their point of view on the legal grounds that the court has invoked ex officio. If necessary, the court must reopen the oral hearings.[55]

45. The obligation of the court to ex officio consider and apply the law assumes that the facts necessary to apply a rule are sufficiently covered by the allegations of the parties. After all, rules apply to specific facts and if the facts necessary to apply a rule have not been advanced by the parties, the court cannot apply this rule. In this way, even though the courts are not as such bound by the legal argumentation of the parties, the (factual) allegations of the parties affect the legal rules applied by the courts. Pursuant to the case law of the Court of Cassation, the court is only obliged to invoke ex officio such legal grounds of which the application is warranted by the facts that the parties have specifically advanced ('*faits spécialement invoqués*') in support of their claims. Facts that have only been mentioned casually or incidentally ('*faits adventices*') do not trigger the obligation of the court to apply the law ex officio. In such circumstances, the ex officio application of the law is a mere (discretionary) power of the court.[56]

C. Oral and Written Procedure

46. The civil procedure is, in principle, written as well as oral. The proceedings will be initiated by a writ of summons (or other written request – *see infra*, paragraphs 241–254), following which a preliminary hearing takes place (*see infra*, paragraphs 258–263). After this preliminary hearing, written pleadings are exchanged (*see infra*, paragraphs 264–269). After the exchange of the written pleadings, there is an oral hearing (*see infra*, paragraphs 270–275).

53. Court of Cassation 23 January 2014, C.12.0467.N; Court of Cassation 28 September 2012, C.12.0049.N.

54. Court of Cassation 5 December 2014, *Rechtspraak Antwerpen Brussel Gent* 2015, 397; Court of Cassation 14 December 2012, C.12.0018.N; Court of Cassation 2 April 2010, C.09.0204.F.

55. Article 774, para. 2, Judicial Code; *see* Court of Cassation 20 April 2009, S.08.0015.N; Court of Cassation 7 December 2006, C.04.0501.F; Court of Cassation 23 November 2006, C.06.0006.F.

56. Court of Cassation 10 February 2014, C.13.0381.N; Court of Cassation 31 October 2013, C.13.0005.N; Court of Cassation 2 April 2010, C.09.0204.F; Court of Cassation 20 April 2009, S.08.0015.N; Court of Cassation 16 March 2006, C.04.0267.N; Court of Cassation 14 April 2005, C.03.0148.F.

II. Fundamental Guarantees

A. *Establishment of Courts by Law*

47. Article 146 of the Constitution provides that no court or any other entity capable of rendering judgment may be established otherwise than by statute, voted in Parliament.

B. *General Principles Governing the Proper Administration of Justice*

48. There are a number of binding principles relating to the proper administration of justice that are applicable to each judicial body. Some of these principles are explicitly recognised in Article 6.1 of the ECHR and Article 14.1 of the CCPR.

1. Principles Recognised as Being 'General'

a. Access to Justice

49. The right to bring a dispute before court is a fundamental right recognised under national as well as international law. It has, *inter alia,* been derived by the European Court of Human Rights (ECtHR) from Article 6.1 of the ECHR.[57]

50. This fundamental right consists of two components. First of all, there is the right of access to a court, meaning that for each dispute concerning civil rights, a possibility of recourse to a court – established by law – should be provided. As a result, the State should establish a system of legal aid for those with limited resources (*see infra*, paragraphs 231–234 and 419–432).[58] Furthermore, the access to justice should not be prevented by the complexity or obscureness of the procedural rules[59] or excessive formalism in the application or interpretation of those rules.[60] Second, the right of recourse to judicial remedies requires a minimal jurisdiction on behalf of the judge.[61] Regarding purely private matters, the courts should be able to determine with full jurisdiction the rights and duties of the parties.

51. The 'right to a court' is, however, not an absolute one. It may be subject to legitimate and proportional limitations. Legitimate restrictions to the right of access to justice are, for example, legal certainty, a proper functioning of the judiciary and measures which aim at reducing the courts' workload. The requirement that the limitations must be proportional means that they must not restrict or reduce the access

---

57. *Stanley Golder/United Kingdom*, ECtHR No. 4451/70 of 21 February 1975, §36; *see* also Article 14.1 CCPR; Article 47 of the Charter of the Fundamental Rights of the European Union and Article 13 of the Belgian Constitution, which states that nobody can be held from the judge attributed to him by law.
58. *Airey/Ireland*, ECtHR No. 6289/73 of 9 October 1979, §§20–28.
59. *Faniel/Belgium*, ECtHR No. 11892/08 of 1 March 2011, §30; *de Geouffre de la Pradelle/France*, ECtHR No. 12964/87 of 16 December 1992, §§33–35.
60. *Dattel/Luxembourg,* ECtHR No. 18522/06 of 30 July 2009, §§38–47.
61. *Sigma Radio Television Ltd./Cyprus*, ECtHR No. 32181/04 and 35122/05 of 21 July 2011, §157; *Obermeier/Austria*, ECtHR No. 11761/85 of 28 June 1990, §70.

left to the individual in such a way or to such an extent that the very essence of the right is impaired.[62]

b. Fair Trial

52. The right to a fair trial, as safeguarded by Article 6.1 of the ECHR and Article 14.1 of the CCPR essentially corresponds with the right of defence, which is recognised by the Court of Cassation as a general principle of law.[63]

53. The most important component of the right of defence is the right to an adversary treatment of the case. The right to an adversary treatment of the case implies that each party must be afforded a reasonable opportunity to present his case – including his evidence – under conditions that do not place him at a substantial disadvantage *vis-à-vis* his opponent.[64] Each party must have the opportunity to have knowledge of and comment on all evidence adduced or observations filed.[65]

54. The right to adversarial proceedings is often named together with the right to equality of arms, another long established element of fairness, in the sense of a 'fair balance' between the parties.[66]

c. Independence

55. The right to an independent judge is safeguarded constitutionally by Article 151 of the Constitution.[67] It implies that the judge should be able to render judgment according to his conscience, independently of any outside influence and without being accountable to the government or other forces.[68]

56. The independence of the judge is guaranteed by his appointment for life, the existence of incompatibilities, and the objective nature of the conditions for nomination to the courts (*see also infra*, paragraphs 104–121).

d. Impartiality

57. The right to an impartial judge implies that the judge must act with an open mind, free of bias and without prejudice to any of the parties or their dispute. Additionally, the judge's behaviour should be free of any sign or appearance of partiality: 'Justice

---

62. *Stanev/Bulgary*, ECtHR No. 36760/06 of 17 January 2012, §§230 and 241; *Brualla Gómez de la Torre/Spain*, ECtHR No. 26737/95 of 19 December 1997, §33; *de Geouffre de la Pradelle/France*, ECtHR No. 12964/87 of 16 December 1992, §28.
63. Court of Cassation 2 May 1961, *Pasicrisie belge* 1961, I, 926.
64. *Kress/France*, ECtHR No. 39594/98 of 7 June 2001, §§72–76; *Dombo Beheer B.V./Netherlands*, ECtHR No. 14448/88 of 27 October 1993, §33.
65. *K.D.B./Netherlands*, ECtHR No. 80/1997/864/1075 of 27 March 1998, §44; *Mantovanelli/France*, ECtHR No. 21497/93 of 18 March 1997, §33; *Vermeulen/Belgium*, ECtHR No. 19075/91 of 20 February 1996, §33.
66. *Nideröst-Huber/Switzerland*, ECtHR No. 18990/91 of 18 February 1997, §23.
67. It should be noted, however, that Article 151 of the Constitution is criticised for lacking sufficient guarantees as to the (institutional) independence of the judiciary *vis-à-vis* the other state powers (I. Dupré, 'De Hoge Raad voor de Justitie', *Rechtskundig Weekblad* 1998–1999, 1508–1510).
68. *H./Belgium*, ECtHR No. 8950/80 of 30 November 1987, §51.

must not only be done, but also seen to be done'. In its famous *Spaghetti* case the Court of Cassation established very clearly that even the appearance of the lack of independence or impartiality must be avoided.[69]

58. The Judicial Code provides for a special procedure whereby a party may prevent a judge, whose impartiality may be legally questioned, from sitting on the bench in a given case (*see infra*, paragraphs 402–410).[70]

e. Treatment of the case within a Reasonable Delay

59. The right to a treatment of the case within a reasonable delay must be assessed on a case-by-case basis, taking into account all the relevant factors in each individual case.[71] It requires that a careful balance is struck between the interest of the parties in obtaining a decision as soon as possible and the requirement to comply with the fundamental principles of due process.

f. Reasons for the Decision

60. Article 149 of the Constitution requires the court to state the reasons on which its decision is based, in order to avoid any sign of unfairness and to enable review by a higher court. According to the Court of Cassation, Article 149 of the Constitution should be regarded as a merely formal obligation; it can be considered to be complied with if the court has indicated the (legal and factual) reasons founding its decision, irrespective of the legal validity of these reasons.[72] On the other hand, the fact that the (substance of the) decision seems legally justified may still constitute a violation of Article 149 of the Constitution if the court failed to answer to all pleas and arguments raised by the parties.[73]

---

69. Court of Cassation 14 October 1996, P.96.1267.F: during the investigation of the abovementioned *Dutroux* case the investigating judge was invited by the parents of the victims for a 'spaghetti evening', held to raise funds to cover the costs of the trial. The acceptance of the invitation and a small gift from the participants by the judge was considered as sufficient grounds to doubt the judge's neutrality. *See* also *De Cubber/Belgium*, ECtHR No. 9186/80 of 26 October 1984, §26: '(...) any judge in respect of whom there is a legitimate reason to fear a lack of impartiality must withdraw. What is at stake is the confidence which the courts in a democratic society must inspire in the public (...)'.
70. *See* Articles 828–847 Judicial Code ('Challenge of Judges and Abstention').
71. *Siegel/France*, ECtHR No. 36350/97 of 28 November 2000; *Frydlender/France*, ECtHR No. 30797/96 of 27 June 2000; *König/Germany*, EctHR No. 6232/73 of 28 June 1978, Series A, Vol. 27, §99; Court of Cassation 30 June 2000, C.98.0484.N; Court of Cassation 5 May 1987, AR 1059.
72. Court of Cassation 14 January 1997, P.97.0005.N; Court of Cassation 3 January 1995, P.93.1560.N. This is subject, however, to the condition that review by the Court of Cassation does not become impossible by the lack or deficiency of the reasoning (Court of Cassation 19 October 2000, C.00.0164.F).
73. Court of Cassation 5 October 1998, S.98.0032.N.

2. Features Not Considered as Being 'General Principles of Law'

61. Some features, although they do appear in many cases, are not considered to be general principles of law since they are not generally applicable to all courts and cases.

a. The Public Nature of the Trial

62. The public nature of the trial[74] is meant to avoid abuses by offering to the press and to the public the opportunity of a certain 'supervision' regarding the administration of justice.

63. According to the Court of Cassation the public nature of court hearings is not a general principle of law. It only needs to be assured when provided by an international treaty, the Constitution or a statutory provision.[75]

b. The Right to Appeal

64. The right to appeal is not constitutionally guaranteed, nor does it amount to a general principle of due process in civil matters.[76] Nevertheless, Article 616 of the Judicial Code provides, as a general rule, that each judgment rendered in first instance may be subject to appeal.

---

74. *See* Article 148 Constitution and Article 757 Judicial Code.

75. Court of Cassation 9 October 1959, with opinion of Solicitor General R. Hayoit de Termicourt, *Arresten van het Hof van Cassatie* 1960, 115.

76. ECtHR 23 July 1968, 'Belgian linguistic case', §9: the Court held that Article 6 of the ECHR does not require any right of appeal, but if there is an appeal, the guarantees of said Article 6 apply; *see* also Constitutional Court No. 96/2016 of 16 June 2016, §B.6.1.; Court of Cassation 21 January 1983, AR 3621, *Arresten van het Hof van Cassatie* 1982–1983, 675, *Pasicrisie belge* 1983, 594, and K. Broeckx, *Het recht op hoger beroep en het beginsel van de dubbele aanleg in het civiele geding*, Antwerp-Apeldoorn, Maklu, 1995, 413 et seq.

Part I. Structure of the Judiciary

Chapter 1. Structure of the Court System

§1. Institutional versus Functional Meaning of the Notion 'Judiciary'

65. The organisation of the court system has remained a federal matter. Article 40, paragraph 1, of the Constitution stipulates that the judicial power is exercised by the ordinary courts, which constitute the judiciary in the institutional meaning of the word, i.e., the judicial branch of government. The notion judiciary, however, also has a functional meaning, in the sense of the judicial function as such, i.e., the settling of disputes by a judicial body. This judicial function is not only exercised by the ordinary courts, but also by other bodies, such as the Constitutional Court (*see infra*, paragraphs 96–99) and the administrative courts, of which the most important one in Belgium is the Administrative Jurisdiction Section of the Council of State (*see infra*, paragraphs 100–103).

66. The figure below shows the structure of the Belgian judiciary (in its functional meaning) in a simplified manner.

Figure 1. Structure of the Belgian Court System

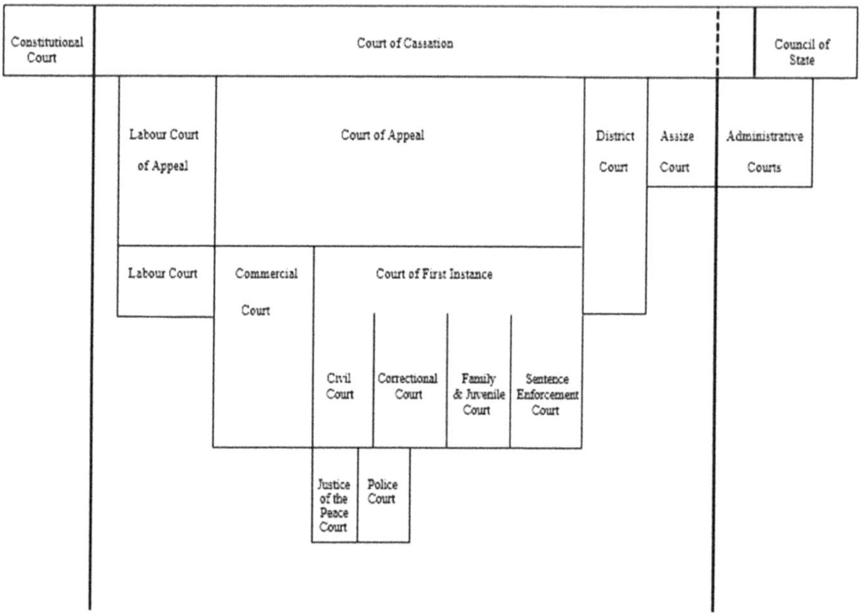

§2. Organisation and Composition of the Different Courts

I. Complex Structure

67. The structure of the Belgian (civil) judiciary is rather complicated, which may be explained by four reasons.

68. First of all, the territorial spread of the courts. The judicial organisation rests on a division of the national territory into several areas.

The sub-districts or cantons (*canton – kanton*) are the smallest geographical subdivision, of which there are currently 187.[77] There is one Justice of the Peace Court (*justice de paix – vredegerecht*) in each sub-district.

The sub-districts are grouped into judicial districts (*arrondissement*), of which there are currently twelve. The districts' borders correspond with the borders of the provinces Antwerp, Limburg, Walloon Brabant, East Flanders, West Flanders, Luxembourg, Liège, Namur and Hainaut. There are, however, separate districts for

77. The 187 judicial sub-districts are listed in Article 1 of the Supplement to the Judicial Code (*annexe au Code judiciaire – bijvoegsel bij het Gerechtelijk Wetboek*).

Brussels, Louvain and Eupen. In principle,[78] each district encompasses one Police Court (*tribunal de police – politierechtbank*) and one Court of First Instance (*tribunal de première instance – rechtbank van eerste aanleg*). It also accommodates a District Court (*tribunal d'arrondissement – arrondissementsrechtbank*), which is not a permanent court, but only convenes in case of certain jurisdictional disputes (*see infra*, paragraphs 178–179).

Until 1 April 2014, there were twenty-seven districts, which had each at least one Police Court, a Court of First Instance, a Labour Court (*tribunal de travail – arbeidsrechtbank*) and a Commercial Court (*tribunal de commerce – rechtbank van koophandel*). As part of the 2014 reform, the number of districts was reduced from twenty-seven to twelve (*see supra*, paragraph 25). Furthermore, the Labour Courts and Commercial Courts are now organised at the level of the Courts of Appeal, which is called the 'judicial area' (*ressort – rechtsgebied*) and of which there are five: Antwerp, Brussels, Ghent, Liège and Mons.[79] The former locations of these courts (in the twenty-seven judicial districts), however, are maintained as local divisions of these five centralised courts where hearings are held, in order to preserve the proximity of justice. The idea is that each local division offers the 'basic judicial services', whereas the cases that require more specialised skills or knowledge are assigned to one of the divisions for the whole district or area.[80] The allocation of cases to the divisions is laid down in a 'case allocation regulation' (*règlement de répartition des affaires – zaakverdelingsreglement*) per judicial district or area.[81] This should allow the divisions to achieve specialisation in a particular type of cases. Another objective of the restructuring of the judiciary is to facilitate mobility of the judges and court staff so

---

78. An exception is made for Brussels, Mons and Eupen. As to Brussels, note that the scale operation of the districts was crisscrossed with the reform of the judicial district of Brussels by the Act of 19 July 2012 (*Belgian Official Gazette*, 22 August 2012 (ed. 1)), which entered into force on 31 March 2014. The reform of the judicial district of Brussels entailed that some courts (i.e., Court of First Instance, Commercial Court, Labor Court and District Court) were 'duplicated' in the sense that both a Dutch-speaking and a French-speaking court were installed, each competent for the entire judicial district of Brussels. Consequently, there are two Courts of First Instance in Brussels: a Dutch-speaking Court of First Instance and a French-speaking Court of First Instance. In principle, cases are allocated between the Dutch- and French-speaking courts according to the previously existing rules regarding the allocation of cases between the former Dutch- and French-language chambers of the Brussels Court. As to the Police Courts in Brussels, there are four in total: a Dutch- and French-speaking Police Court of Brussels, a Police Court of Halle and a Police Court of Vilvoorde.
79. Article 156 Constitution and Article 5 Judicial Code Supplement.
80. Article 186, para. 1, Judicial Code enumerates the types of 'specialised cases' that are eligible for exclusive allocation to one of the divisions.
81. This regulation cannot give rise to any jurisdictional disputes, as it is merely a matter of internal allocation of cases (Article 186, para. 2, Judicial Code).

that they can be better deployed according to the districts' workload (quantitative goal) and their specialisation (qualitative goal).[82]

The maps below illustrate the current shape of the judicial landscape.

Figure 2. The Judicial Districts After the 2014 Reform[83]

82. The scale operation in itself automatically resulted in a greater mobility of the judges as their working area has been enlarged. In addition, other measures of 'internal' and 'external' mobility were implemented. Internal mobility means that judges are appointed alternatively in other districts or sub-districts of the judicial area so that their consent is not needed to transfer them to those other districts or sub-districts. External mobility implies that judges may be transferred to courts in which they have not been appointed primarily or alternatively, provided that their consent has been obtained. Said external mobility may be horizontal (transfer to a court of the same level) or vertical (transfer to a court of a higher or lower level).

83. Source: www.justitie.belgium.be (accessed September 2017).

Figure 3. The Five Judicial Areas[84]

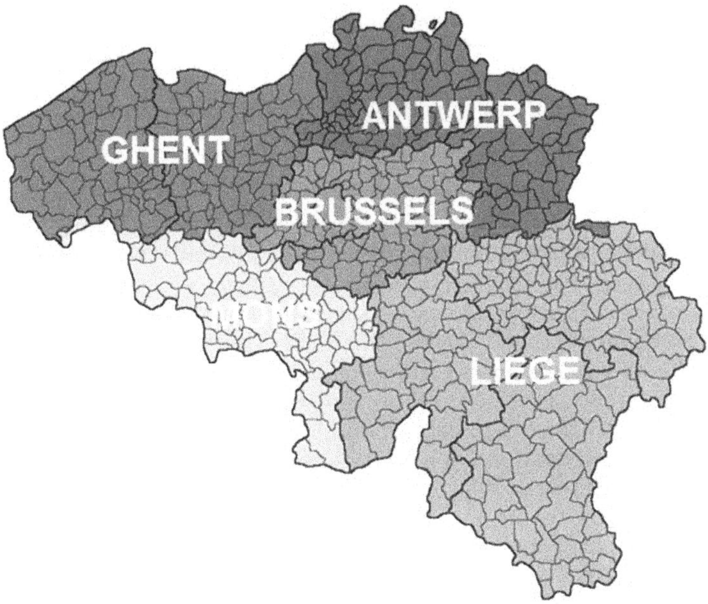

69. A second explanation for the complexity of the judicial structure is the distribution of powers between the courts. Each court has jurisdiction over particular types of cases (*see infra*, paragraphs 147–172).

70. Third, Belgian procedural law recognises, as a general rule, that each judgment rendered in first instance may be subject to appeal.[85] Appeals against judgments of the Justice of the Peace Court or the Police Court (in civil matters) are brought before the Court of First Instance. Appeals against judgments rendered by the Court of First Instance or the Commercial Court are lodged before the Court of Appeal (*cour d'appel – hof van beroep*). Appeals against judgments of the Labour Court must be filed with the Labour Court of Appeal (*cour du travail – arbeidshof*).

71. A final explanation for the complexity of the judicial structure is that the Belgian legal system provides for a further (extraordinary) legal remedy against judgments rendered in last instance, i.e., the petition for cassation (*pourvoi en cassation – cassatieberoep*), which is to be filed before the Court of Cassation.

84. Source: www.justitie.belgium.be (accessed September 2017).
85. Article 616 Judicial Code.

II. Overview of the Composition of the Different Courts

72. Belgium has a traditionally shaped judiciary. At the bottom there are five first instance courts: Justice of the Peace Courts, Police Courts, Courts of First Instance,[86] Labour Courts and Commercial Courts.

73. The Justice of the Peace Court consists of a single courtroom, presided by a single judge.

74. The Police Court is also a single-judge court, but may consist of several divisions, called 'chambers' (*chambre – kamer*).

75. The Court of First Instance is divided into three or four sections (*section – sectie*): (1) the Civil Court (*tribunal civil – burgerlijke rechtbank*), (2) the Family and Juvenile Court (*tribunal de la famille et de la jeunesse – familie- en jeugdrechtbank*), (3) the Criminal Court (*tribunal correctionel – correctionele rechtbank*) and (4) the Sentence Enforcement Court (*tribunal de l'application des peines – strafuitvoeringsrechtbank*). Only the Courts of First Instance that are located in the same city where a Court of Appeal is vested, are comprised of said fourth section, which has jurisdiction over the enforcement of criminal penalties (e.g., parole issues).[87]

Each of the sections of the Court of First Instance is composed of one or more chambers, presided by one or three judges.[88]

With the entry into force of the Act of 19 October 2015 (the so-called Potpourri I Act), the system of the single judge has been extended to all types of cases. The previously existing (limited) statutory exceptions to the single-judge rule have been abolished, as well as the possibility for the parties to request the handling of the case by three judges.[89] Only the president of the Court of First Instance is empowered to deviate from the single-judge rule on a case-by-case basis upon request of the judge who is handling the case, under the condition that the complexity or importance of the case or other special and objective reasons give cause to do so.[90]

The Family and Juvenile Court is a newly established section within the Court of First Instance (operational since 1 September 2014),[91] which comprises of juvenile chambers (Juvenile Court), family chambers and, within the latter, chambers for amicable settlement (*chambre de règlement à l'amiable – kamer voor minnelijke schikking*) (Family Court). The chambers for amicable settlement are presided over by a judge who received specific training in the amicable settlement of disputes.[92] Furthermore, every Court of First Instance has one or more judges of attachments[93] (*juge des saisies – beslagrechter*), dealing with the enforcement of judgments (*see infra*, paragraphs 502–547) and pre-trial attachments (*see infra*, paragraphs 473–501).

86. The Court of First Instance also serves as an appellate court for judgments rendered in first instance by the Justice of the Peace Court and the Police Court (in civil matters).
87. Article 76, para. 1, Judicial Code.
88. Article 78, para. 1, Judicial Code.
89. Article 91 Judicial Code.
90. Article 92, para. 1/1, Judicial Code.
91. Before 1 September 2014, there was only a Juvenile Court.
92. Article 78, para. 5, Judicial Code.
93. Article 79, para. 1, Judicial Code.

Finally the president of the Court of First Instance can give preliminary rulings (*see infra*, paragraphs 316–321).[94]

76. The Labour Court is composed of several chambers. Normally, each chamber is presided by one professional judge, assisted by two (exceptionally four) lay judges, one from the side of the employers and one from the side of the employees or the self-employed, depending on the litigating parties.[95] Lay judges are appointed on the recommendation of the various representative organisations of employers, employees and self-employed people.

77. The Commercial Court consists of several chambers, presided by one professional judge and two (assisting) lay judges, the latter being appointed on the recommendation of the various associations representing commerce and industry.[96]

78. Courts of Appeal and Labour Courts of Appeal are organised on the level of each of the five judicial areas.

In the Court of Appeal there are chambers for civil matters, chambers for juvenile matters, chambers for family matters (and within the latter, chambers for amicable settlement) and chambers for criminal matters.[97] Every chamber is presided over by one or three judges.[98] Until recently, the cases on appeal were, in principle, distributed to a chamber with three judges. Since the entry into force of the aforementioned 'Potpourri I Act', this rule has been reversed. Cases relating to civil matters are dealt with by a single judge on appeal.[99] Only the first president of the Court of Appeal is empowered to deviate from the single-judge rule upon request of the judge who is handling the case, under the condition that the complexity or importance of the case or other special and objective reasons give cause to do so.[100]

The Labour Court of Appeal is composed of professional and lay judges on appeal, similarly to the Labour Court.[101]

79. Finally, on top of the pyramid, there is the Court of Cassation, Belgium's Supreme Court of the judiciary, of which there is only one, located in Brussels.[102] There are three chambers: one for civil cases, one for labour and social security cases and one for criminal cases.[103] Each chamber consists of a Dutch- and French-speaking department.

80. The figure below summarises the abovementioned principles in a simplified manner.

---

94. Article 584 Judicial Code.
95. Articles 81 and 197–202 Judicial Code. Contrary to the rule, the chamber deciding on collective debt settlement cases is composed of a single professional judge in the Labour Court (Article 81, para. 2, Judicial Code).
96. Articles 84 and 203–205 Judicial Code.
97. Article 101, para. 1(1), Judicial Code.
98. Article 101, para. 2(2), Judicial Code.
99. Article 109*bis*, §3 Judicial Code.
100. Article 109*bis*, §3 Judicial Code.
101. Article 104 Judicial Code.
102. Article 147(1) Constitution.
103. Article 133 Judicial Code.

Figure 4. Structure of the Belgian Judiciary (Ordinary Courts)

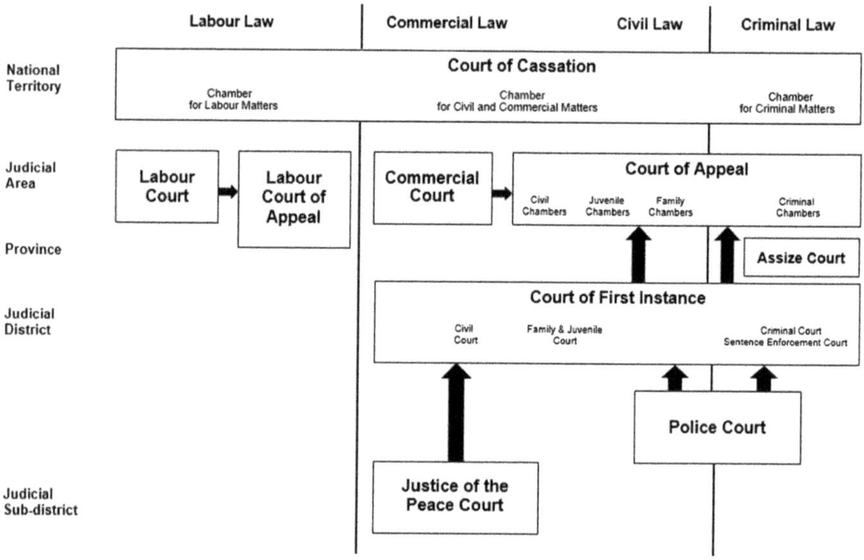

Chapter 2. Administration of the Court

81. The court's caseload is distributed in accordance with two regulations: the case allocation regulation (*see also supra*, paragraph 68) and the internal regulation (*règlement particulier – bijzonder reglement*) of the court. The case allocation regulation is established by Royal Decree. It concerns the distribution of the cases to the divisions of the court.[104] The internal regulation is established by decision of the president of the court. This regulation provides for the division of the court in chambers, as well as their competences, and the time schedule of the chambers' hearings. The president of the court is responsible for the organisation of the court's workload and the allocation of the cases, according to the court's case allocation regulation and internal regulation.[105]

82. The regulation regarding the allocation of civil cases to a certain division, section, chamber or judge cannot give rise to any jurisdictional disputes, as it is merely a matter of internal allocation of cases. Disputes regarding the allocation of cases are settled in accordance with the (simple) procedure laid down in Article 88, §2, of the Judicial Code. The dispute has to be raised by one of the parties '*in limine litis*' (meaning in the first pleadings, before any other plea or defence), or by the judge ex officio at the start of the oral hearings, otherwise the allocation of the case will be considered definitive.[106] The president of the court considers the request and decides whether or not to refer the case to another division, section, chamber or judge. This decision may be appealed only by the public prosecutor at the Court of Appeal, who can initiate proceedings before the Court of Cassation.

83. From 1 July to, and including, 31 August, judicial holidays take place.[107] During this period there are no regular court sessions. However, every court has special 'holiday chambers' that deal with urgent matters.[108]

84. In administrative and organisational matters, the judge is assisted by the court registrars (*greffier – griffier*) (*see infra,* paragraph 124).

---

104. Article 186 Judicial Code.
105. Articles 90 and 109 Judicial Code.
106. Court of Cassation 1 June 1990, *Arresten van het Hof van Cassatie* 1989–1990, 1262.
107. Article 340 Judicial Code.
108. Articles 334–339 Judicial Code.

Chapter 3. The Public Prosecutor's Office

85. In Belgium, a distinction is made between 'sitting magistrates', who adjudicate the cases that are brought before them and who are judges, and 'standing magistrates',[109] who serve in the public prosecutor's office (*ministère public – openbaar ministerie*). There is a public prosecutor's office within each court, except for the Justice of the Peace Court, the Police Court, the Commercial Court and the District Court.[110]

86. The public prosecutor's legal status differs from the judiciary. Officials of the public prosecutor's office are not appointed for life, but can be dismissed.[111] Further on, they are subject to the supervision of the Minister of Justice, who has the right to order the public prosecutor's office to take action in a certain case. Nevertheless, they also enjoy a constitutionally guaranteed independence.[112] They are also independent *vis-à-vis* the sitting judge and the parties to the case.

87. The public prosecutor's office fulfils a number of tasks in both criminal and civil cases.

88. Only in criminal cases it really prosecutes (or acts within the meaning of 'public prosecution' in common law), except before the Court of Cassation.

89. In civil cases, the public prosecutor's task is threefold. First of all, it can initiate (remedy) proceedings on its own initiative in circumstances provided for by statute or whenever public policy reasons so require.[113] In this case, the public prosecutor acts as a party to the proceedings, which are subject to the general rules applicable to adversary proceedings. Second, it may order certain police and executive measures for reasons of public policy.[114] Finally, it acts as an advisor to the court in the circumstances provided for by statute or whenever it considers its advice to be useful (*see also infra*, paragraphs 276–279).[115] Said advice is not binding on the court and the court is not obliged to respond to it.[116] The advice of the prosecutor at the Court of Cassation, however, which is mandatory in all cases,[117] often has an important influence on the

109. So named because they stand up when addressing the court.
110. Where the office of the public prosecutor is performed by the public prosecutor's office within the Court of First Instance (Article 150, §1 para. 2, Judicial Code).
111. Article 153 Constitution.
112. Article 151, §1, para. 1, of the Constitution stipulates that the public prosecutor's office is independent in the exercise of its functions, without prejudice to the right of the competent minister to order prosecutions and to prescribe binding directives on criminal policy, including policy on investigations and prosecutions.
113. For example, Article. 652 of the Judicial Code enables the public prosecutor to initiate proceedings before the Court of Cassation in order to withdraw the case from the judge if the latter did not render judgment within six months after the closing of the oral hearings.
114. Two cases are expressly provided for in the Judicial Code: the public prosecutor in the Labour Court can request certain information from public authorities (Article 138*ter* Judicial Code) and, upon the request of an individual, the public prosecutor may order the intervention of a bailiff or the police force when a judgment has to be enforced (Article 139 Judicial Code).
115. Article 138*bis juncto* Articles 764–768 Judicial Code.
116. Court of Cassation 4 December 1987, *Arresten van het Hof van Cassatie* 1987–1988, 449.
117. Article 1107, para. 2, Judicial Code.

Court's judgment. The advice will be given in writing or orally during the hearing.[118] In any event, the parties have the right to reply.

118. Article 767 Judicial Code.

Chapter 4. The High Council of Justice

90. The considerable public criticism that was expressed in the aftermath of the case of Dutroux in the mid-1990s gave rise to several major reforms of the judiciary and the law enforcement agencies, thereby focusing on a more qualitative, efficient, transparent and humane system (*see also supra*, paragraphs 23–24). One of the measures adopted in the aftermath of these events was the establishment of the High Council of Justice on 31 December 1999 (operational since 2 August 2000).[119]

91. The High Council of Justice does neither belong to the judiciary, nor to the other branches of government. It is an independent constitutional body that serves as an intermediary, or a bridge, between the judiciary on the one hand and the legislative and executive on the other hand. Its constitutional foundations are laid down in Article 151 of the Constitution, while detailed rules on its composition and functions are elabourated in Article 259*bis*/1–22 of the Judicial Code.

92. The High Council consists of two joint committees – a Dutch-speaking and a French-speaking committee – which are comprised of eleven judges[120] and eleven non-judges. The group of non-judges needs to consist of at least four members of each sex and at least four attorneys with ten years of experience at the bar, three university professors and four persons with a university or equivalent degree, having at least ten years of relevant professional experience. The judges are elected by their peers; the non-judges are appointed by the federal Senate.[121]

93. Two commissions are assembled from among each committee: a nomination and appointment commission[122] (*commission de nomination et de désignation – benoemings- en aanwijzingscommissie*) and an advisory and investigation commission[123] (*commission d'avis et d'enquête – advies- en onderzoekscommissie*). These commissions are equally composed of judges and non-judges. In a number of cases, the respective Dutch-speaking and French-speaking commissions have to act together, in which case they are referred to as the joint nomination and appointment commission[124] (*commission de nomination et de désignation réunie – verenigde benoemings- en aanwijzingscommissie*) and the joint advisory and investigation commission[125] (*commission d'avis et d'enquête réunie – verenigde benoemings- en aanwijzingscommissie*).

94. The nomination and appointment commissions have certain powers in relation to the nomination, appointment, evaluation and initial and in-service training of members of the judiciary. They are responsible, for instance, for the preparation and organisation of the exams which provide (alternative) access to the magistracy,

---

119. For further information, *see* also the High Council's website: www.hrj.be (accessed September 2017).
120. Each linguistic committee needs to consist of at least one judge and one official of the public prosecutor's office.
121. Article 259*bis*/1, §1, Judicial Code, which brings the total number of members of the High Council of Justice on 44.
122. Article 259*bis*/8 Judicial Code.
123. Article 259*bis*/11 Judicial Code.
124. Articles 259*bis*/9–10 Judicial Code.
125. Articles 259*bis*/12–14 Judicial Code.

i.e., the competitive entrance exam for admission to the judicial traineeship; the exam of professional aptitude and the oral evaluation exam (*see also infra*, paragraphs 104–108).[126] They are also entrusted with the recommendation of candidates for the nomination as judge and the appointment of judges in executive or managerial functions (e.g., as president of a court), or to carry out a special mandate (e.g., as a liaison judge in juvenile matters or as a federal judge),[127] as well as with the establishment of general guidelines for the initial and in-service training of judges and of judicial trainees. Since 2009, a new independent body – the Institute for Judicial Training (*Institut de Formation Judiciaire – Instituut voor Gerechtelijke Opleiding*) – is charged with the implementation of the training programmes.[128]

95. The advisory and investigation commissions' primary task is to prepare (non-binding) recommendations and opinions regarding the general functioning of the judiciary,[129] as well as to investigate complaints in this respect.[130] Its most far-reaching power is the possibility of initiating an investigation on the functioning of the judiciary upon request of the Minister of Justice or the majority of the Chambers of Parliament or on its own motion, upon prior approval by a majority of the members of the joint advisory and investigation commission.[131]

126. Article 259*bis*/9 Judicial Code.
127. Article 259*bis*-10, §1, 1° Judicial Code.
128. Act of 31 January 2007 on the Judicial Training and the Establishment of the Institute for Judicial Training (*Belgian Official Gazette*, 22 February 2007).
129. Article 259*bis*/12 Judicial Code.
130. Article 259*bis*/15 Judicial Code. On the understanding, however, that the High Council cannot interfere in the handling of a particular (court) case.
131. Article 259*bis*/16 Judicial Code.

Chapter 5. The Constitutional Court

96. Traditionally, the Belgian judiciary has held the position that it does not have the power to review the validity of statutes under the Constitution. This power of judicial review rests exclusively with the Constitutional Court (*Cour constitutionnelle – Grondwettelijk Hof*), which is not part of the judiciary, the judicial branch of government (*see supra*, paragraph 65).

97. The Constitutional Court owes its existence to the development of the Belgian State from a unitary state into a federal state. Major reforms since 1970 have resulted in the establishment of a federal state within which the legislative power is divided between the federation and the federated entities according to a system in which each legislative body has exclusive powers (*see also supra*, paragraphs 11–12). The statutes of the federation and the decrees and ordinances of the federated entities (the regions and communities) have the same force of law. The division of the legislative power between different legislatures brought with it the risk of conflicts of legislative jurisdiction. In this context, the constitutional legislature of 1980 decided to establish a new adjudicative body, the Court of Arbitration (*Cour d'arbitrage – Arbitragehof*), which was entrusted with the task of demarcating the boundaries of each authority's legislative power. For this purpose, it was given the power to nullify any statutes, whether federal or regional, promulgated in breach of the division of legislative jurisdiction that has been established by or in pursuance of the Constitution. Since then, however, the jurisdiction of the Court has been gradually extended to include the review of federal and regional statutes on their compliance with other articles of the Constitution.[132] Accordingly, the name of the Court of Arbitration was changed into Constitutional Court in 2007.

98. There are two ways in which a case can be brought before the Constitutional Court: in the form of an action for annulment, which may be instituted by certain government authorities as well as by any (natural or legal) person declaring a justifiable interest, or in the form of a preliminary question referred by another court (if a question comes up in a court regarding the compatibility of federal statutes or regional decrees and ordinances with the Constitution, that court must in principle address a preliminary question to the Constitutional Court).

99. The Court's constitutional foundations are laid down in Article 142 of the Constitution, while detailed rules on its organisation, functioning, procedure as well as the effects of its judgments are elabourated in the (repeatedly amended) Special Act of 6 January 1989.[133]

---

132. To date, the Court's competence has been extended to section II of the Constitution, which relates to rights and freedoms (Articles 8–32), as well as to Article 143, para. 1 (the principle of federal loyalty), Article 170 (the legality principle in tax matters), Article 172 (the equality principle in tax matters) and Article 191 (the protection of foreign nationals) of the Constitution.

133. An (unofficial) English version of these texts is available on the Constitutional Court's website under the heading 'Basic Texts', at www.const-court.be (accessed September 2017).

Chapter 6. The Council of State

100. The Council of State (*Conseil d'Etat – Raad van State*) is the highest (i.e., supreme) administrative court in Belgium, established by the Act of 23 December 1946.[134] As such, it is not part of the judiciary, the judicial branch of government (*see supra*, paragraph 65). It encompasses, within a single institution, both an advisory body (the Legislative section) and an adjudicating body (the Administrative Section).[135]

101. The Legislative Section (*section de legislation – afdeling wetgeving*) delivers legal advisory opinions on draft statutory texts, in order to verify whether these texts are in conformity with the applicable (international and Belgian) rules of law, as well as to check on their wording and whether the official Dutch and French text versions are consistent with each other. Although these opinions are not binding upon the authorities requesting the advice, in practice they have great moral authority.

102. Besides its advisory role regarding legislation, the Council also has a jurisdictional role, providing legal recourse to citizens being wronged by government actions. For this purpose, the Administrative Section (*section du contentieux administrative – afdeling bestuursrechtspraak*) is given the power to suspend and annul (individual and legislative) administrative acts, i.e., acts performed by an administrative authority.[136] It is not authorised to annul or suspend legislative acts, as this power belongs exclusively to the Constitutional Court (*see infra*, paragraphs 96–99). It is also authorised to review and, as the case may be, suspend and/or annul decisions rendered by a lower-ranking administrative court. In the latter case, the Administrative Section of the Council of State functions as an administrative court of cassation, and thus as a Supreme Court. Over the years, the Administrative Section has been provided with new and additional powers, confirming its important and unique role in safeguarding the legal rights of citizens *vis-à-vis* the administration. In 2014, for instance, Article 144 of the Constitution was amended with a view to provide the Council of State with the power to rule upon the (private) civil law consequences of its decisions (which are of an objective nature) (*contentieux de l'indemnité réparatrice – schadevergoeding tot herstel*). At the choice of the citizen demanding the annulment of the administrative act, he can either claim full compensation for the loss he suffered before the (ordinary) civil courts of the judiciary based on general civil liability law, in which case he has to prove that the administration committed a fault, or he can claim reasonable compensation based on this administrative principle before the Council of State, in which case the unlawfulness of the act suffices so no fault of the administration has to be shown, but in which case only partial compensation could be awarded if private or public interests related to the case so require.

---

134. Before then, the legal protection of citizens against the administration was ensured by the ordinary (civil) courts, which were also authorised to settle administrative disputes.

135. Therefore, the Council of State is said to be situated on the junction of the three traditional powers of state (M. Van Damme, *The Council of State: Institution on the Junction of the Three Traditional Powers of State*, in *The Principle of Equality: A South African and Belgian Perspective* 71-88 (J. Vande Lanotte ed., Maklu 2001).

136. This kind of disputes forms about 98% of the Council's caseload.

103. The Council's constitutional foundations are laid down in Article 160 of the Constitution, while detailed rules on its composition, authority and functioning are elabourated in the (repeatedly amended) Coordinated Act on the Council of State.[137]

137. Royal Decree of 12 January 1973, *Belgian Official Gazette*, 21 March 1973.

Part II. Participants in the Judicial System

Chapter 1. Members of the Judiciary

§1. Judges

I. Nomination and Appointment

104. Until the 1990s the criteria for the appointment of judges were rather opaque. It was not transparent whether access to the position of judge was based solely on the qualifications and merits of the candidate. A first step towards greater objectivity and transparency in the appointment of judges was made with the Act of 18 July 1991.[138] A second decisive step in that direction was realised as part of the Octopus Reform of 1998 (*see supra*, paragraphs 23–24 and 90). One of the central points of these reforms was the elimination of the so-called political appointments whereby, next to capacity and suitability to carry out the office, political support from a political party was indispensable to be appointed as a magistrate. To this end, Article 151 of the Constitution was amended, which now stipulates that judges are appointed by the King pursuant to their reasoned nomination by the respective nomination and appointment commission of the High Council of Justice, by a majority of two-thirds in accordance with the terms specified by the law and after evaluation of their qualifications and aptitude. The nomination can be rejected only in the manner specified by statute and with adequate justification.[139] In addition, Article 151 of the Constitution was revised in order to 'reaffirm' the principle of judicial independence.[140]

105. There are actually three alternative ways of entering the judiciary: (1) the judicial traineeship; (2) the professional aptitude exam; and (3) the oral evaluation exam. The first way of access is designed for candidates with little working experience. It includes a judicial traineeship, which may be commenced only after the candidate has passed a (written and oral) competitive entrance exam. Candidates must have performed at least two years at the bar or similar legal function in a period of four

138. *Belgian Official Gazette*, 26 July 1991.
139. Article 151, para. 4, Constitution.
140. Article 151, para. 1, Constitution: 'Judges are independent in the exercise of their jurisdictional competences.'

years preceding the exam.[141] The second way of access is intended for candidates with a larger professional experience. In addition to a required minimum of four years of working experience in a legal function, candidates need to pass the 'professional aptitude exam', giving immediate access to a vacancy.[142] The third way of access includes the successful completion of an oral evaluation exam, also giving instant access to a vacancy, which is reserved to candidates who have acquired many years of professional experience.[143] These different ways of access aims at balancing the number of young and more experienced judges.

106. All candidates must be the holder of a Master or Doctor of Law degree. Except for the appointment as judge in the Justice of the Peace Court and Police Court,[144] there is no age requirement.

107. The nomination and appointment commissions of the High Council of Justice are responsible for the preparation and organisation of the exams, as well as the nomination for appointment of candidates for a vacancy for a position of judge (*see supra*, paragraph 94). These commissions are also in charge of the nomination of candidates for an appointment by the King to the positions of first president of the Court of Cassation, first president of the appellate courts, president of the lower courts, and head of the public prosecutor's office.[145]

108. It should be pointed out that the nomination process is still criticised for not having completely excluded any potential political and ideological influence. The composition of the High Council, half of its members being appointed by the Senate (*see supra*, paragraph 92), remains a matter of concern.[146] Former members of the High Council rebut this criticism, stating that they have never observed any political or ideological influence by the politically appointed members. In any event, it is probably safe to say that the balanced composition of the High Council serves as a safeguard in this respect.[147] The requirement that each nomination has to be supported by two thirds of the votes cast in the respective nomination and appointment commission serves the same goal.[148]

---

141. Article 190, para. 1 *juncto* Article 259*octies* Judicial Code.
142. The required working experience depends on the type of judicial function (*see* Articles 186*bis*–206 Judicial Code).
143. Articles 187*bis*, 191*bis* and 194*bis* Judicial Code.
144. Candidates must be at least 35 years old.
145. Article 151, paras 3–5 Constitution, and Article 259*bis*-10 Judicial Code.
146. B. Allemeersch, A. Alen & B. Dalle, *Judicial Independence in Belgium*, in *Judicial Independence in Transition. Strengthening the Rule of Law in the OSCE Region* 320 (A. Seibert-Fohr ed., Springer 2011).
147. S. Voet & M. Storme, *Institutional Judicial Reform Experiences in Belgium: New Bodies Governing the Judiciary*, in *Judicial Reforms in Luxembourg and Europe* 153 (B. Hess ed., Studies of the Max Planck Institute Luxembourg for International, European and Regulatory Procedural law, Vol. 1, Nomos, 2014).
148. Article 259*ter*, para. 4, Judicial Code.

II. Incompatibilities

109. The Judicial Code provides for a series of incompatibilities, aimed at safeguarding the impartiality and independence of judges.[149] Most incompatibilities relate to the simultaneous exercise of the judicial function and certain offices and professions, such as the office of notary public, bailiff, attorney, political and military offices and clergy, as well as any other remunerated public office, with the exception of certain academic functions. Other rules provide for incompatibilities in case of kinship.

110. In addition to compliance with the rules on incompatibilities, judges must refrain from dealing with a case as soon as there can be reasonable doubt about their independence or impartiality, in the absence of which their authority can be challenged[150] or they can be withdrawn from the case.[151]

III. Rights and Duties

111. In relation to the judge's responsibilities, a distinction must be made between the duties concerning his office as such and his general duty to refrain from any acts which could harm the honour and dignity of his office.

112. As to the first category of duties, the judge's main task is to adjudicate on the case brought before him. The judge may not refuse to render judgment, as that would amount to a 'denial of justice'.[152] The refusal of any judge to decide in a case which has been lawfully subjected to his jurisdiction is punishable under Article 258 of the Criminal Code. Any such judge would also be liable for civil claims under Article 1140 of the Judicial Code (*see infra*, paragraph 119).

The demarcation of the task of the judge versus the role of the parties to the proceedings is explained in detail under paragraphs 34–45.

113. The judge's general duty to uphold the dignity of his office means, for instance, that he must lead an irreproachable and indisputable private life, be reserved in his opinions and not search for publicity, especially not by openly taking position in controversial matters. Although the Judicial Code does not contain any (specific) ethical rules of conduct for judges, the High Council of Justice and the Advisory Council for the Magistracy (*see infra*, paragraph 122) published a 'Guide for Judges' in 2012.[153] This guide is not to be considered as a binding code of discipline, but includes recommendations, statements and key principles on how judges should act

149. Articles 292–304 Judicial Code. *See* also Article. 155 Constitution, which stipulates that 'a judge cannot accept a salaried position from a government, unless this position is exercised free of charge, and even then, such a position must not entail an incompatibility as determined by the law'.
150. Articles 828–850 Judicial Code.
151. Articles 648–659 Judicial Code.
152. Article 5 Judicial Code.
153. The guide is available in both Dutch and French, at http://www.csj.be/en/content/guide-judges (accessed September 2017).

in certain situations. The guidelines are inspired by and based on the Judicial Ethics Report 2009–2010 of the European Network of Councils for the Judiciary.[154]

IV. Evaluation and Discipline

114. Article 151, §6, paragraph 1, of the Constitution states that judges are subject to an evaluation. This evaluation entails a periodic internal quality assessment with respect to the way in which the office is exercised, but cannot relate to the (quality of the) content of a court decision. The evaluation procedures are described in Articles 259*novies-undecies* of the Judicial Code. The evaluation criteria and their weightings are set by the King, upon a proposal from the High Council of Justice.[155]

115. Article 152, paragraph 2, of the Constitution stipulates that no judge can be deprived of his office or suspended otherwise than by way of a (disciplinary) court decision. Judges who neglect their duties or damage the dignity of their office through their behaviour may be subject to light or severe disciplinary sanctions. Disciplinary sanctions of the first category are a warning or reprimand.[156] Regarding severe disciplinary sanctions, a further distinction is made between severe disciplinary measures of the first degree (i.e., deduction from wage, withdrawal of an adjunct or special mandate and suspension) and severe disciplinary measures of the second degree (i.e., downgrade in salary scale, retraction of the latest salary increase, dismissal and removal).[157]

116. The disciplinary rules for judges[158] have been changed considerably by the Act of 15 July 2013.[159] The new rules should make disciplinary proceedings quicker, simpler and more transparent and, above all, they should guarantee – more so than before – the independence and impartiality of the disciplinary authorities. On the latter point, the pivotal role of the direct hierarchical superior of the judge concerned was especially considered to be problematic. Some disciplinary investigations seemed like personal vendettas, whilst other investigations lacked effectiveness because of the reluctance of the superior to take action.[160] The creation of two independent (non-permanent) disciplinary courts (one for the Dutch-speaking region and one for the French- and German-speaking region) should remedy these deficiencies.

---

154. *See* https://www.encj.eu/images/stories/pdf/ethics/judicialethicsdeontologiefinal.pdf (accessed September 2017). This report was approved by the General Assembly of ENCJ during its London meeting on 2–4 June 2010.
155. Article 259*nonies*, §1, para. 6, Judicial Code.
156. Article 405, §1, para. 1, Judicial Code.
157. Article 405, §1, para. 2, Judicial Code.
158. Which are not only applicable to judges, but also to officers of the public prosecutor's office, legal secretaries and court registrars.
159. *Belgian Official Gazette*, 25 July 2013. The new rules are laid down in Articles 404–423 of the Judicial Code.
160. S. Voet & M. Storme, *Institutional Judicial Reform Experiences in Belgium: New Bodies Governing the Judiciary*, in *Judicial reforms in Luxembourg and Europe* 166 (B. Hess ed., Studies of the Max Planck Institute Luxembourg for International, European and Regulatory Procedural law, Vol. 1, Nomos 2014).

117. Article 410, §1, of the Judicial Code lists all persons having capacity to bring disciplinary proceedings. In addition, disciplinary proceedings can always be initiated by the public prosecutor's office.[161] The basic rules of fair trial are to be respected during the disciplinary proceedings, i.e., the judge is heard[162] and the hearing is, in principle, public.[163] Further on, the person involved has a right to consult his file, and may be assisted by a person of his choice.[164] Decisions of the disciplinary courts may be subject to appeal before the disciplinary courts of appeal.[165]

118. As to the judge's criminal liability, note that judges do not have immunity from criminal jurisdiction. Nevertheless, they enjoy the privilege of being tried directly by the Court of Appeal for offences they have allegedly committed within or outside the exercise of their office (*privilège de jurisdiction – voorrang van rechtsmacht*).[166] The Court of Appeal renders judgment 'at first and final instance', meaning that its decision is not appealable.[167]

119. At the civil level, negligence in the performance of his duties will only trigger the judge's liability in the circumstances provided for in Article 1140 of the Judicial Code, e.g., in case of refusal to render judgment or in case of deceit. In this event, proceedings can be initiated against the judge before the Court of Cassation.[168] Outside these cases, the Belgian State may be held responsible for damage caused by the careless and negligent behaviour of judges in the exercise of their duties, in accordance with the general rules on civil liability.[169]

V. End of Functions

120. Although Article 152, paragraph 1, of the Constitution provides that judges are appointed for life, retirement is mandatory at the age of sixty-seven.[170] Judges approaching their retirement age may, however, at their own request, be authorised by the King to continue exercising their office until they have reached the age of seventy.[171]

161. Article 410, §2, Judicial Code.
162. Court of Cassation 22 October 2009, D.09.0018.N.
163. Article 416, para. 1, Judicial Code.
164. Articles 417–418 Judicial Code.
165. Article 420 Judicial Code.
166. Articles 479–483 Criminal Code.
167. When other persons are tried together with the judge before the Court of Appeal, they will not be able either to lodge an appeal against the judgment. According to the Constitutional Court this does not constitute an unequal treatment (Constitutional Court No. 66/94 of 14 July 1994, *Belgian Official Gazette*, 17 August 1994).
168. Article 1143 Judicial Code.
169. Articles 1382–1383 Civil Code.
170. Article 383, §1, para. 3, Judicial Code. The age limit for judges and officers of the public prosecutor's office in the Court of Cassation is seventy (Article 383, §1, para. 2, Judicial Code).
171. Article 383*ter* Judicial Code. The age limit for post-retirement exercising of their office by judges and officers of the public prosecutor's office in the Court of Cassation is set at seventy-three.

Retired judges may also be appointed as a 'substitute judge'[172] at their own request. Retired judges who have been appointed as substitute judge may even continue exercising this office after the age of seventy as far as it is considered useful for the requirements of the service.[173]

121. Retired judges receive a pension equalling the average amount of their wage over the last five years of their office. This rule is intended to ensure that judges can rely on equal financial means as before, thus guaranteeing their independence during their time in the office.[174]

VI. Interest Groups and Networks

122. There exist several national organisations that promote the collective interests of (part of) the Belgian magistracy, of which the most important one is the Advisory Council for the Magistracy (*Conseil consultatif de la magistrature – Adviesraad van de magistratuur*).[175] The Council's members represent all branches of the judiciary and are elected by their peers. The Council's mission is to give advisory opinions to the Minister of Justice, the federal Parliament, i.e., the Chamber of Representatives and the Senate, and to consult with them, on topics relating to the status, rights and duties, as well as the working conditions of judges and officers of the public prosecutor's office. Since 2006, the Council has rendered about thirty advisory opinions in various domains. An initiative that caught the eye of the Belgian media, was its abovementioned 2012 deontological guide for magistrates, which it drafted in cooperation with the High Council of Justice (*see supra,* paragraph 113).

123. Another important (European) initiative is the European Judicial Network in civil and commercial matters, which facilitates relations between the national judicial authorities of the respective Member States through a network of national contact points, thereby furthering cooperation in cross-border cases.[176]

§2. Court Registries

124. Every court has a registry (*greffe – griffie*), which serves as the court's secretariat and is headed by a chief registrar (*greffier en chef – hoofdgriffier*).[177] There may be one or more court registrars (as well as additional administrative staff) in every

172. Substitute judges may be appointed in order to replace judges that cannot attend a court session (due to, illness or holidays, for instance) or to lend a hand in handling the court's caseload. Substitute judges are chosen among retired judges, but also (well-experienced) attorneys, public notaries and law professors.
173. Article 383, §2, Judicial Code.
174. Article 391 Judicial Code.
175. The Council was established by the Act of 8 March 1999 (*Belgian Official Gazette*, 19 March 1999) and is operational since 14 May 2006.
176. *See* https://e-justice.europa.eu/content_about_the_network-431-en.do (accessed September 2017).
177. Article 157 Judicial Code.

registry, depending on the size of the court. The court registrars are members of the judiciary; they fulfil a judicial function, but have no adjudicating authority. They assist the judges in the exercise of their office. In principle, a court registrar must be present at every hearing.[178] The registrar acts as an independent and impartial observer; he takes minutes of the hearing and ensures that the applicable rules are complied with.

§3. Legal Secretaries

125. The abovementioned court registrars (*see supra*, paragraph 124) may not be confused with other (legal) professionals by whom the judges are assisted, such as legal secretaries (*référendaire – referendaris*).[179] Legal secretaries assist the judges in the drawing-up of the judgment. They study the case file and carry out legal research on the instructions and under the supervision of one or more judges. The legal secretaries at the Court of Cassation are also responsible for the translation and publication of the Court's decisions.

178. Article 168 Judicial Code.
179. Articles 135*bis* and 162 Judicial Code.

Chapter 2. Attorneys

§1. Exercise of the Profession

I. Conditions for Admission

126. Attorneys (*avocat – advocaat*) exercise a liberal profession. They pursue a self-employed activity, according to their own private conscience. They do not belong to any of the state powers. Nevertheless, their profession is closely regulated by rules and regulations.

127. The conditions for admission to the profession are elabourated in Articles 428–438 of the Judicial Code. Next to diploma[180] and nationality[181] requirements, candidate attorneys must be enrolled on the list of trainees. Trainee attorneys are fully qualified attorneys, but are subject to certain training obligations. After having completed three years of training under the supervision of an experienced attorney, one may apply for admission to the bar (*tableau*).

II. Rights and Duties

128. Attorneys are professionally engaged in the defence of private interests. At all times and under all circumstances, they are at the service of parties seeking justice. This mission statement includes legal counselling and legal representation in court. Attorneys may also provide assistance in alternative dispute resolution procedures, such as arbitration and mediation. Furthermore, they may act as arbitrator or mediator themselves.

---

180. A Master or Doctor degree in law is required (Article 428 Judicial Code). A degree from another European Member State can be considered to be equivalent under the conditions laid down in the European Directive 2005/36/EC of 7 September 2005 on the recognition of professional qualifications (*Official Journal* L255/22 of 2005), and provided that such degree demonstrates that the person concerned is qualified to be admitted to practice law in a EU Member State. Foreign EU attorneys are also required to pass an aptitude test if their training differs fundamentally from the areas covered by a Belgian law degree (Article 428*bis* Judicial Code).
181. One must have the Belgian nationality or the nationality of an EU Member State (Article 428 Judicial Code). For non-EU members, the King can allow for an exception to the nationality requirement, after receiving the opinion of the Bar Associations (Article 428, para. 2, Judicial Code). *See* also Articles 477*bis*–477*quater* of the Judicial Code, which provide for the conditions under which an attorney of another EU Member State can temporarily exercise his profession in Belgium (implementing European Directives 77/249/EEC of 22 March 1977 to facilitate the effective exercise by lawyers of freedom to provide services (*Official Journal* L078 of 1977) and 98/5/EC of 16 February 1998 to facilitate practice of the profession of lawyer on a permanent basis in a Member State other than that in which the qualification was obtained (*Official Journal* L077 of 1998).

129. Attorneys have the right to plead and represent their client before all ordinary civil courts, without the need of a specific power of attorney.[182] The mere declaration of acting on behalf of their client serves as a presumption of lawful representation.[183] As with any mandate, mistakes or negligence of the attorney, which fall within the limits of the representation, are considered to be the mistakes or negligence of the principal, i.e., the client, and cannot give rise to force majeure.[184]

130. As legal representation is not compulsory in Belgium, parties have the right to choose to appear and plead in person, without a legal representative. Only in exceptional circumstances, proceedings may not be initiated without the intervention of a (specialised) attorney. For instance, in civil matters, only attorneys who are admitted to practice before the Court of Cassation may plead and represent their clients before this Supreme Court.[185] In addition, Article 758, paragraph 2, of the Judicial Code provides that, when a party is unable to present its arguments in a calm and clear manner to the court, the judge may interrupt the pleadings and ask that the party presents its case through a legal representative.

131. In principle, only attorneys have the right to speak on behalf of the parties in court.[186] In some (lower) courts, however, parties may be assisted or represented by their spouse or close relatives.[187] In the Labour Courts, parties may be assisted or represented by a representative of a trade union.[188]

132. With the exception of attorneys taking on (state-funded) *pro bono* cases (*see infra*, paragraph 431), attorneys are paid by their clients, irrespective of the outcome of the proceedings.[189] The 'winning' party, however, may recover (part of) his attorney's fees from the 'losing' party. The compensation for attorney's fees and expenses is limited to a fixed lump sum indemnification (*indemnité de procedure – rechtsplegingsvergoeding*), which is awarded by the court to the prevailing party (*see also infra*, paragraph 436). Hence, an entire recovery of the attorney's fee is not always

182. Article 440, para. 2, Judicial Code; *see* also Court of Cassation 12 February 2016, F.14.0223.F. For the performance of certain procedural acts, however, a special authorisation from the client is required. For instance, to waive a claim or to agree to settle with the court's decision. In this event, the burden of proof lies with the party who wishes to rely on the attorney's authority (Court of Cassation 6 April 2016, P.16.0299.F).
183. The Judicial Code provides for a special procedure enabling parties to rebut that presumption (Articles 849–850 Judicial Code – *see* further *infra* , paras 415–418).
184. Court of Cassation 3 May 2011, P.10.1865.N; Court of Cassation 27 April 2010, P.10.0512.N; compare with Court of Cassation 9 November 2011, P.11.1027.F.
185. Article 478 *juncto* Article 1080 Judicial Code. Their number is limited to twenty. They are appointed by the King upon recommendation of an advisory commission that may present for each vacancy a list of three candidates for appointment. Candidates must have at least ten years professional experience at the bar and have passed an exam organised by the bar of the Court of Cassation (Articles 478*bis* and 478*ter* Judicial Code). They are neither employees of the Court of Cassation, nor are they part of it. They serve as a filter, ensuring the high quality standard of the cassation appeals.
186. Article 440, para. 1, Judicial Code. *See* also Article 728, §4, Judicial Code.
187. Article 728, §2, Judicial Code.
188. Article 728, §3, Judicial Code.
189. As of 1 January 2014, attorneys are subject to VAT, so parties are also charged with the VAT (at a rate of 21%) owed on the attorney's fees.

guaranteed. The part not covered by the fixed lump sum indemnification remains at the expense of the party.

133. Article 446*ter* of the Judicial Code states that attorneys shall estimate their fees with the modesty that may be expected from their profession. Factors that may influence the calculation of fees are, *inter alia*, the size of the case, the nature of the tasks performed and the complexity of the issue in question. If the attorney's fees exceed the boundaries of fair moderation, the competent bar council (*see* further *infra*, paragraph 139) may reduce them, without prejudice to the right of the party to submit the case to the competent court.

134. Article 446*ter* of the Judicial Code prohibits contingency fee based agreements. This prohibition must be interpreted narrowly to target only such arrangements whereby the very existence of any kind of fee is made dependent upon the outcome of the litigation ('no cure, no pay') and whereby, if the case is won, the calculation of the fee is based exclusively on the level of damages awarded. The reason for this prohibition is that such agreements affect the attorney's independence in the handling of the case because he acquires a personal interest in its outcome.

III. Discipline

135. The ethical rules of conduct for attorneys are laid down in (binding) regulations issued by the bar associations and local bars. These rules consider, for instance, the attorney's independence, the obligations of integrity, discretion and confidentiality, etc.

136. Disciplinary sanctions are imposed by a disciplinary board. There is a disciplinary board in every judicial area (*see supra*, paragraphs 67 et seq.). The disciplinary rules are described in Articles 456–477 of the Judicial Code.

137. Complaints are to be filed with the president of the bar of which the attorney concerned is a member. The president may also initiate investigations ex officio.[190] If the president finds that there are reasons to summon the attorney before the disciplinary board, the case is referred to the disciplinary board. If the president considers the complaint to be inadmissible or ill-founded, no further action will be taken. Both the attorney and the complainant are informed of the decision to dismiss the complaint. The complainant can challenge this decision within a period of three months.[191]

138. Disciplinary sanctions vary from a simple warning to a suspension for a year and the removal from the bar.[192] The decisions of the disciplinary boards can be reviewed by the disciplinary boards of appeal.[193]

190. Article 458, §1, para. 1, Judicial Code.
191. Article 458, §2, Judicial Code.
192. Article 460 Judicial Code.
193. Of which there are two: one for the appeals against the decisions of the Dutch-speaking disciplinary boards and one for the appeals against the decisions of the French- and German-speaking disciplinary boards (Articles 464–468 Judicial Code).

§2. Organisation of the Profession

139. Every attorney must be member of a local bar (*Ordre des Avocats – Orde van Advocaten*). Until recently, there used to be a local bar in every judicial district.[194] When the judicial districts were merged in 2014 (*see infra*, paragraphs 25 and 68), the bar associations were left the choice whether they wanted to join in on the merger. Only a few associations have merged so far.[195]

140. Every bar elects a bar council (*Conseil de l'Ordre – Raad van de Orde*) and a president (*bâtonnier – stafhouder*) from among its members for a term of one year. The bar council is responsible for the general management of the bar, which includes, *inter alia*, the organisation of the legal aid system in its territory, the enrolment of (trainee) attorneys and the mitigation of exaggerated fees. The president is responsible for the day-to-day management of the bar. He also considers complaints about the attorneys of his bar (*see supra*, paragraph 137).

141. All local bars of the Dutch-speaking community are grouped into the Flemish Bar Association (*Orde van Vlaamse Balies*), whereas the French and German Bar Association (*Ordre des barreaux francophones et germanophone – Kammer der französischsprachigen und deutschsprachigen Rechtsanwaltschaften)* encompasses the French- and German-speaking local bars. The role of the respective associations is to promote the collective interests of its members, as well as to issue regulations regarding the legal profession (including disciplinary and deontological rules), which are binding upon its members (*see supra*, paragraph 135).

194. The attorneys who are admitted to practice before the Court of Cassation have their own bar.
195. For instance, on 1 September 2016, the bars of Hasselt and Tongeren were merged into the bar of Limburg.

Chapter 3. Bailiffs

§1. Exercise of the Profession

142. Bailiffs (*huissier de justice – gerechtsdeurwaarder*) have a dual professional identity: on the one hand, they are public officials, appointed by the King; on the other hand, they are practitioners of a self-employed activity. They are public officials because a share of official authority has been delegated to them. Only bailiffs have the authority to carry out the service of writs of summons, as well as the enforcement of judgments, court orders and other enforceable titles, including the seizure of property.[196] Bailiffs are also called upon to establish certain material facts at the request of private persons. For instance, in the context of divorce proceedings, the most secure way to establish adultery is through a bailiff's writ.[197]

143. The bailiffs' office is said to be mandatory, i.e., they are obligated to deliver their services when requested, unless there are legal reasons not to do so.[198] Bailiffs may only act within the judicial district in which they are appointed by the King.[199] Any acts performed outside of the district's border are considered to be null and void.

144. The legal status of the bailiffs was changed considerably by the Act of 7 January 2014,[200] which aimed at attaining greater objectivity as to their appointment,[201] as well as their disciplinary system.[202]

§2. Organisation of the Profession

145. There is a bailiff's district chamber (*chambre d'arrondissement des huissiers de justice – arrondissementskamer van gerechtsdeurwaarders*) in every judicial district,[203] which is composed of all the bailiffs stationed in that district. The chamber is managed by a council, which is presided over by a syndic.[204] The council's tasks are described in Article 552 of the Judicial Code and include, *inter alia*, the maintenance of good order and discipline among its members and the prevention and settlement of any disputes that may arise between them.

---

196. Article 519, §1, para. 1, Judicial Code.
197. Article 1016*bis* Judicial Code.
198. Article 519, §1, para. 1, Judicial Code.
199. Article 516 Judicial Code.
200. *Belgian Official Gazette*, 22 January 2014.
201. Articles 510–515 Judicial Code. A candidate bailiff must hold a Master's or Doctor's degree in law and must have completed a two-year training period in a bailiff's office.
202. Articles 533–548 Judicial Code.
203. Article 549, §1, Judicial Code. There is, however, a joint chamber for the districts of Verviers and Eupen.
204. Article 551 Judicial Code.

146. There is also a Belgian National Association of Bailiffs (*Chambre nationale des huissiers de justice de Belgique – Nationale Kamer van Gerechtsdeurwaarders*), which is a national representative organisation that promotes and defends the collective interests of the bailiffs.

Part III. Jurisdiction

Chapter 1. Jurisdiction

§1. Subject Matter Jurisdiction

I. Factors to Be Taken into Account

A. General, Specific and Exclusive Jurisdiction

147. The courts' subject matter jurisdiction is dependent on four factors: the nature of the claim, its (economic) value, its urgency and the legal status of the parties involved.[205] Most courts have a general jurisdiction, in addition to some specific or exclusive competences. Whereas the value of the claim is decisive with regard to a court's general jurisdiction, the specific and exclusive competences are mainly determined by the nature of the claim. The urgency of the claim is only relevant with regard to summary proceedings. The parties' legal status is an element of the Commercial Court's general jurisdiction.

148. The value of the claim is determined by the amount of money claimed in the act instituting the proceedings.[206] If the value of the claim is modified in the course of the proceedings, this will not affect the jurisdiction of the court before which the case is pending. If there is more than one claim or claimant, all claims are joined together in order to determine the value of the claim.[207] If, however, the claim is part of a larger debt of the defendant, the jurisdiction of the court is determined on the basis of the amount of the entire debt.[208]

B. Functionality, Specialisation and Public Policy

149. The distribution of powers between the courts is functional. Its goal is to safeguard the sound administration of justice, by ensuring that disputes are adjudicated by their 'natural judge', i.e., a judge who has the expertise and know-how required to

205. Article 9 Judicial Code.
206. Article 557 Judicial Code.
207. Articles 558 and 560 Judicial Code.
208. Article 559 Judicial Code.

deal with the case. The judiciary's pyramidal structure is inherently characterised by specialisation: each court has jurisdiction over specific types of cases: civil, criminal, commercial or labour. Over the years, the courts have been assigned additional specific competences. Reasons relating to substantive law, as well as reasons of expertise or location of the court are at the root of these additional competence allocations. This is, for example, the case for the courts of Brussels. The Brussels courts have exclusive jurisdiction (for the whole country) over several kinds of specific claims and procedures, such as claims regarding nuclear and oil pollution liability and consumer class action procedures (as for the latter, *see infra*, paragraph 328). In some cases, however, the allocation of jurisdiction has been nothing more than an arbitrary shift of caseload, thereby compromising the intended specialisation and transparency of the rules of jurisdiction. A textbook example of this is the shift of jurisdiction regarding collective debt settlement procedures from the judge of attachments to the Labour Court (*see also infra*, paragraphs 559–563).

150. The subject matter jurisdiction of the courts is a matter of public policy. Any deviating agreements between the parties are to be considered null and void. The court's lack of jurisdiction may be raised at any moment in the course of the proceedings, either on the court's own motion or at the initiative of the parties.[209] It is also a ground for appeal and further appeal.

II. Main Claims and Ancillary Claims

A. Main Claims

151. The subject matter jurisdiction is determined by the main claim (*demande principale – hoofdvordering*), i.e., the claim made by the plaintiff in the act instituting the proceedings.

B. Ancillary Claims

152. Ancillary claims (*demande incidente – tussenvordering*) are claims brought before the court in the course of the proceedings with the view to change the initial claim, to initiate a new claim (by either of the parties) or to involve third parties in the dispute.[210] These ancillary claims may influence the court's (initial) jurisdiction.

1. Extension or Modification of the Original Claim

153. An extension or modification of the original claim does not affect the jurisdiction of the court before which the case is pending, provided that the court's jurisdiction has been determined on the basis of the value of the initial claim, and the modified or new claim is also expressed in terms of money, and no rules of specific or exclusive jurisdiction are applicable to the new (modified) claim (*see also supra*, paragraph 148).

---

209. Article 854 Judicial Code.
210. Article 13 Judicial Code.

2. Counterclaim

154. The defendant can initiate a counterclaim (*demande reconventionelle – tegenvordering*). The initial court has jurisdiction with regard to this counterclaim under the circumstances described in Article 563 of the Judicial Code:

1° The Court of First Instance has jurisdiction over all counterclaims, irrespective of their nature or value, except when the counterclaim pertains to the exclusive jurisdiction of another court.

- The Labour Court, the Commercial Court, the Justice of the Peace Court and the Police Court have jurisdiction over all counterclaims if the subject of the counterclaim, irrespective of its value, falls within the scope of the court's general jurisdiction or ensues from the same contract or the same set of facts underpinning the initial (main) claim.
- All courts have jurisdiction over counterclaims asserting the reckless and provocative nature of another party's claim.

3. Claim in Intervention

155. Claims in intervention (*demande en intervention – vordering tot tussenkomst*) aim at involving a third party to the pending proceedings. The intervention of the third party can happen voluntarily (i.e., at the third party's initiative) or compulsory (i.e., at the initiative of (one of) the original parties).[211]

156. Claims in intervention always belong to the jurisdiction of the court before which these claims are made.[212]

C. Parallel Proceedings (Lis Pendens)

157. The rule of *lis pendens* (*litispendance – aanhangigheid*) states that where two claims involving the same parties, the same cause of action, and the same set of facts are being considered by two different courts, one of these courts must, either on its own motion or at the request of one of the parties, refer the case in favour of the other court.[213]

158. Article 565, paragraph 2, of the Judicial Code sets up a priority system for determining the competent court:

1° The Family Court has priority in all matters referred to in Article 629bis, §1, of the Judicial Code (this is the priority of the Family Court before which a family-related claim regarding the same family has previously been filed – see also infra, paragraph 176);

---

211. Article 813 Judicial Code.
212. Article 564 Judicial Code.
213. Article 29 *juncto* 565, para. 1, Judicial Code.

2° The Justice of the Peace Court has priority in all matters referred to in Articles 628, 3° and 629quater of the Judicial Code (this is the priority of the Justice of the Peace Court of the place of residence or habitual domicile of the unqualified person or underage child for claims regarding that person or child);

3° The court that has already rendered a (substantive) judgment with regard to the case has priority;

4° The Court of First Instance has priority over the other courts;

5° The Labour Court has priority over the Commercial Court;

6° The Labour Court and the Commercial Court have priority over the Justice of the Peace Court;

7° The Justice of the Peace Court has priority over the Police Court;

8° The court first seized has priority over the court before which the claim was brought later, upon the condition that both courts rank equally,[214] otherwise the priority rules of Article 565, paragraph 2, 1°-7° of the Judicial Code remain applicable.

If, however, one of the claims pertains to the exclusive jurisdiction of one of the courts seized, the claims must be joined before this court.[215]

D. Related Actions

159. The rule regarding related actions (*connexité – samenhang*) states that where two or more claims are closely related (but not identical), it is appropriate to consolidate them in order to avoid conflicting judgments.[216]

160. Two situations can be distinguished:

1. Two or More Claims Pending Before Different Courts

161. One of the parties can raise the issue of the close correlation between the claims and ask the court to refer the case to the other court, taking into account the

214. Court of Cassation 10 May 1979, *Arresten van het Hof van Cassatie* 1978–1979, 1084.
215. Article 565, para. 3, Judicial Code.
216. Article 30 *juncto* Article 566 Judicial Code.

priority rules of Article 565, paragraph 2, 1°– 2° and 4°–8° of the Judicial Code (*see supra*, paragraph 158).

2. Two or More Claims Pending Before the Same Court

i Initiated by the Same Act

162. The act instituting the proceedings may contain several claims, provided that they are closely related and taking into account the abovementioned priority rules.[217]

ii Initiated by Different Acts

163. The consolidation of the claims can be ordered ex officio by the court.[218]

III. Overview of the Jurisdiction of the Different Courts

A. First Instance Courts

164. Belgium has five first instance courts: Justice of the Peace Courts, Police Courts, Courts of First Instance, Commercial Courts and Labour Courts.

165. The Justice of the Peace Court is a small claims court. It has general jurisdiction over all claims that do not exceed EUR 2,500,[219] provided that these claims do not belong to the specific or exclusive jurisdiction of another court. The Justice of the Peace Court is also regarded as a proximity court, due to its accessibility and informal atmosphere. Therefore, it has a specific jurisdiction over certain disputes, irrespective of the amount of the claim,[220] such as disputes regarding immovable property (such as lease and the use and administration of jointly owned property), neighbour disputes and actions regarding the protection and guardianship of unqualified (i.e., mentally disabled) persons.

166. The Police Court is a traffic court. In addition to its traditional criminal jurisdiction regarding traffic offences, it has been provided with exclusive jurisdiction in civil matters for all compensatory claims, irrespective of their value, relating to traffic accidents.[221] It also has a specific jurisdiction with regard to certain matters, such as the hearing of appeals against municipal administrative sanctions.[222]

---

217. Article 701 Judicial Code.
218. Article 856 Judicial Code.
219. Article 590 Judicial Code. The statutory limit was recently expanded from € 1,860 to € 2,500 in order to re-balance the workload after the transfer of the Justice of the Peace Court's jurisdiction over family-related disputes to the newly established Family Court.
220. Articles 591 and 594 Judicial Code.
221. Article 601*bis* Judicial Code.
222. Article 601*ter* Judicial Code.

167. The Court of First Instance consists of three (or four)[223] branches or sections, two of which deal with civil matters: the Civil Court and the Family and Juvenile Court.[224]

The Civil Court has the power to adjudicate all civil claims, except for the ones that pertain to the exclusive jurisdiction of another court or that are to be brought directly before the Court of Appeal or the Court of Cassation. This implies that the Civil Court can judge cases belonging to the general or specific subject matter jurisdiction of another court, as well as cases for which no other court has jurisdiction. Therefore, the Civil Court is said to dispose of a full general jurisdiction (*plénitude de jurisdiction – volheid van bevoegdheid*).[225] The full general jurisdiction of the Civil Court is limited, however, by the possibility for the defendant to dispute the jurisdiction of the Civil Court and request that the case be referred to the court which has the general or specific jurisdiction over the case. This request must be made in the first pleadings.[226] In addition, the Civil Court also has exclusive jurisdiction over a number of claims, such as requests for the granting of a declaration of enforceability (exequatur) in respect of foreign judgments.[227]

The Family and Juvenile Court consists of chambers for juvenile matters, which constitute the Juvenile Court, and chambers for family matters (including amicable settlement chambers), which constitute the Family Court. The Juvenile Court handles juvenile matters.[228] The Family Court is a newly established section within the Court of First Instance (operational since 1 September 2014) that has a specific jurisdiction over family-related disputes in the broadest sense, regardless of the value of the claim.[229] Prior to the establishment of the Family Court, the jurisdiction regarding family matters used to be scattered across multiple courts. By creating the Family Court the Belgian legislature wanted to bring an end to this fragmentation, as well as to allocate all family-related disputes to a specialised judge.

Every Court of First Instance also accommodates one or more judges of attachments, who have exclusive jurisdiction over attachments for sale (*see infra*, paragraphs 502–547) and preliminary seizures (*see infra*, paragraphs 473–501).[230]

It should be stressed that the different sections of the Court of First Instance, as well as the judge(s) of attachments, form part of one and the same court. Hence,

223. As explained above, there is a fourth branch or section in the Courts of First Instance that are located in the same city where a Court of Appeal is vested, i.e., the Sentence Enforcement Court (*see supra* , para. 75).
224. Note, however, that the Criminal Court is competent to rule over the civil law consequences of the criminal offence in question.
225. Article 568, para. 1, Judicial Code.
226. Article 568, para. 2, Judicial Code. *See* also Court of Cassation 16 November 2012, C.08.0589.N.
227. Articles 569–571 Judicial Code. However, the granting of a declaration of enforceability of foreign judgments concerning insolvency matters, belongs to the jurisdiction of the Commercial Courts (Article 121 Code of Private International Law *juncto* Article 570, para. 2, Judicial Code).
228. Within the meaning of the Act of 8 April 1965 on the protection of young persons, the care for minors who have committed an act that qualifies as an offence and the reparation of damages caused by that offence (*Belgian Official Gazette*, 15 April 1965).
229. Article 572*bis* Judicial Code.
230. Article 1395 Judicial Code.

disputes regarding the distribution of powers between the different sections (or between one of them and the judge of attachments) are not jurisdiction conflicts, but are merely a matter of internal allocation of cases. Hence, the addressed judge cannot decline its jurisdiction, but the 'allocation dispute' is settled in accordance with the (simple) procedure laid down in Article 88, §2, of the Judicial Code (*see supra*, paragraph 82).

168. The Labour Court has specific jurisdiction with regard to matters of individual labour law and social security law, regardless of the value of the claim.[231] In principle, it has no jurisdiction with regard to matters of collective labour law, being conflicts that go beyond the individual employer-employee relationship (such as a strike or lockout). The Belgian legislature preferred that these disputes would be solved by means of negotiations and has therefore decided to keep those disputes away from the judiciary as a whole.

The Labour Court has also been provided with jurisdiction over a specific type of insolvency proceedings, namely the collective debt settlement procedure (*règlement collectif de dettes – collectieve schuldenregeling*). This procedure gives over-indebted private individuals the opportunity to reorganise their finances and re-establish their economic capability under the supervision of a court-appointed debt mediator (*see infra*, paragraphs 559–563).[232]

169. The Commercial Court has general jurisdiction to adjudicate all disputes between enterprises – defined as entities durably pursuing an economic goal – in relation to an action that was performed in pursuance of that goal, irrespective of the monetary value of the claim.[233] It also has exclusive jurisdiction over insolvency proceedings for enterprises, such as bankruptcy and judicial reorganisation. The latter aims at rescuing enterprises with difficulties by means of a recovery plan drawn up under court supervision.[234]

B. Appellate Courts and Court of Cassation

170. The courts of appeal have jurisdiction to hear appeals against judgments rendered in first instance by the Courts of First Instance and by the Commercial Courts.[235] The Labour Courts of Appeal hear appeals against judgments rendered in first instance by the Labour Courts.[236] Decisions rendered in first instance by the Justice of the Peace Courts and Police Courts are to be appealed, however, before the Court of First Instance (and not before the (Labour) Court of Appeal).[237]

---

231. Articles 578–583 Judicial Code.
232. Article 578, 14°, Judicial Code.
233. Article 573, para. 1, 1°, Judicial Code. The term 'enterprises' is to be interpreted broadly and also includes, among others, the liberal professions (e.g., attorneys) and non-profit organisations (e.g., hospitals, nursing homes). *See* B. Allemeersch & T. Reingraber, 'De bevoegdheids(her) verdeling' in B. Allemeersch, P. Taelman, P. Van Orshoven & B. Vanlerberghe (ed.), *Nieuwe Justitie*, Antwerp-Cambridge, Intersentia, 2014, 47–80.
234. *See* the Continuity of Enterprises Act of 31 January 2009 (*Belgian Official Gazette*, 9 February 2009).
235. Article 602, 1° and 2° Judicial Code.
236. Article 607 Judicial Code.
237. Article 577 Judicial Code.

171. The Court of Cassation is Belgium's judicial Supreme Court. It has jurisdiction over further appeals, i.e., appeals against judgments rendered in last instance.[238] It also deals with certain specific procedures, such as conflicts of attribution (i.e., jurisdictional conflicts between the ordinary and administrative courts), requests for annulment of regulations of the bar associations[239] and the removal of a judge from the case.[240]

172. The scope of the review of the appellate courts and the Court of Cassation, as well as the procedure before these courts, is discussed further below (*see infra*, paragraphs 350–378).

§2. Venue (Territorial Jurisdiction)

I. Factors to Be Taken into Account

A. General (Default) Rules

173. As mentioned above, the civil courts are spread throughout the national territory (*see supra*, paragraph 68). Every court's power to adjudicate disputes is limited by the boundaries of the area which has been conferred to it by law.[241] Hence, the plaintiff must not only determine which is the materially competent court, but he must also identify that court's location.

174. In principle, the rules governing the courts' territorial jurisdiction are supplementary rules of law, meaning that they can be overridden by contract or other legally effective agreement. It is common practice in Belgium to insert choice of forum clauses in (standard) contracts. In the absence of such forum selection agreement, the plaintiff has the choice to initiate his claim before the court of: (1) the domicile of the defendant or one of them, if there are multiple defendants; (2) the place where the disputed contract has been concluded or has been or must be performed; (3) the place that has been chosen for the performance of the contract; or (4) the place where the bailiff has served the writ of summons in the event that the defendant does not have a known domicile in Belgium or abroad.[242]

B. Specific (Mandatory and Public Policy) Rules

175. In some cases, the court's territorial jurisdiction is governed by mandatory rules of law. In this event, the parties can still conclude an agreement with respect to

---

238. Article 608 Judicial Code.
239. Article 501 *juncto* Article 611 Judicial Code.
240. Articles 609–615 Judicial Code.
241. Articles 10 and 622 Judicial Code.
242. Article 624 Judicial Code. These rules do not apply in case of summary proceedings. As these proceedings are, by their nature, urgent, they may be instituted before the president of the court located in the place where the (future) decision has to be executed (Court of Cassation 22 December 1989, AR 6707, *Rechtskundig Weekblad* 1989–1990, 1087).

the competent court, but only after the dispute has arisen.[243] The mandatory jurisdiction rules are laid down in Articles 627–629*quater* of the Judicial Code. The venue is often linked to the place where a certain fact has happened or a certain act was performed (e.g., the court of the employee's workplace has jurisdiction with regard to disputes between employer and employee). In other cases, the venue is determined in accordance with a certain person's domicile or place of residence (e.g., claims regarding maintenance obligations towards an underage child are to be brought before the Family Court of that child's domicile or habitual place of residence, provided that no Family Court has previously been seized with a family-related claim regarding the same family and parties have not concluded any forum selection agreement).

176. Only in exceptional cases, the court's territorial jurisdiction is a matter of public policy, in which event the parties may not under any circumstance choose their own forum (and the court must examine its jurisdiction on its own motion). These rules are elabourated in Articles 631–633*decies* of the Judicial Code. For example, any claims between parties who are (or have been) married or are (or have been) legal cohabitants and claims for maintenance obligations relating to their children are to be made to the Family Court before which a family-related claim regarding that same family has previously been filed. The underlying idea of this jurisdiction rule is that, as soon as a certain Family Court has been seized, the same court should retain jurisdiction for all (future) disputes regarding the same family. This is the principle of the so-called territorial immutability of the Family Court, which is a matter of public policy.[244]

II. Main Claims and Ancillary Claims

177. The rules set out above with regard to the courts' subject matter jurisdiction apply accordingly (*see supra*, paragraphs 151–163).[245]

§3. (Resolution of) Jurisdiction Conflicts

I. Jurisdiction Conflicts at the First Instance Level

178. Jurisdiction conflicts are time-consuming and are therefore to be resolved as quickly as possible. The Belgian civil justice system provides for a special non-permanent court, namely the District Court, which has as its only task to resolve jurisdiction conflicts. The District Court is composed of four members: the president

243. Whereas the default rules can be overridden prior to the arising of any dispute.

244. Upon request of a party or the public prosecutor's office, the Family Court can refer the case to the Family Court in another judicial district where a youth record of one of the persons involved in the pending family dispute has been opened. Moreover, the Family Court can, on its own motion, for reasons of good administration of justice decide to refer the case to the Family Court in another judicial district (Article 629*bis*, §7 Judicial Code).

245. Article 634 Judicial Code.

of the Court of First Instance, the president of the Labour Court, the president of the Commercial Court and the president of the Justice of the Peace Courts and the Police Courts or a judge appointed by one of them, with an alternating presidency.[246] In case of equalling of votes, the vote of the judge presiding the District Court will be decisive. The District Court only convenes when it is asked to rule about a jurisdiction conflict. Its decisions are not appealable. Only the public prosecutor at the Court of Appeal may lodge an appeal with the Court of Cassation.[247]

179. A court's jurisdiction may be challenged by one of the parties or by the court on its own motion. The latter is only possible if the relevant jurisdiction rule is a matter of public policy and has not been invoked by one of the parties. If the jurisdiction issue is raised by the court on its own motion, the issue is referred to the District Court.[248] The District Court's decision is binding on the court to which the case is remanded. The same applies if the jurisdiction issue is raised by one of the parties,[249] provided that the opposite party requests that the issue is referred to the District Court. In all other cases, for instance, in the absence of any response from the opposite party, the jurisdiction issue is settled by the court itself, which shall, if necessary, refer the case to the competent court. The latter is bound by the referral and cannot decline its jurisdiction.[250]

II. Jurisdiction Conflicts at the Appellate Level

180. If a jurisdiction issue is raised at the appellate level, the Court of Appeal or Labour Court of Appeal itself will decide upon the issue and, as the case may be, refer the case to the competent appellate court.[251]

In case a jurisdiction conflict is raised before the Court of First Instance, acting as an appellate instance over a decision rendered in first instance by a Justice of the Peace Court or a Police Court, the rules explained above under paragraphs 178–179 are applicable.

246. Article 74 Judicial Code.
247. Article 642 Judicial Code.
248. Article 640 Judicial Code.
249. The jurisdiction issue must, in principle, be raised in the party's first pleadings. If the issue, however, relates to jurisdiction rules which are considered to be of public policy, it can be raised at any stage of the trial (Articles 854–855 Judicial Code).
250. Article 639 Judicial Code.
251. Article 643 Judicial Code.

Chapter 2. International Jurisdiction

181. Whether or not the Belgian courts have jurisdiction over a cross-border dispute is determined by the *lex fori*, i.e., the laws of the jurisdiction where the legal action is brought, which consists of treaties, regulations and national (private international) rules of law.

182. Roughly speaking,[252] the rules of international jurisdiction may be governed by (1) EU Regulations, of which the most important one in this area is the Regulation No. 1215/2012 of 12 December 2012 on Jurisdiction and the Recognition and Enforcement of Judgments in Civil and Commercial Matters;[253] (2) bilateral and international treaties, which have lost most of their importance due to the introduction of the aforementioned European instruments; or (3) the Belgian Code of Private International Law of 2004,[254] for cases in which neither the EU regulations nor any other international instrument do apply.

§1. Rules Applicable in the Absence of a Treaty

183. The Code of Private International Law introduced a complete system of grounds for international jurisdiction for claims introduced in Belgium after 1 October 2004.

184. The general rule is that the Belgian courts have jurisdiction if the defendant has his domicile or habitual place of residence in Belgium at the time of the initiation of the proceedings.[255] If, however, the substance of the claim is covered by an EU regulation, the defendant's domicile in Belgium will normally trigger the application of the EU regulation. Hence, this *forum rei* rule is of limited scope in practice.

185. The Code allows for forum choice agreements conferring jurisdiction on the Belgian courts.[256] The Belgian courts, however, may deny their jurisdiction if any relevant connection with Belgium is lacking (this is the forum non conveniens principle).[257]

186. The parties may also agree to exclude the jurisdiction of the Belgian courts by giving jurisdiction to one or more foreign courts. In this event, the Belgian court before which the case is pending must declare itself without jurisdiction unless it is foreseeable that the foreign court's decision would not be eligible for recognition and enforcement in Belgium.[258]

252. *See* for a more detailed account: J. Erauw, *Private International Law*, in *Introduction to Belgian Law* 413–448 (M. Kruithof & W. De Bondt eds, Kluwer Law International 2017).
253. *Official Journal* L351/1 of 2012.
254. Introduced by the Act of 16 July 2004 and entered into force on 1 October 2004.
255. Article 5 Code of Private International Law.
256. Article 6, §1, Code of Private International Law.
257. Article 6, §2, Code of Private International Law.
258. Article 7 Code of Private International Law.

187. The Code also provides that the Belgian courts have jurisdiction to grant urgent or interlocutory relief with respect to persons or property located in the Belgium, even if they would not have jurisdiction to adjudicate on the merits of the case.[259]

188. Furthermore, the Code introduced the novelty that the Belgian courts can take up jurisdiction based on the notion of the 'necessity to intervene', i.e., if litigating abroad would be impossible or if it would be unreasonable to demand that the procedure is conducted before a foreign court.[260] This may be the case if it is highly likely that litigating before the foreign court will not ensure that justice is done, for instance, due to wide-spread corruption or civil war.

189. In the event that the Belgian courts have international jurisdiction, the court's local jurisdiction is established in accordance with the general rules of the Judicial Code (*see supra*, paragraphs 173–176).[261]

§2. International Treaties

190. The rules of the Code of Private International Law apply only when a dispute does not fall within the scope of one of the EU Regulations or bilateral and international treaties. As to the latter, Belgium is still party to a few treaties containing jurisdiction rules, for example, the bilateral treaties concluded with France, the Netherlands, Germany and Italy (which are still applicable, but only within the (narrow) margin left by the EU Regulations) and some multilateral treaties in the field of transportation, air-travel and international law of the sea.

191. As far as the EU Regulations are concerned, it is a clear purpose and goal of the European Union to establish more judicial cooperation in civil matters.[262] This cooperation seeks to eliminate obstacles deriving from incompatibilities between the various legal systems, and thus facilitate access to justice. Its cornerstone is the principle of mutual recognition and enforcement of judgments and of decisions resulting from extrajudicial cases (*see infra*, paragraphs 556–558).

192. In the area of international jurisdiction, the most important EU instrument is the abovementioned Regulation No. 1215/2012 of 12 December 2012 on Jurisdiction and the Recognition and Enforcement of Judgments in Civil and Commercial Matters. This is the so-called Brussels I*bis*-Regulation, which is a recast of the Brussels I-Regulation No. 44/2011 of 22 December 2000.[263] The general rule is that jurisdiction is conferred upon the courts of the Member State in which the defendant is domiciled, regardless of his nationality.[264] Articles 62 and 63 of the Regulation set out the criteria

259. Article 10 Code of Private International Law.
260. Article 11 Code of Private International Law.
261. Article 13 Code of Private International Law.
262. *See* Title V of the Treaty on the Functioning of the European Union. *See* also 'The Stockholm Programme. An open and secure Europe serving and protecting citizens', *Official Journal* C115/1 of 2010 and Decision No. 1149/2007/EC of 25 September 2007 establishing for the period 2007–2013 the Specific Programme 'Civil Justice' as part of the General Programme 'Fundamental Rights and Justice', *Official Journal* L257/16 of 2007.
263. *Official Journal* L12/1 of 2001.
264. Article 4 Regulation No. 1215/2012.

for determining whether the defendant's domicile is located in the country of a given Member State. Parties may, however, deviate from this general rule by concluding forum choice agreements, which take priority over the general rule, provided that the dispute does not fall within the list of topics mentioned under Article 24, for which mandatory and exclusive fora are imposed.

193. For some areas, specific EU regulations have been issued:

- Regulation No. 2015/848 of 20 May 2015 on Insolvency Proceedings:[265] this regulation establishes a common framework for insolvency proceedings in the EU, the purpose of which is to avoid assets being transferred from one Member State to the other in order to obtain a more favourable legal position, to the detriment of the creditors; in general, jurisdiction is conferred on the courts of the Member State where the debtor has his centre of main interests.
- Regulation No. 2012/650 of 4 July 2012 on Jurisdiction, Applicable Law, Recognition and Enforcement of Decisions and Acceptance and Enforcement of Authentic Instruments in Matters of Succession and on the Creation of a European Certificate of Succession:[266] an effort was made in order to obtain a parallel between competent forum and applicable law, so that the court having jurisdiction can apply its national law as the singular law of the succession.
- Regulation No. 4/2009 of 18 December 2008 on Jurisdiction, Applicable Law, Recognition and Enforcement of Decisions and Cooperation in Matters relating to Maintenance Obligations:[267] this regulation provides for a series of measures aimed at facilitating the payment of maintenance claims (arising from a family relationship, parentage, marriage or affinity) in cross-border situations; as a main rule, jurisdiction lies with the court of the place where either the defendant or creditor is habitually resident, or with the court which has jurisdiction for the proceedings over the status or the matter relating to parental responsibility to which the maintenance obligation is related.
- Regulation No. 2201/2003 of 27 November 2003 concerning Jurisdiction and the Recognition and Enforcement of Judgments in Matrimonial Matters and the Matters of Parental Responsibility ('Brussels IIa-Regulation'):[268] this regulation established a full and separate system of jurisdictional rules in matters of marriage (annulment, divorce) and parental authority (custody, rights of access, guardianship, protection of a child or its property and child abduction); in general, matters relating to parental responsibility come under the jurisdiction of the courts of the Member State of habitual residence of the child; where a child's habitual residence cannot be established, the Member State in which the child is present will assume jurisdiction by default.

---

265. *Official Journal* L141/19 of 2015.
266. *Official Journal* L201/107 of 2012.
267. *Official Journal* L7/1 of 2009.
268. *Official Journal* L338/1 of 2003.

Part IV. Actions and Claims

Chapter 1. Actions

§1. Definition

194. The party's right to take legal action against another party requires the existence of a subjective right underpinning that action. The legal action (*actio*) enables the party to safeguard and enforce his subjective rights.

§2. Admissibility

195. The admissibility of the legal action is examined by the court before which the action is initiated.

196. Articles 17–18 of the Judicial Code provide for only two admissibility requirements: the party initiating a claim must have legal standing (*qualité – hoedanigheid*) and must demonstrate a legitimate, personal and immediate interest in bringing the case before the court (*intérêt – belang*).

197. Legal standing means that a party must have the power to initiate the action (this is the so-called *ius agendi*). A litigating party has legal standing if he is the holder of the contested subjective right. If, however, the holder of the contested right is represented in the proceedings by a third person (such as parents acting in respect of the person or goods of their underage children), said third person must prove that he has legal standing to defend the interests of the actual interested party.

198. The interest requirement means that the party bringing the action must show that the action may grant him a certain (material or moral) advantage. The interest has to be legitimate, personal and immediate. The latter implies that the interest must be more than merely possible; there must be a real ongoing dispute between the parties for the plaintiff to have an interest in having his rights recognised by the court. Exceptionally, an action regarding a (possible) future dispute may be admissible if it aims at preventing the violation of a 'seriously threatened right' ('*actio ad futurum*').

The requirement that the interest must be personal means that the party bringing the action must have a direct and individual right that he wants to see enforced. The protection of a general interest (e.g., the protection of 'the environment' or 'the consumer') is therefore not admissible. This requirement prevents organisations representing collective interests from taking legal action, as the mere fact that an organisation acts in order to promote its statutory goal does not amount to a personal and direct interest.[269] The legislature, however, has given the power to certain (public and private) organisations, that meet certain criteria, to bring injunctive or declaratory actions on behalf of the persons whose interests they represent. These actions only exist in a limited number of legal fields: consumer protection, environment, discrimination and racism. The group action, however, does not allow the 'group members', on whose behalf the action is brought, to recover their individual damages. If such a member wants damages, he will have to initiate an individual civil action. Furthermore, as of 1 September 2014, a collective mass claims settlement procedure has been made available in certain consumer law disputes. It allows a class representative to introduce an action for collective redress where a group of consumers has suffered harm. A notable feature of the procedure is that the interests of the individual consumers – who are not involved as parties in the procedure as such – are represented by a class representative. The (positive or negative) outcome of the procedure, however, will be binding on the individual consumers (*see infra*, paragraph 328).

199. A third important admissibility requirement is that the party bringing the action must have legal capacity (*capacité – bekwaamheid*) to do so. In principle, every person (whether a natural person or a legal entity) has capacity unless a statutory exception applies. A textbook example of a person lacking legal capacity is an underage child. The action will have to be brought by (or against) the child's legal representative, i.e., his parents.

§3. Vexatious Litigation

200. The sound administration of justice requires that a careful balance is struck between the right of access to justice on the one hand and the prevention (and sanctioning) of the misuse of the justice system on the other hand. Proceedings are vexatious if instituted maliciously and without probable cause.[270] Furthermore, a party's procedural behaviour as such, i.e., irrespective of the substance and/or the merits of the case, may also be considered as reckless or provocative.

201. Article 780*bis* of the Judicial Code provides that the party who has used the justice system for clearly wrongful or delaying purposes may be sentenced to a civil fine up to EUR 2,500, without prejudice to the right of the other party to submit a civil claim for damages.

269. Court of Cassation 25 October 1985, *Arresten van het Hof van Cassatie* 1985–1986, 249.
270. Court of Cassation 2 March 2015, C.14.0337.F; Court of Cassation 16 March 2012, C.08.0323.F-C.09.0590.F.

Chapter 2. Claims and Defences

§1. Definition

202. A claim, c.q., defence consists of three identifying elements: its object, its cause and the parties involved.

203. The object or '*petitum*' (*objet – voorwerp*) of the claim is the (material, moral or psychological) result or advantage that the parties seek to obtain.[271] The parties are responsible for specifying the relief sought; the court cannot ex officio change the object of the claim, nor can it grant a claim that was not expressed or grant more than was claimed (*see supra*, paragraph 34). The court may, however, ask questions to further clarify the parties' (factual and legal) allegations and claims.[272] The court's right to ask questions may – to a certain extent – influence the substantive outcome of the case, as the information resulting from the court's questioning may induce the parties to alter the object of their claim or introduce new claims.[273] Such alteration of the object of the claim or the introduction of new claims (if allowed in that stage of the proceedings), however, still has to be formally introduced by one of the parties.

204. The cause (*cause – oorzaak*) of the claim refers to the facts relied upon by the parties to substantiate the relief sought. The parties are responsible for providing the factual allegations on which their claim (or defence) is based. The court may not introduce new facts on its own motion. The court, however, has far-reaching powers with regard to the administration of evidence. The Belgian Judicial Code contains a wide range of techniques on the delivery and gathering of evidence with which facts asserted by the parties can be proven (such as the forced submission of documents, witness depositions, expert investigations, etc.). If the parties fail to produce (sufficient) evidence, the court may order, even on its own initiative, any investigation measure that can provide it with more certainty as to the substance of the claim. By doing so, however, the court may indirectly interfere with the cause of the claim, as new facts may 'result' from the court-ordered investigation measure. Provided that the court respects the rights of defence, it can base its decision on these facts, even though they have not been formally taken up by one of the parties.[274]

---

271. K. Broeckx, *Het recht op hoger beroep en het beginsel van de dubbele aanleg in het civiele geding*, Antwerp, Maklu, 1995, 283; J. Van Compernolle & G. Closset-Marchal, 'Examen de jurisprudence (1985–1996) – Droit judiciaire privé', *Revue Critique de Jurisprudence Belge* 1997, 535.
272. E. Krings, 'Het ambt van de rechter bij de leiding van het rechtsgeding', *Rechtskundig Weekblad* 1983–1984, 351 and 362.
273. G. de Leval, 'L'action en justice', in G. DE LEVAL (ed.), *Droit judiciaire*, II, *Manuel de procédure civile*, Larcier, 2015, 124.
274. W. Van Eeckhoutte, 'Schuifelen op de rechterstoel – De taak van de rechter in het belgisch privaatrechtelijk procesrecht: een kwestie van moeten of mogen', in VVSRBN (ed.), *Preadviezen 2015*, Boom, Den Haag, 2015, 289–295.

205. It is clear from the foregoing that the object and the cause of claim are essentially factual concepts. In accordance with the maxims of '*iura novit curia*' ('the court knows the law') and '*da mihi factum dabo tibi jus*' ('give me the facts and I shall give you the law'), it is up to the court to independently, i.e., regardless of the legal arguments of the parties (if any), and ex officio consider which legal rules are relevant and applicable to the case (*see supra*, paragraphs 43–45).

§2. Distinction

I. Different Kinds of Claims

206. Roughly, there are two kinds of claims: (1) the main claims, i.e., the claims made by the plaintiff in the act instituting the proceedings; and (2) the ancillary claims, i.e., the claims initiated in the course of the proceedings.

207. As to the ancillary claims, a further distinction is made on the basis of the object of the ancillary claim. There are ancillary claims which aim at (1) modifying or extending the initial claim; (2) initiating new claims (by either of the parties; if such new claim is initiated by the defendant, it is called a counterclaim); or (3) involving third parties to the proceedings (claims in intervention, which can be voluntarily (at the third party's initiative) or compulsory (at the initiative of (one of) the original parties) (*see also supra*, paragraphs 152–156).

208. The distinction between the various types of claims is important with regard to their admissibility, the court's jurisdiction (*see supra*, paragraphs 152–156) and the formal requirements to be complied with.

209. Article 807 of the Judicial Code stipulates that, in adversarial proceedings, the original claim can be extended or modified if the new or modified claim ensues from the same contract or the same set of facts underpinning the original claim.[275] Claims aiming at recovering interests, rent and other amounts of money that may fall due in the course of the proceedings may be initiated at any stage of the proceedings, even in case of default of the defendant.[276]

210. The conditions of Article 807 of the Judicial Code do not apply to counterclaims.[277] This means that a counterclaim is possible, even if it does not relate to the subject of the original (main) claim. If, however, the counterclaim could

275. Article 807 of the Judicial Code is to be considered as a supplementary statutory rule, meaning that the defendant can (tacitly or explicitly) approve an extension or modification of the claim that does not ensue from the same contract or the same set of facts underpinning the initial claim. The inadmissibility of such new or modified claim cannot be raised by the court ex officio.

276. Article 808 Judicial Code.

277. Court of Cassation 3 November 1972, *Arresten van het Hof van Cassatie* 1973, 218; Court of Cassation 26 May 1976, *Arresten van het Hof van Cassatie* 1976, 1067; Court of Cassation 30 March 1979, *Arresten van het Hof van Cassatie* 1978–1979, 900.

considerably delay the handling of the original claim, each claim is to be considered separately.[278]

211. Extensions or modifications of the original claim, as well as counterclaims are initiated by means of written pleadings, without the need for a (new) writ of summons.[279]

212. According to Article 812 of the Judicial Code, interventions are possible as long as the hearings have not been closed.[280] The intervention, however, may not prejudice the rights of defence of the intervening party. To this end, the court may order that certain investigation measures be carried out again. Furthermore, the intervention may not delay the handling of the original claim.[281] Voluntary claims in intervention are initiated by means of petition; compulsory claims in intervention require a (new) writ of summons.[282]

II. Different Kinds of Defences

213. The defendant may contest the claim made against him on its merits or by way of a plea. He can also introduce a counterclaim (*see supra*, paragraphs 154 and 210).

214. In a defence on the merits (*défense au fond – verweer ten gronde*), the defendant tackles the subject matter of the case by rebutting the (factual and/or legal) allegations and claims made by the plaintiff. This type of defence may be instituted at any stage of the proceedings and may, if successful, result in the definite end of the dispute.

215. The defendant who raises a plea does not object the merits of the claim at issue, but (only) the way in which the claim is brought before the court. If successful, a plea will prevent the court from an examination of the merits of the case.

216. A distinction is made between pleas that are purely procedural (*exception – exceptie*) and pleas that relate to the admissibility of the legal action (*fin de non-recevoir – middel van niet-toelaatbaarheid*). The first category of pleas may aim at merely suspending the proceedings (until certain (procedural) requirements are fulfilled)[283] or terminating them for procedural reasons. In the latter case, however, the authority of res judicata of the judgment is limited and does not prevent the plaintiff from initiating the same claim. Most procedural pleas must be raised before any other plea or defence ('*in limine litis*').[284] Pleas concerning the admissibility of the legal action, for instance, the plaintiff's lack of legal standing or the lack of a legitimate,

278. Article 810 Judicial Code.
279. Article 809 Judicial Code.
280. Claims in intervention aimed at obtaining an order against the intervening party, however, may not occur in appeal for the first time (Article 812, para. 2, Judicial Code).
281. Where appropriate, the plaintiff may ask the court to render judgment on the initial claim first and defer the claim in intervention to a later hearing (Article 814 Judicial Code).
282. Article 813 Judicial Code.
283. The failure of a party to disclose the documents on which he wishes to rely, for instance, may result in a staying of the proceedings (Article 736 Judicial Code).
284. Articles 854, 864 and 868–869 Judicial Code

personal and immediate interest of the plaintiff in bringing the case before the court (*see supra*, paragraphs 195–199), may usually be raised at any stage of the proceedings, but not for the first time before the Court of Cassation.[285]

285. Court of Cassation 18 October 2012, C.11.0761.F; compare with Court of Cassation 14 February 2014, C.12.0522.F.

Chapter 3. Sanctions on Procedural Irregularities

217. Two kinds of procedural irregularities (and their respective sanctions) are explicitly provided for in the Judicial Code, namely (1) the non-compliance with formal requirements; and (2) the non-compliance with time limits.

§1. Formal Requirements

218. The sanction for infringement of a formal requirement is the 'nullity' of the procedural act (*nullité – nietigheid*). This means that the procedural act is declared invalid and cannot produce any legal effects.

219. The essential feature of the sanction system, which is laid down in Articles 860–866 of the Judicial Code, is that the non-compliance with a procedural requirement should not automatically result in the imposing of sanctions. Sanctions may be imposed only where provided for by statute.[286] Furthermore, the court will ascertain the severity of the procedural irregularity and will impose a sanction only if the party entering the plea proves that his procedural interests (for instance, his rights of defence) have been harmed by the formal deficiency.[287] This implies that the court cannot sanction the procedural irregularity on its own motion, but only at the request of one of the parties. In addition, the plea for nullity must be raised before any other plea or defence.[288]

220. In an (ongoing) effort to speed up and simplify civil proceedings, the legislature has recently modified Article 863 of the Judicial Code. Said article provides that, whenever a signature is missing on a procedural document, the court shall order that the irregularity is corrected, but no sanction is imposed.

221. If procedural acts performed by public officials, such as bailiffs or notaries public, are declared null, the resulting costs are to be borne by the official concerned.[289] To all other persons, including attorneys, the general rules on civil liability are applicable.

§2. Time Limits

222. Court proceedings must be dealt with as quickly and efficiently as possible. To achieve this, the Judicial Code provides for most procedural acts to be performed within a certain time limit. The non-compliance with time limits may be sanctioned by the nullity of the procedural act (*see supra*, paragraphs 218–221), the loss of the right to perform the procedural action (*déchéance – verval*), or have no consequence at all.

286. Article 860 Judicial Code.
287. Article 861 Judicial Code.
288. Article 864 Judicial Code.
289. Article 866 Judicial Code.

I. Calculation

223. Generally, time limits are calculated starting from the day after the day of the act or event that triggers the running of the time limit (*dies a quo*)[290] until and including the last day, i.e., the day on which the time limit elapses (*dies ad quem*).[291] Time limits are calculated from midnight to midnight, respecting, however, the opening hours of the court registry.[292]

224. The Judicial Code applies a dual-date system for the calculation of a period which starts to run as of the notice or service of a paper-based document.

With regard to the addressee, the time limit is calculated with effect from (and unless the law stipulates otherwise): (1) the first day following that on which the judicial registered letter (i.e., a special type of registered letter with acknowledgement of receipt sent by the court registry)[293] or the registered letter with acknowledgment of receipt is presented at the place of residence of the addressee or, where applicable, at his domicile or address for service where service is effected by such letter; (2) the third working day following that on which the registered letter or ordinary letter is presented to the postal service, except where the addressee provides evidence to the contrary, where service is effected by such letter.

With regard to the person transmitting the document, the date of transmission (or the date of presentation of the document to the postal service or to the court registry) is regarded as the date of service.[294]

225. For time limits indicated in years or months, one must count from the day after the *dies a quo* until the day before such day in the next year or month.[295] For instance, when the event starting the time limit takes place on 15 February, the time limit itself will start on 16 February (the day after the *dies a quo*) and end on 15 March (the day before such day in the next month).

226. When the time limit expires on a Saturday, a Sunday or a public holiday,[296] it will be prolonged until the next working day.[297]

227. There exist a few exceptional circumstances in which the time limit may be prolonged (for instance, in favour of the party who has no place of residence or domicile in Belgium[298]), or suspended (for instance, due to the death of a party[299] or force majeure) (*see also infra*, paragraph 352). In addition, when the time limit begins

---

290. Article 52, para. 1, Judicial Code.
291. Article 53, para. 1, Judicial Code.
292. This restriction does not apply when procedural documents are transmitted electronically to the court registry (Article 52, para. 2, Judicial Code).
293. Article 46 Judicial Code.
294. Article 53*bis* Judicial Code.
295. Article 54 Judicial Code.
296. The public holidays are: 1 January (New Year's Day); Easter Sunday and Easter Monday (variable dates); 1 May (Labour Day); Ascension Day (sixth Thursday after Easter Sunday); Whitsun and Whit Monday (seventh Sunday and Monday after Easter Sunday); 21 July (national holiday); 15 August (Assumption); 1 November (All Saints Day); 11 November (Armistice WW I); 25 December (Christmas).
297. Article 53, para. 2, Judicial Code.
298. Article 55 Judicial Code. *See infra* para. 255.
299. Article 56 Judicial Code.

and ends during the judicial holidays (1 July-31 August[300]), it is (automatically) extended until the fifteenth day of the new judicial year (15 September).[301]

II. Sanctions

228. When time limits are sanctioned by the nullity of the procedural act in question, the conditions set out above with respect to formal deficiencies apply accordingly, meaning that the non-compliance with the time limit will only result in the nullity of the procedural act if the party raising the plea proves that his procedural interests have been prejudiced (*see supra*, paragraphs 218–221).

229. Time limits may also be sanctioned by the loss of the right to perform the procedural action in question. These are called peremptory time limits (*délai de forclusion – vervaltermijn*). This is the case for all time limits applicable to appellate remedies, which are provided for by law under the penalty of inadmissibility, which must be pronounced by the court *sua sponte*.[302]

230. In other cases, the Judicial Code does not provide for a sanction in case of non-compliance with a time limit. In this event, it is not clear which kind of sanction – if any – should be imposed.

300. Article 334 Judicial Code.
301. Article 50, para. 2, Judicial Code.
302. Article 860, para. 2, *juncto* Article 865 Judicial Code.

Part V. Proceedings

Chapter 1. Pre-trial Proceedings

§1. Access to Justice: Legal Aid and Legal Assistance

231. The Belgian justice system provides for several mechanisms available to people who do not have the resources needed to cover the costs of litigation. These mechanisms are available to both claimants and defendants.

A distinction must be made between legal aid and legal assistance.

232. Legal aid means that a person with limited resources is (entirely or partially) exempt from the payment of certain litigation costs (with the exception of attorney's fees), such as the various court fees, costs for the intervention of public officials, such as bailiffs, and expenses concerning investigation measures. The request for legal aid has to be made to the court that is competent to rule on the merits of the case. Within every court there is a bureau for legal aid (*bureau d'aide juridique – bureau voor rechtsbijstand*), i.e., a special chamber presided by a single judge that decides on the requests for legal aid. In the Justice of the Peace Court and the Police Court, however, where there is no such bureau, it is the judge himself who decides whether or not to grant the request.

233. Legal assistance means, *inter alia*, that a person with limited resources and in need for legal counsel is appointed an attorney whose services are paid (in full or in part)[303] by the Belgian State. The application for legal assistance has to be made to one of the bureaus for legal assistance, which are established within every local bar under the auspices of the respective bar councils.

234. For further information on legal aid, legal assistance and legal costs, *see* Part VI.

§2. Formal Notice

235. It is a general principle of Belgian law that the creditor should send a notice (*mise en demeure – ingebrekestelling*) to the debtor if he wants the debtor to carry out his obligations, at least if performance is still possible and useful for the creditor.

303. People whose resources are above a certain threshold have to pay a small non-refundable contribution.

§3. Pre-trial Settlement

236. Before initiating formal proceedings, one party may invite the other to an amicable settlement before the judge.[304] The request is made in writing or orally at the court registry, which will notify the parties of the date on which they are expected to appear in court for the settlement hearing. The court will then try to achieve an amicable settlement by assisting the parties towards an agreement. If a settlement is reached, the judge shall incorporate the details of the settlement in a formal statement, which is binding on the parties and can be enforced against them in the event of non-compliance. If the conciliation attempt fails (or if one of the parties does not show up), the judge does not have the power to adjudicate the dispute. Any party, however, has the right to initiate formal proceedings after a failed attempt at conciliation. The pre-trial reconciliation attempt is voluntary, unless it is required by statute.[305]

237. In family cases, there are specific chambers within the Family Court before which the amicable settlement is conducted and which are presided by a judge who received special training in the amicable settlement of disputes.

238. In addition, if the parties reach a settlement in the course of court proceedings, they may always ask the judge to take notice of that agreement, in which case he will render a 'consent judgment' (*jugement d'accord – akkoordvonnis*).[306]

239. In any event, the judge merely acts as a notary public, taking notice of the parties' agreement. He does not interfere in, or rule on, the content or fairness of the settlement, unless rules of public policy are violated.

304. Articles 731–733 Judicial Code.
305. In land rent cases, for instance, the claimant is obliged to undertake a pre-trial settlement attempt before the court prior to the initiation of formal proceedings (Article 1345 Judicial Code).
306. Article 1043 Judicial Code.

Chapter 2. Proceedings in First Instance

§1. Ordinary Proceedings

I. Initiation of Proceedings

A. Language

240. Belgium has three official languages: Dutch, French and German. The language of civil proceedings is, in principle, determined by the language of the court before which the claim is to be initiated. The courts are, in principle, unilingual. Whether proceedings are conducted in Dutch, French or German is subject to the rules laid down in the Act of 15 June 1935 on the Use of Languages in Judicial Matters.[307] Proceedings before courts situated in a unilingual region are usually conducted in the language of that region. Put simply, proceedings in the southern region of Belgium (Wallonia) are in French, whereas those in the northern region (Flanders) are in Dutch. Proceedings before courts situated in the German-speaking community (the district of Eupen, within Wallonia) are conducted in German. A special regime applies to Brussels, where the rules governing the use of languages will not only determine the language of the proceedings but also the competent court (*see supra*, paragraph 68). The Language Act of 15 June 1935 also comprises a certain number of rules regarding the possibility to request a language change.

B. Notice to Appear Before Court

1. Writ of Summons

241. The most common way to initiate civil proceedings is by way of a writ of summons (*citation – dagvaarding*), i.e., an official document that is served on the defendant by a bailiff at the request of the claimant.[308]

242. The writ of summons must meet the formal and substantive requirements of Articles 43, 45 and 702 of the Judicial Code. The writ must, for instance, mention the full name and domicile (or place of residence) of both plaintiff and defendant, as well as the object of the claim, i.e., the relief sought, and a brief description of the facts relied upon to substantiate the claim. Any irregularity or omission may cause the nullity of the writ, provided that the conditions of Articles 860 et seq. are fulfilled (*see supra*, paragraphs 218–221).

243. The writ of summons is usually drafted by (the attorney of) the plaintiff and completed by the bailiff. The bailiff, however, has the sole authority to serve the writ on the defendant (*see supra*, paragraphs 142–143).

307. *Belgian Official Gazette*, 22 June 1935.
308. Article 700 *juncto* Articles 32–45 Judicial Code.

244. The bailiff hands over a certified copy of the document to the defendant who signs the original as proof that the act has been served. When the defendant refuses to accept the certified copy, the bailiff shall record this refusal on the original, but the servicing of the document will be considered as completed.[309]

245. Hereafter, the original is filed with the court's registrar, which will register the case on the court's docket (*see* further *infra*, paragraph 256).

246. If the bailiff can locate the defendant, the writ of summons should be served on him personally, whatever place he is to be found in.[310] When the defendant is a legal entity, the writ is served on the physical person who is authorised, pursuant to the entity's articles of association, to represent the entity in legal proceedings.[311]

247. If the bailiff is unable to locate the defendant, the writ may be served at the defendant's domicile or place of residence and delivered to a relative or employee of the defendant, on the condition that such relative or employee must be at least sixteen years of age.[312] If this is not possible either (for instance, because there is nobody at home), the bailiff may leave a copy of the writ at the defendant's domicile or place of residence. In this case, the bailiff shall send the defendant a registered letter stating that the writ has been served. The letter also mentions the possibility for the defendant to get a copy of the writ at the bailiff's office.[313] If the bailiff is unable to identify or locate the physical person who is authorised to represent the legal entity, the writ may be served at the entity's registered office or corporate headquarters.[314]

248. Article 39 of the Judicial Code provides that each party may choose his domicile at the address of a mandatory, usually an attorney or bailiff. In this event, all writs and other documents may be served at this address. The bailiff may, however, still serve writs or other documents at the defendant's (actual) domicile or registered office,[315] unless the defendant's (actual) domicile or registered office is located abroad and he has a chosen domicile in Belgium. In this event, the bailiff must serve the writ at the chosen domicile.[316]

249. When the defendant has neither a known (elected) domicile nor place of residence in Belgium, the writ of summons has to be served abroad. With regard to service to defendants with a known (elected) domicile or place of residence abroad, three situations must be distinguished. The service may be governed by (1) the EU Regulation No. 1397/2007 of 13 November 2007 on the Service in the Member States of Judicial and Extrajudicial Documents in Civil or Commercial Matters (Service of Documents), and repealing EU Regulation No. 1348/2000;[317] (2) the Hague Convention of 15 November 1965 on the Service Abroad of Judicial and Extrajudicial Documents

309. Article 33, para. 3, Judicial Code.
310. Article 33 Judicial Code.
311. Article 34 Judicial Code.
312. Article 35, paras 2 and 3, Judicial Code. The bailiff is authorised to ask for an identity card in order to verify the identity of the receiver of the writ (Article 1, para. 3, Royal Decree of 25 March 2003 concerning identity cards (*Belgian Official Gazette*, 28 March 2003 (ed. 4)).
313. Article 38 Judicial Code.
314. Article 35, para. 1, Judicial Code.
315. Situated in Belgium (Court of Cassation 10 May 2012, C.11.0556.N).
316. Article 40, para. 4, Judicial Code; Court of Cassation 9 January 1997, *Arresten van het Hof van Cassatie* 1997, 52.
317. *Official Journal* L324/79 of 2007.

in Civil or Commercial Matters (ratified in Belgium by the Act of 24 January 1970);[318] or (3) Article 40 of the Judicial Code, where neither the EU Regulation nor the Hague Convention do apply.

The EU Regulation No. 1397/2007 provides for several means of service and notification of judicial documents.[319] The most frequently used method is regulated in Articles 4–11 of the Regulation. In this case, the transmitting agency competent under the law of the Member State in which the documents originate shall transmit the documents to be served in another Member State to the competent receiving agency of that Member State. In Belgium, the following judicial officers are designated as competent transmitting agencies: (1) the court registries; (2) the public prosecutor's office and (3) the bailiffs.[320] The transmission of documents includes a (certified) copy of the writ of summons drafted in or accompanied by a translation thereof in one of the languages provided for in Article 8 of the Regulation (i.e., a language which the addressee understands or the official language of the Member State addressed or, if there are several official languages in that Member State, the official language or one of the official languages of the place where service is to be effected), as well as a request drawn up using the standard form (set out in Annex I of the Regulation) and completed in the official language of the Member State addressed or, if there are several official languages in that Member State, the official language or one of the official languages of the place where service is to be effected, or in another language which that Member State has indicated it can accept. Depending on the agency effecting the transmission of documents, the translation is the responsibility of the court registries, the public prosecutor's office or the bailiff. The costs of translation shall be borne by the applicant, without prejudice to any possible subsequent decision by the court or competent authority on liability for such costs.[321] The receiving agency[322] shall itself serve the document or have it served, either in accordance with the law of the Member State addressed or by a particular method requested by the transmitting agency, unless that method is incompatible with the law of that Member State. The receiving agency shall take all necessary steps to effect the service of the document as soon as possible, and in any event within one month of receipt.[323] When the formalities concerning the service of the document have been completed, a certificate of completion of those formalities shall be drawn up in the standard form (set out in Annex I of the Regulation) and addressed to the transmitting agency, together with a copy of the document served if requested by the transmitting agency.[324] With respect to the addressee, the date of service of the document is determined by the law of the Member State addressed (*see supra*, paragraph 224).

318. *Belgian Official Gazette*, 9 February 1971.
319. *See* for a more detailed account: P. Gielen & K. Dockers, *De Europese burgerlijke procedure: stand van zaken doorheen het Belgisch recht*, Herentals, Knops Publishing, 2014.
320. *See* European Judicial Atlas in Civil Matters, at http://ec.europa.eu/justice_home/judicialatlascivil/html/ds_transmitting_be_en.htm (accessed September 2017).
321. Article 5, para. 2, Regulation No. 1397/2007.
322. For Belgium, the receiving agency is the National Association of Bailiffs.
323. Article 7 Regulation No. 1397/2007.
324. Article 10, para. 1, Regulation No. 1397/2007.

The Hague Convention, which binds sixty-nine countries, organises the service of judicial documents through national central authorities, which communicate by using standard multilingual forms. Each contracting state must designate a central authority[325] which will undertake to receive requests for service coming from other contracting states. The authority or judicial officer competent under the law of the state in which the documents originate shall forward to the central authority of the state addressed a request conforming to the Convention model.[326] The document to be served or a copy thereof shall be annexed to the request.[327] The standard terms in the model shall in all cases be written either in French or in English. They may also be written in the official language, or in one of the official languages, of the State in which the documents originate.[328] The corresponding blanks shall be completed either in the language of the state addressed or in French or in English.[329] The central authority of the state addressed shall itself serve the document or shall arrange to have it served by an appropriate agency, either by a method prescribed by its internal law for the service of documents in domestic actions upon persons who are within its territory or by a particular method requested by the applicant, unless such a method is incompatible with the law of the state addressed.[330] The central authority may require the document to be written in, or translated into, the official language or one of the official languages of the state addressed.[331] This is the responsibility of the competent transmitting agency. With respect to the addressee, the date of service of the document is the date of the actual receipt thereof by the addressee.[332]

Where no regulation or treaty applies, the service of judicial documents to an addressee with a known (elected) place of residence or domicile abroad is regulated by Article 40 of the Judicial Code, which states that the bailiff sends a transcript of the original of the writ to the (elected) place of residence or domicile of the addressee abroad, by registered mail or by airmail if the place of destination is not located in a neighbouring country. The document is deemed to have been served as soon as the bailiff delivers it to the post office in return for a receipt (*see supra*, paragraph 224). Article 40 of the Judicial Code does not provide for any language or translation requirements.

250. The Belgian Judicial Code provides for two exceptional cases of 'fictitious service', i.e., situations in which the writ of summons is not factually served on the defendant. First, if the defendant has no known (elected) domicile or place of residence in Belgium or abroad, the writ is sent to the public prosecutor.[333] The applicant is, however, required to prove that he has taken all reasonable measures to retrieve the defendant's (elected) domicile or place of residence (in Belgium or abroad).[334] Second,

325. In Belgium, this is the National Association of Bailiffs.
326. Article 3, para. 1, Hague Convention.
327. Article 3, para. 2, Hague Convention.
328. Article 7, para. 1, Hague Convention.
329. Article 7, para. 2, Hague Convention.
330. Article 5, para. 1, Hague Convention.
331. Article 5, para. 3, Hague Convention.
332. Court of Cassation 21 December 2007, C.06.0155.F.
333. Article 40, para. 2, Judicial Code.
334. Court of Cassation 8 October 2015, C.12.0565.N.

if it is physically impossible to leave a copy of the writ at the place where the service should be accomplished, the writ is also sent to the public prosecutor.[335]

251. On 31 December 2016, the electronic service of judicial documents was – finally (!) – recognised under Belgian procedural law.[336] The (new) Articles 32*quater*/1–3 of the Belgian Judicial Code provide that every physical and legal person is given an email address for judicial purposes. Depending on the circumstances of the case, the bailiff decides whether to serve the document personally or by electronic means.

2. Other Means of Notice

252. In some cases, proceedings may be initiated by means of a petition (*requête contradictoire – verzoekschrift op tegenspraak*), which is a written request directly addressed to the court by the plaintiff (or his legal counsel), which is subsequently notified to the defendant by the court registry. The petition must meet the formal and substantive requirements provided for in Articles 1034*bis*-1034*sexies* of the Judicial Code, on pain of nullity. The plaintiff, for instance, must attach an up-to-date certificate of domicile of the defendant to his petition. This certificate can be obtained from the local authorities. Apart from its form, the petition has the same legal effects as the writ of summons, but it is a more informal and less expensive manner to launch (adversarial)[337] legal proceedings. The petition may, however, be used only if expressly provided for by law.[338]

253. If both parties agree on presenting their dispute to the judge, they may file a joint petition declaring their voluntary appearance (*comparution volontaire – vrijwillige verschijning*).[339] Although this option presents many advantages (it is a fast and cheap way to initiate proceedings and it mitigates the 'civilised violence' that is inherent to every court proceeding), it is seldom used in practice.

254. Exceptionally, proceedings may be initiated by registered mail, oral request or telegram.

3. Waiting Period

255. Regardless of the way in which the proceedings are initiated, the defendant is, in any event, granted a minimum period of eight days between the day of the service or notification of the act instituting the proceedings and the day of the preliminary

335. Article 38 Judicial Code.

336. A recent Royal Decree of 14 June 2017 (*Belgian Official Gazette*, 22 June 2017) implements some aspects of these new rules, but it will still take some time before the electronic service of judicial documents becomes (fully) operational.

337. This petition is to be distinguished from the unilateral petition that is used to initiate ex parte proceedings.

338. Especially in those areas of law where the legislature held the opinion that access to justice should be made easier, the petition has become the ordinary way of initiating proceedings. For instance, all disputes before the Labour Court (Article 704, §1, Judicial Code) and the Family Court (Article 1253*ter* Judicial Code) may be initiated by means of a petition.

339. Article 706 Judicial Code. Voluntary appearance is only possible before the Court of First Instance, the Labour Court, the Commercial Court, the Police Court and the Justice of the Peace Court.

hearing, in order to allow him to prepare his defence and consult an attorney.[340] The waiting period may be shortened by the court in case of urgency. It may be extended if the defendant has no (elected) domicile or residence in Belgium. The period is extended by fifteen days if the defendant resides in France, Luxembourg, the Netherlands, Germany or the United Kingdom; by thirty days if he resides in another European country and by eighty days if he resides in another part of the world.[341]

C. Registration by the Court

256. After the payment of an enrolment fee, the court registrar will register the case on the court's docket. This is a public register in which all cases submitted to the court are registered under a serial number, thus identifying the case.

257. Next to the court's docket, there are two other types of dockets. The particular docket of each chamber contains the cases which have been referred to that particular chamber while the docket of the hearing is basically the agenda of each hearing; it contains the list of cases to be heard.[342]

II. Progress of Proceedings

A. Adversary Proceedings

1. Preparatory Measures

a. Preliminary Hearing

258. The preliminary hearing (*audience introductive – inleidingszitting*), the date of which is determined in the act instituting the proceedings, can be considered as a first case management hearing where the judge will decide on the further course of the case.

259. Two categories of cases can be distinguished: cases that only require short hearings and more complex cases. The first category of cases are immediately resolved at the preliminary hearing or at a hearing at a nearby date,[343] whereas the second category of cases are generally handled in accordance with a procedural calendar, which is either agreed upon by the parties or, in the absence of such agreement, imposed by the judge.[344] The procedural calendar fixes the deadlines that need to be respected by the parties with regard to the filing and exchange of their written pleadings and

340. Article 708 Judicial Code.
341. Article 709 *juncto* Article 55 Judicial Code.
342. Articles 711–719 Judicial Code.
343. Article 735 Judicial Code.
344. Articles 747–748 Judicial Code.

supporting documents.[345] It also provides for the trial date, which is determined by the judge. If all parties agree, the case may also be referred to the court's docket. In this event, no procedural calendar is made up (the parties mutually agree upon the exchange of their pleadings), nor is the trial date fixed at this stage (when the case is ready to be argued before court, the parties can request the court to set a trial date). Another possibility is that the case is postponed (as far as circumstances allow) for hearing at a later date.

260. In principle, parties are required to appear in person or through their legal representative at the preliminary hearing.[346] In some (lower) courts, parties may be assisted or represented by their spouse or close relatives.[347] In the Labour Courts, parties may be assisted or represented by a representative of a trade union.[348]

261. In certain disputes, such as some family law cases, the parties have a legal obligation to appear in person at the preliminary hearing.[349] The parties' personal appearance must allow the court to attain a clear understanding of the situation and to explore whether, and to what extent, the parties would be able to come to an agreement. Furthermore, the legislature wanted parents to take responsibility in procedures concerning their children. Where appropriate, the case may be referred to the chambers for amicable settlement. If the claimant does not appear in person, the court may dismiss the claim (in which case the claimant has to start over) or refer the case to the court's particular docket (in which case the proceedings shall only continue after the (simple) request of one of the parties). If the defendant fails to appear in person, the court may render a judgment by default or order the postponement of the case to a later hearing. In the latter case, the court registry will notify the defendant of the date of the second hearing by judicial letter. If the defendant does not appear in person at the second hearing, the judge shall pronounce a judgment that is deemed to have been rendered after trial (adversarial proceedings), i.e., that is not susceptible to opposition.[350]

262. Only attorneys have the right to agree upon a written appearance instead of the personal appearance.[351]

263. In the event that one of the parties is not present or validly represented, the other party can ask that a default judgment is pronounced (*see infra*, paragraphs 309–315).

---

345. The procedural calendar is determined by the agenda of the court, in the sense that the parties' deadlines are fixed in accordance with the earliest date on which the hearing of the case can take place. After all, it would not be useful to determine very tight deadlines if the hearing can only take place at a much later stage.
346. Article 728, §1, Judicial Code.
347. Article 728, §2, Judicial Code.
348. Aticle 728, §3, Judicial Code.
349. Articles 1253*ter*/2 and 1253*ter*/4 Judicial Code. If the dispute relates to maintenance obligations towards underage children, the parties must not only appear in person at the preliminary hearing, but also at the hearing(s) dealing with issues regarding the children (Article 1253*ter*/2, para. 2, Judicial Code). In the event of exceptional circumstances, however, the court may decide that the appearance in person is not necessary (Article 1253*ter*/2, para. 3, Judicial Code).
350. Article 1253*ter*/2, para. 4, Judicial Code.
351. Article 729 Judicial Code.

b. Exchange of Written Pleadings and Evidence

264. Parties must set out their claims and defences, as well as the (numbered) arguments in support thereof, in written pleadings. The original pleadings are filed with the court's registry; simultaneously, a copy must be sent to the opposite party.[352]

265. The written pleadings must meet the formal and substantive requirements of Articles 743 and 744 of the Judicial Code. As part of a recent reform of the Judicial Code, written pleadings now need to be drafted in accordance with a predetermined structure: (1) Relevant facts; (2) Specification of the relief sought; (3) Factual and legal argumentation; and (4) The decision requested from the court. If not, the court is not held to respond to the pleadings.

266. The last written pleadings of each party are deemed to replace all previous pleadings; hence, they must be comprehensive and contain all (well-structured) claims, defences and (numbered) arguments the parties maintain and submit to the court for decision.[353] This should facilitate the task of the court, because it is only held to decide on claims, defences and arguments which have been presented by the parties in their last written pleadings.[354]

267. Unlike before, the time limits for the filing of the written pleadings (as laid down in the procedural calendar) are mandatory. Pleadings filed after the expiration of the deadlines, will be disregarded by the court, unless parties mutually agree that the late pleadings are not to be excluded from the proceedings.[355] Parties may request the court to be allowed to file additional pleadings upon discovery of a new fact or document that is essential to the case.[356]

268. Next to the exchange of written pleadings, parties must communicate to each other all documents on which they rely. Failure to disclose will result in a stay of the proceedings.[357] In principle, documents only have to be submitted if they are referred to in the pleadings or if the claim or defence is based on them. There is no obligation to submit documents that are harmful to a party's case (or support the opponent's case). If, however, a party is shown to hold a document which could prove or disprove a fact that is relevant to the case, the court may order that party to submit that document (*see also infra*, paragraphs 451 and 454–455).

269. Recently, a new ICT tool, called 'E-Deposit', has been made available in some courts, which allows for the electronic filing of written pleadings and supporting

352. The pleadings will be disregarded by the judge when a party has filed his pleadings on time with the court's registry, but has forgotten to send a copy to the opposite party within the fixed term (Court of Cassation 26 September 2008, *Rechtskundig Weekblad* 2010–2011, 538) or *vice versa* (Court of Cassation 21 April 2017, C.16.0418.N).

353. Article 748*bis* Judicial Code.

354. Article 780, para. 1, 3° Judicial Code. According to the Court of Cassation, the court is even forbidden from deciding on claims or defences that were expressed in previous pleadings, but not reiterated in the last pleadings (Court of Cassation 19 November 2015, C.15.0198.N).

355. Article 748, §1, Judicial Code. The agreement on late pleadings can be concluded tacitly (Court of Cassation 6 April 2001, C.98.0358.N).

356. Article 748, §2, Judicial Code.

357. Article 736 Judicial Code.

documents.[358] This is a first step towards the complete digitalisation of the judicial procedure. Article 32*ter* of the Judicial Code provides that the use of the E-Deposit application can be made mandatory for some or all (professional) participants in the judicial system.

2. Trial

270. On the trial date, the case will be presented orally to the court. Parties may plead in person or through their legal representative. If, however, a party is unable to present its arguments in a calm and clear manner to the court, the court – which has the power to maintain law and order during the hearing – may interrupt the pleadings and ask that the party presents its case through an attorney.[359] In practice, the oral pleadings are mostly done by lawyers.[360] Generally, the claimant presents his oral arguments and evidence first, followed by the defendant's oral arguments and evidence. The parties may also agree to replace the traditional pleadings with an interactive debate, which is presided over by the judge.[361]

271. When the case cannot be dealt with in one hearing, the court will adjourn the case to an additional hearing, which is to be attended by the same judges.[362]

272. The importance of the oral pleadings should not be exaggerated as the court is not held to answer claims and arguments that have only been put forward at the occasion of the oral pleadings. The court is not prohibited, however, from taking into account arguments that ware only made orally at the trial date, provided that the rights of defence of the opposite party are respected.[363]

273. Apart from the exceptions provided for by law, the hearings are open to the public.[364]

274. There is no jury trial in civil cases.

275. Oral pleadings are not a must. The parties (or their counsels) may agree to a purely written procedure whereby the judge will decide the case on the basis of the written pleadings and supporting documents. The judge may summon the parties to clarify their position on certain issues orally.[365]

3. Opinion of the Public Prosecutor's Office

276. Some types of claims, such as claims regarding maintenance obligations towards underage children, must be communicated for advice to the public prosecutor's

358. As of 2 July 2016, this tool is used in the Courts of Appeal, the Labour Courts of Appeal and the Commercial Courts. The FPS Justice intends to roll out this application to the other courts in the next few years.
359. Article 758, para. 2, Judicial Code.
360. An exception to this is the Justice of the Peace Court, where *pro se* litigants are common.
361. Article 756*ter* Judicial Code.
362. Article 779 Judicial Code; *see* also Court of Cassation 22 February 2013, C.02.0309.N.
363. Court of Cassation 18 March 2011, C.10.0382.N.
364. Article 148 Constitution and Article 757, §1, Judicial Code. Article 757, §2, of the Judicial Code contains a list of claims, such as family-related maintenance claims, which are not open to the public, unless the court decides otherwise.
365. Article 755 Judicial Code.

office. This communication is mandatory on pain of nullity of the judgment.[366] In principle, the public prosecutor's office freely decides whether or not to render its advice. The Board of Prosecutor's General, however, may issue binding guidelines in order to ensure some uniformity in this respect.[367]

277. In other cases, when considered useful, the public prosecutor's office can ask to be involved in the case and give an advice, whereas the judge can also request the public prosecutor's advice ex officio.[368]

278. The advice will be given in writing after the closing of the hearing or orally during the hearing.[369] In any event, the parties have the right to reply.

279. The advice is not binding on the court and the court is not obliged to respond to it.[370]

4. Judgment

a. Deliberation

280. After the closing of the hearings and, as the case may be, the delivery of the opinion of the public prosecutor's office (*see supra*, paragraphs 276–279), the court takes the case into deliberation. A written judgment should normally[371] be rendered within one month, but in practice, this may take longer. No sanction is provided if the one-month deadline is not observed. A list of delayed cases must, however, be sent to the president of the court and the public prosecutor every month. If no judgment is rendered within three months after the closing of the hearings, the judge must inform his hierarchical superior. One of the parties may also take the initiative on this.[372] If the court has not rendered judgment within six months, the case can be withdrawn from this court (*see also infra*, paragraphs 411–414).[373]

281. When the case is handled by three judges, the decisions are taken by majority vote.

282. As long as the judgment has not been rendered, the parties may request the court to reopen the proceedings upon discovery of a new fact or document that is essential to the case.[374] The court may also ex officio decide to reopen the proceedings, for instance if it has additional queries that were not answered in the parties' written

366. Articles 764, para. 1 and 765/1 Judicial Code.
367. Article 764, para. 5, Judicial Code. On 10 December 2015, the Board of Prosecutor's General issued a circular 13/2015 that enumerates the types of cases in which the public prosecutor's office shall, in principle, render (or not render) an advice (*see* http://www.om-mp.be/?q=nl/meer-weten/omzendbrieven (accessed September 2017)).
368. Articles 764, para. 2, and 765 Judicial Code.
369. Article 767 Judicial Code.
370. Court of Cassation 4 December 1987, *Arresten van het Hof van Cassatie* 1987–1988, 449.
371. When the hearings are closed in June (i.e., the month prior to the judicial holidays (*see supra* para. 227)), the time limit for rendering the judgment is prolonged with an extra month (Article 770, para. 1, Judicial Code).
372. Article 770, §1, para. 1, Judicial Code.
373. Article 652 Judicial Code.
374. Articles 772–773 Judicial Code.

and oral pleadings.[375] Moreover, it is under an obligation to do so if it considers dismissing the claim on the basis of a legal reason that has not been addressed by any of the parties.[376]

After the reopening of the proceedings, the parties can submit new pleadings and supporting documents.

If the reopening of the proceedings has been ordered in order to give the parties the occasion to file pleadings with regard to a new relevant fact or document, the court must be composed of the same judges who attended the previous hearings. If this should not be possible (for instance, due to illness, retirement or maternity leave of one or more judges), the proceedings must be repeated from the very beginning before the newly composed court, on pain of nullity of the judgment, unless the parties agree to deviate from this rule.[377] If, however, the reopening of the hearings has been ordered with regard to completely new issues, which have not been discussed during previous hearings, there is no need for maintaining the identical composition of the court.[378]

b. Different Kinds of Judgments

283. Article 19 of the Judicial Code distinguishes between 'final decisions' (*décision définitif – eindbeslissing*), in which the court settles a dispute on the merits or a procedural issue (for instance, regarding the court's jurisdiction or a procedural irregularity), and 'decisions before adjudicating' (*décision avant dire droit – beslissing alvorens recht te doen*), in which the court does not decide on the subject matter of the dispute but orders certain measures in order to investigate the dispute (such as decisions ordering an investigation measure) or provisionally arrange the (legal) situation of the parties (such as decisions ordering the defendant to pay provisional damages). The latter must be distinguished from decisions concerning the administration of the trial (*mesure d'ordre – maatregel van inwendige aard*), which are administrative measures ordered by the court with respect to the administration and the progress of the proceedings, such as decisions fixing the terms to file pleadings or the trial date.[379]

284. The distinction between final decisions, decisions before adjudicating and decisions concerning the administration of the trial is particularly important with regard to the available appellate remedies (*see infra*, paragraphs 339 and 351).

285. Further on, a distinction is made between 'final judgments' (*jugement définitif – eindvonnis*) and 'interlocutory judgments' (*jugement incident – tussenvonnis*). In practice, it often happens that the court settles the dispute by one or several interlocutory judgments (which may contain final decisions and/or decisions before adjudicating), and eventually a final judgment in which the remaining points at issue are settled, and which makes a definite end to the trial.

375. Article 774, para. 1, Judicial Code.
376. Article 774, para. 2, Judicial Code.
377. Article 779 Judicial Code.
378. Court of Cassation 13 December 1990, *Arresten van het Hof van Cassatie* 1990–1991, 415; Court of Cassation 28 November 1991, *Arresten van het Hof van Cassatie* 1991–1992, 286; Court of Cassation 15 June 1993, *Pasicrisie belge* 1993, I, 571.
379. Article 1046 Judicial Code.

c. Formal Aspects

286. In theory, the judgment should be read aloud to the parties during a public court hearing.[380] This rule is, however, not applied (anymore) in practice.

287. The judgment's formal requirements are elabourated in Articles 780–782*bis* of the Judicial Code. Besides the identification of the court and the litigating parties, each judgment must contain a description of the subject matter of the dispute, as well as the court's answer to the claims, defences and (factual and legal) arguments which have been presented in the parties' last pleadings.

288. The judge(s) who rendered the judgment, as well as the assisting court registrar sign the original of the judgment, which is kept at the court registry.[381] The court registry sends an unsigned (free) copy of the judgment by ordinary mail to each of the parties or their counsel.[382]

289. The non-compliance with the formal requirements results in the nullity of the judgment, meaning that the judgment is void and cannot produce any legal effects. Pursuant to Article 20 of the Judicial Code, the judgment is, however, not automatically null and void; the nullity must be established and pronounced by a court in the context of review proceedings.

d. Res Judicata

290. The authority of res judicata (*autorité de la chose jugée – gezag van gewijsde*) is an inherent feature of final judicial decisions, meaning that what has been decided, cannot be questioned anymore.[383] On the one hand, it indicates that the judgment is conclusive as to the rights and obligations of the parties; on the other hand, it prevents any subsequent action by the same parties regarding the same claim.[384]

291. Each final decision (*see supra*, paragraph 283) has the authority of res judicata.[385] Decisions before adjudicating have no such authority. Interim decisions (ordered by the president of the court; *see infra*, paragraphs 316–320) have a limited authority of res judicata; the president of the court cannot render a new interim decision, but the court that has to judge on the merits is not bound by the interim decision.

292. The authority of res judicata exists from the moment the judgment is rendered until the judgment is successfully challenged through a legal remedy.

293. The plea of res judicata must be entered by the defendant. The court is prohibited from raising the issue on its own motion.[386] The plea can be entered at any stage of the proceedings, but not for the first time in proceedings before the Court of

---

380. Article 148 Constitution.

381. Recently, the FPS Justice introduced the VAJA-database. In the (distant) future, a digitalised copy of all judgments pronounced by the Belgian judicial courts will be (electronically) stored in this database.

382. Article 792, para. 1, *juncto* Article 46/1 Judicial Code.

383. *See* for a more detailed account: P. Taelman, *Het gezag van het rechterlijk gewijsde – Een begrippenstudie*, Diegem, Kluwer, 2001.

384. Article 25 Judicial Code.

385. Article 24 Judicial Code.

386. Article 27 Judicial Code.

Cassation. The plea will be granted if it is clear that both actions are identical, meaning that they concern the same parties (acting in the same capacity), the same subject and the same (factual) cause, irrespective of the legal ground(s) invoked by the parties or the judge.[387]

294. The authority of res judicata has a relative effect, meaning that the judgment is only binding for the litigating parties.[388] The rights and obligations arising out of the judgment can only be enforced by and against the litigating parties. Despite this relative effect, third parties have to accept the existence of the judgment and the effects this judgment has between the litigating parties. Furthermore, the judgment has a certain (refutable) evidential value.[389] If a third party's rights are adversely affected by a judgment, an extraordinary legal remedy is available to him (*see infra*, paragraphs 379–384).

295. If the time for initiating ordinary legal remedies – i.e., opposition and appeal – has elapsed, the decision acquires the force of res judicata (*force de la chose jugée – kracht van gewijsde*).[390] This implies that it is definite and can only be challenged through extraordinary judicial means.

e. Notice and Service

296. A distinction is made between the service (*signification – betekening*) and the notification (*notification – kennisgeving*) of the judgment. In essence, service refers to the delivery of a document by writ via a government judicial official. In Belgium, this judicial official is the bailiff. Notification is effected by the court registry (on rare occasions by the public prosecutor's office) by so-called judicial mail (which is a special type of registered letter with acknowledgement of receipt (*pli judiciaire – gerechtsbrief*)), registered mail or ordinary mail.

297. In all cases, the court registry sends an unsigned (free) copy of the judgment by ordinary mail to each of the parties or their counsel.[391] This notice is given for information purposes only and does neither make the judgment enforceable against either party, nor does it trigger the running of the term of appeal (or any other appellate remedy). In the near future, it should be possible to effect this notice via a new ICT tool, called 'E-box'. This tool should allow electronic correspondence between all judicial authorities, attorneys, notaries public and bailiffs. Article 32*ter* of the Judicial Code provides that the use of this application can be made mandatory for some or all (professional) participants in the judicial system.

298. In most cases, if a party wants a judgment to be enforceable against the other party, it needs to be served on that other party.[392] This means that the party wanting the judgment to be enforced must request the court registry to deliver a copy thereof with an order for enforcement[393] and request the bailiff to serve the judgment on his

387. Article 23 Judicial Code.
388. Court of Cassation 20 June 1996, C.93.0183.N.
389. Court of Cassation 12 May 2016, C.14.0561.N.
390. Article 28 Judicial Code.
391. Article 792, para. 1, *juncto* Article 46/1 Judicial Code.
392. Article 1495, para. 1, Judicial Code.
393. Article 1386 Judicial Code.

opponent(s). Normally, the service of the judgment constitutes the starting point of the term of appeal (and other appellate remedies).[394]

299. In some exceptional cases, the Judicial Code requires the court registry to notify the decision to the parties by judicial mail, in which case this notification is the starting point of the term of appeal (for both parties).[395] This notification needs to contain information on the appellate remedies, their time limit and the competent court. The absence of this information results in the nullity of the notification, meaning that the notification is void and cannot produce any legal effects.

300. The service or notification to addressees with a known (elected) place of residence or domicile abroad is subject to the applicable regulations and treaties (*see supra*, paragraphs 248–249).

f. Interpretation, Rectification and Supplementation[396]

301. In principle, the court has no power to change or supplement its judgment after having rendered a final decision (*litis finiri oportet*).[397]

302. Nevertheless, the court may explain its decision to the extent that it is ambiguous or unclear.[398] The court may also correct clerical errors (such as calculation and typographical errors) in its decisions.[399] The court must, however, make sure that such interpretation or rectification does not alter the substance of its decision.

303. Recently, the court's power to finetune its decisions was expanded. The court may now also 'supplement' its decisions. This means that the court may render an additional judgment, insofar as it has neglected to render judgment on one (or more) of the claims presented by the parties (*infra petita*).[400]

304. The interpretation and rectification of the judgment may occur at the initiative of the court (ex officio) or at the initiative of the parties (or one of them). The supplementation of the judgment is, however, always party-driven.[401]

305. Interpretation, rectification and supplementation of the judgment is no longer possible if an appeal has been lodged against the judgment. Moreover, one has to wait the expiry of the term for lodging an appeal or further appeal prior to the filing of a request for interpretation, unless the parties agree to deviate from this rule.[402]

g. Penalty in Case of Non-compliance

306. To ensure the effective compliance with a judgment ordering the debtor to perform or refrain from a certain action, the creditor can request the court to impose

394. Article 57, para. 1, Judicial Code.
395. Article 792, paras 2 and 3 *juncto* Articles 46, §2, and 57 Judicial Code. *See supra* para. 288.
396. *See* for a more detailed account: C. Van Severen, *Uitlegging, verbetering en herstel van rechterlijke uitspraken*, Mechelen, Kluwer, 2016.
397. Article 19, para. 2, Judicial Code.
398. Article 793 Judicial Code.
399. Article 794 Judicial Code.
400. Article 794/1 Judicial Code.
401. Articles 796–797 Judicial Code.
402. Articles 798–799 Judicial Code.

a non-compliance penalty (*astreinte – dwangsom*) to be paid in the event that the debtor does not voluntarily comply with the judgment.[403] The penalty is an additional conviction, serving as an incentive for the debtor to execute his main conviction.

307. The court can impose a periodical penalty (due per time unit, e.g., EUR 100 for each day the judgment is not complied with, or per established breach) or a lump sum (which is due at once). The court cannot impose a non-compliance penalty on its own initiative, but it may ex officio raise or lower the amount requested by a party, depending on what it considers being appropriate under the circumstances.

308. The penalty is collected by the party to whom it has been granted. It can be requested in all cases, except where the main claim relates to the performance of a labour contract or the payment of a sum of money. In the latter case, the creditor may proceed to the attachment of the debtor's property (*see infra*, paragraphs 502–547).

B. *Default Proceedings*

1. Conditions for Rendering a Judgment by Default

309. Each judgment indicates whether it is rendered by default (*par défaut – bij verstek*) or after adversarial proceedings (*contradictoire – op tegenspraak*).[404] It is up to the court to verify whether the conditions for rendering a judgment by default are fulfilled.[405]

310. A judgment can only be rendered by default when one of the parties does not appear at the preliminary hearing and the other party asks a default judgment to be pronounced.[406] The judge cannot, under any circumstances, deliver a default judgment ex officio. The party who is present at the hearing can also request the court to adjourn the case.[407] In this event, the court registry will notify the defaulting party of the date of the second hearing upon receipt of a written request in this respect from the other party.[408] If the defaulting party is absent again at the second hearing, the other party may request that a default judgment is rendered.[409]

---

403. The rules regarding the non-compliance penalty, which are elaborated in Articles 1385*bis* et seq. of the Judicial Code, originate from the Benelux Convention of 26 November 1973 on the Uniform Law on Penalty Payments. Accordingly, the case law of the Benelux Court of Justice is of utmost importance for the application and interpretation of the rules.

404. The judgments of the Court of Cassation are an exception to this rule, as they are always deemed to have been rendered after trial (Article 1113, para. 1, Judicial Code).

405. The court's assessment is, however, not decisive with regard to the question whether or not opposition is possible against the judgment (opposition is only available to persons who were convicted by default). The real nature of the judgment (i.e., what has actually happened in the proceedings) determines whether or not it is susceptible to opposition or, in other words, whether or not it has been rendered by default or after adversarial proceedings (Court of Cassation 7 May 2010, C.09.0451.F).

406. Article 802 Judicial Code.

407. The reason for this might be that there is some doubt as to whether the absent defendant was duly summoned or notified of the preliminary hearing.

408. Article 803 Judicial Code.

409. Article 804, para. 2, Judicial Code.

311. When none of the parties appear at the preliminary hearing or the party appearing does not request a default judgment or the (re-)summoning of the defaulting party, the court will have to impose a procedural calendar and fix a trial date, in which case the (future) judgment will be deemed to have been rendered after adversarial proceedings.[410]

312. If a party was present at the preliminary hearing, but did not appear at the trial date or a later hearing, a default judgment can be pronounced against that party,[411] unless the absent party has already submitted written pleadings.[412]

2. Assessment of the Judge in Default Proceedings

313. Until recently, the scope of the court's examination of the case if one of the parties does not show up was not laid down in the Judicial Code. Moreover, it was a thorny issue in Belgian jurisprudence and legal doctrine.[413]

314. As of 1 November 2015, the task of the court in case of default by one of the parties is defined in Article 806 of the Judicial Code. Although the wording of said Article 806[414] – 'the judge shall honour the claims or defences of the party that is present, unless the proceedings, those claims or defences violate rules of public policy, including rules which the court has to apply on its own motion' – seems to suggest only a very narrow task for the judge in the event of default by one of the parties, most Belgian courts and legal scholars attribute a broader task to him. Before rendering a judgment by default, the court must first verify whether the defaulting party was duly summoned or notified of the hearing. Second, the court must verify whether it has jurisdiction over the case. As to the merits of the case, the court must *at least* verify whether the claim does not violate any rules of public policy. Moreover, the Court of Cassation has recently confirmed that, for the purposes of Article 806 of the Judicial Code, the concept of 'public policy' is to be interpreted flexibly and evolving. This means, for instance, that the court is authorised to undermine (or tone down) manifestly unfounded or plainly disproportionate claims or excessive interest demands of the party that is present.[415]

410. Article 747, §2, para. 6, Judicial Code.
411. Article 804, para. 1, Judicial Code.
412. Article 804, para. 2, Judicial Code.
413. Some argued that the court must undertake a very broad investigation: the court should apply, on its own motion, all rules that are applicable to the case, meaning not only procedural rules (for instance, regarding the jurisdiction of the court and the admissibility of the claim), but also rules regarding the merits of the claim, whether or not they are of public policy. In other words, the court should investigate any arguments that could have been put forward by the defaulting party. Others were in favour of a narrower task for the court: the court should not undertake an investigation regarding the merits of the claim, but should only verify whether the demand does not violate any (procedural or substantive) rules which are considered to be of public policy.
414. As amended by the so-called Potpourri V Act of 6 July 2017 (*Belgian Official Gazette*, 24 July 2017).
415. Court of Cassation 13 December 2016, P.16.0421.N.

3. Service of the Default Judgment

315. Before 1 November 2015, the default judgment had to be served on the defaulting party within a time limit of one year, in the absence of which the default judgment would be considered 'non-existent'. This implied that the defaulting party could enter a plea in the event that the other party wanted to enforce the judgment after the one-year deadline. The defaulting party could also oppose the judgment in court. However, the procedure prior to the default judgment was preserved, meaning that the party who obtained the 'defunct' judgment, could simply request a new hearing and judgment.

§2. Summary Proceedings

316. The presidents of the Courts of First Instance, Labour Courts and Commercial Courts may provisionally rule on urgent matters which fall within the normal scope of their jurisdiction. The procedure is laid down in Article 584 *juncto* Articles 1035–1041 of the Judicial Code. There are two basic conditions. First of all, the request has to be urgent, meaning that an immediate decision is desirable to prevent (further) harm or serious discomfort.[416] Second, the president can only order interim measures, meaning that he can only act on a temporary basis and cannot decide on (nor cause any prejudice to) the merits of the case.[417] Interim measures may be, for instance, the appointment of a court expert or sequestrator or the issuance of (positive or negative) injunctions.

317. Interim proceedings can be launched either before any procedure on the merits of the case, together with the procedure on the merits or while a procedure on the merits is pending before the court. The latter hypothesis does not constitute a case of *lis pendens*. The court hearing the main action is not bound by the findings of the president (*see also supra*, paragraph 291).

318. In principle, interim proceedings are adversarial proceedings; they are initiated by means of a writ of summons, served upon the defendant to appear before the president of the designated court. The waiting period between the day of service of the writ of summons and the day of the hearing is shortened to at least two days.[418] This term can be shortened even more in case of extreme urgency. The president can even allow that the defendant is summoned to appear at the president's private home (*à l'hôtel du president*), for instance, when the hearing must be held at a time the courthouse is normally closed or on a public holiday.[419]

319. In very urgent cases, a party may apply to the president unilaterally (by using a unilateral or ex parte petition). This exceptional procedure[420] – in which the opponent is not involved and not even summoned – can only be used in case of absolute necessity, which means that the requested provisional measure is of such urgency and/

416. Court of Cassation 23 September 2011, C.10.0279.F; Court of Cassation 11 May 1990, AR 7089; Court of Cassation 21 May 1987, AR 7613.
417. Article 1039, para. 1, Judicial Code.
418. Article 1035, para. 2, Judicial Code.
419. Article 1036 Judicial Code.
420. Which is laid down in Article 584, para. 4, *juncto* Articles 1025–1034 Judicial Code.

or nature that it would be harmful for the plaintiff to rely on the ordinary (adversarial) summary proceedings.

320. Usually, a judgment will be rendered in the days following the hearing, mostly one week later. In very urgent cases, however, the president will render his decision on the same day as the hearing.

321. In this context it should be noted that *any* judge is authorised to order provisional measures in relation to the dispute in the main proceedings (such as investigation measures or measures aimed at the provisional settlement of the dispute).[421] This procedure, which can be used at any stage of the proceedings, is initiated informally by the filing of a simple written request with the court's registry, after which the parties (and their attorneys) are summoned to appear before the court. Contrary to summary proceedings, urgency is not required.

322. In some cases, the Judicial Code provides that a claim is introduced and decided upon 'as in summary proceedings' (*selon les forms du référé – zoals in kort geding*). This means that the court will examine and decide upon the merits of the case, but according to the procedural rules and within the short timeframe applying to summary proceedings.

§3. Ex Parte Proceedings

323. As they undermine the adversarial principle, ex parte proceedings – whereby the opposite party remains virtual and is not involved in the proceedings and not even informed thereof – are available only in cases expressly provided for by statute, as well as in cases of absolute necessity (*see supra*, paragraph 319), or when the identity of the opponent is unknown.[422] The procedure is laid down in Articles 1025–1034 of the Judicial Code. The unilateral petition[423] (*requête unilatérale – eenzijdig verzoekschrift*) must be filed with the court's registry by an attorney, who serves as a filter by ensuring that these kinds of proceedings are used with caution. The court can summon the petitioner in order to hear his arguments or ask for additional information, but this does not happen often in practice. The court's registry shall send the decision to the petitioner. The third party against whom the decision is directed is not notified of the decision. A particular legal remedy is, however, available to the third party whose rights are adversely affected by the judgment, namely third-party opposition, the rules of which are laid down in Articles 1125 et seq. of the Judicial Code (*see infra*, paragraphs 379–384).[424]

421. Article 19, para. 3, Judicial Code.

422. For example, in case of the occupation of property by squatters. Compare with Court of Cassation 25 February 1999, C.96.0409.N.

423. The unilateral petition is to be distinguished from the petition that can be used to introduce adversarial proceedings, which has the same legal effect as a writ of summons (*see supra*, para. 252).

424. Providing for such a legal remedy makes ex parte proceedings compatible with the requirements of Article 6 ECHR (Court of Cassation 14 January 2005, C.02.0221.N).

324. In practice, the preliminary seizure is an important type of ex parte proceedings. Similar to freezing injunctions in common law,[425] the preliminary seizure could be described as the blocking of a debtor's assets without prior notice. It prevents the debtor from disposing freely over his assets, hindering him to dissipate these assets during the pendency of a(n) (upcoming) suit. Normally, the preliminary seizure requires the permission of the judge of attachments,[426] which is requested by means of a unilateral petition (*see* further *infra*, paragraphs 473–501).

325. Another particular type of ex parte procedure is the summary order for payment procedure (*procédure sommaire d'injonction de payer – summiere rechtspleging om betaling te bevelen*),[427] which was introduced in 1967, at the same time of the promulgation of the Judicial Code, in order to provide for a quick and simple procedure for the collection of small and prima facie uncontested monetary claims. In practice, however, the procedure turned out to be burdensome, inefficient, costly and therefore not frequently used by creditors to obtain relief in small and simple matters.[428] In the course of the years, many proposals have been launched in order to amend the summary order for payment procedure, but almost none of these were effectively adopted.[429] To date, a comprehensive reform of the summary for payment procedure has not been realised. Recently, however, a completely new administrative recovery procedure for uncontested claims was introduced. The scope of the new procedure is limited to uncontested (national and cross-border) claims between businesses (B2B) relating to the payment of a sum of money, irrespective of the amount of the claim. In order to surround the out-of-court procedure with necessary guarantees (such as expertise and

425. It is similar to the so-called Mareva Injunction (named for *Mareva Compania Naviera SA v. International Bulkcarriers*, SA [1975] 2 Lloyd's Rep 509), variously known also as freezing order or Mareva Order.

426. This is, however, not the case if the creditor is acting on the basis of an existing judgment or other enforceable title.

427. The procedure is laid down in Articles 1338–1344 of the Judicial Code. *See* for a recent analysis: S. Voet, *Relief in Small and Simple Matters in Belgium*, (4) Erasmus L. Rev. 152–156 (2015).

428. The 2002 Green Paper of the European Commission concluded that 'due to some structural defects (...) the *procédure sommaire d'injonction de payer* procedure has turned out to be more cumbersome than ordinary civil proceedings and has, therefore, not met broad acceptance among legal practitioners' (Green Paper on a European order for payment procedure and on measures to simplify and speed up small claims litigation, COM (2002) 746 final, 9, at http://eur-lex.europa.eu/legal-content/EN/TXT/PDF/?uri=CELEX:52002DC0746andfrom=EN (accessed September 2017)).

429. In 2014, however, this procedure became also applicable for any monetary claim, regardless of its value, belonging to the jurisdiction of the Commercial Court, in an attempt to make the procedure more attractive for business disputes.

independence), a key role is allocated to the bailiffs and the National Chamber of Bailiffs.[430]

326. Besides this administrative recovery procedure, there exists, on the European level, also a European order for payment procedure allowing creditors to recover their uncontested civil and commercial cross-border claims by means of a uniform written procedure that operates on the basis of standard forms.[431] Furthermore, the EU Regulation No. 861/2007 of 11 July 2007[432] introduced a European small claims procedure, which seeks to improve and simplify procedures in civil and commercial matters where the value of the claim does not exceed EUR 2,000 (from mid-2017: EUR 5,000). The small claims procedure is also a purely written procedure that operates on the basis of standard forms.

§4. Collective Redress Proceedings

327. Until recently, Belgium had only very limited tools to resolve mass cases.[433] In addition to joinder of claims (*see supra*, paragraphs 159–163), claims in intervention (*see supra*, paragraphs 155–156 and 212) and the technique of party representation (whereby a person is considered to be authorised to represent a group of individuals provided that he has received an explicit power of attorney from each of them individually), only injunctive or declaratory collective actions were possible. The latter actions, which only exist in a limited number of legal fields (consumer protection, environment, discrimination and racism) allow (public or private) associations or organisations, which meet certain criteria, to bring an injunctive or declaratory action on behalf of a group of individuals. Hence, the group action does not allow the 'group members', on whose behalf the action is brought, to recover their individual damages. If such a member wants damages, he will have to initiate an individual civil action. All of these tools, however, were found to be inadequate for the collective redress of mass claims.

430. The procedure is laid down in Articles 1394/20–27 of the Judicial Code. *See* for a first analysis: D. Mougenot, 'Le recouvrement de dettes d'argent non contestées', in J.-F. Van Drooghenbroeck (ed.), *Le Code judiciaire en pot-pourri: Promesses, réalités et perspectives*, Brussels, Larcier, 2016, 327 et seq.; S. Voet, *Relief in Small and Simple Matters in Belgium*, (4) Erasmus L. Rev. 157 (2015); S. Voet & B. Allemeersch, 'Invordering van onbetwiste geldschulden', in B. Allemeersch & P. Taelman (ed.), *De hervorming van de burgerlijke rechtspleging door Potpourri I*, Bruges, die Keure, 2016, 1 et seq.

431. Regulation No. 1896/2006 of 12 December 2006 creating a European Order for Payment Procedure, *Official Journal* L399/1 of 2006.

432. *Official Journal* L199/1 of 2007.

433. *See* J.-P. Fierens & B. Volders, *Belgium*, in *World Class Actions. A Guide to Group and Representative Actions Around the Globe* 271–285 (P.G. Karlsgodt ed., Oxford University Press 2012) ; P. Taelman & S. Voet, *Belgium and Collective Redress: The Last of the European Mohicans*, in *The Belgian Reports at the Congress of Washington of the International Academy of Comparative Law* 305–346 (E. Dirix & Y.-H. Leleu ed., Bruylant 2011).

328. As of 1 September 2014, a collective mass claims settlement procedure has been made available in consumer law disputes.[434] The procedure is laid down in the Code of Economic Law.[435] It allows a class representative to introduce an action for collective redress where a group of consumers has suffered harm resulting from a company's breach of contract or violation of certain specified statutory provisions and EU regulations relating to consumer protection.[436] According to the Constitutional Court, the limitation of the class action procedure's scope to consumer law disputes is not incompatible with the constitutionally sanctioned principle of equality and non-discrimination. The Court referred, *inter alia*, to the fact that the legislature has announced an evaluation of the procedure in 2017, following which the procedure may be expanded to other fields of substantive law.[437]

329. A notable feature of the procedure is that the interests of the individual consumers – who are not involved as parties in the procedure as such – are represented by a class representative.[438] The (positive or negative) outcome of the procedure, however, will be binding on the individual consumers who have expressly made known their desire to be part of the class action (opt-in system) or have not expressly made known their desire to be excluded (opt-out system). In principle, the competent Belgian court can freely choose between an opt-in or opt-out system, thereby taking into account the underlying facts and claims of the case.[439]

330. Article XVII.39 of the Code of Economic Law states that only consumer associations and authorised non-profit organisations with articles of association specifying a purpose corresponding with the collective harm, have standing to bring a class action.[440] The Constitutional Court, however, annulled said Article XVII.39 of the Code of Economic Law, insofar as it does not provide that representative bodies from Member States of the European Union and the European Economic Area that meet the requirements set forth in paragraph 4 of the Commission Recommendation 2013/396/EU of 11 June 2013 on Common Principles for Injunctive and Compensatory Collective Redress Mechanisms in the Member States concerning Violations of Rights Granted under Union Law[441] may act as group representative.[442]

331. It is required that the class action appears to be more effective than (or superior to) an individual civil action.[443]

---

434. *See* for a thorough analysis: S. Voet, *Belgium's New Consumer Class Action*, in *Multi-party redress mechanisms in Europe: squeaking mice?* 95–109 (V. Harsagi & C.H. Van Rhee ed., Ius Commune Europaeum Series, Vol. 133, Intersentia).
435. Articles XVII.35–69 Code of Economic Law.
436. Articles XVII.36, 1°, and XVII.37 Code of Economic Law.
437. Constitutional Court No. 41/2016 of 17 March 2016.
438. Article XVII.36, 2°, Code of Economic Law.
439. Articles XVII.38, §1, and XVII.43, §2, 3°, Code of Economic Law.
440. Article XVII.39 Code of Economic Law.
441. *Official Journal* L201/60 of 2013.
442. Constitutional Court No. 41/2016 of 17 March 2016.
443. Article XVII.36, 3°, Code of Economic Law.

332. The courts of Brussels have exclusive jurisdiction (for the whole country) over consumer class actions.[444]

444. Article XVII.35 Code of Economic Law. So far, five collective redress actions have been initiated before the (Dutch- or French-speaking) Courts of First Instance or the Commercial Courts in Brussels.

Chapter 3. Review Proceedings

§1. In General

333. Appellate remedies enable the parties to obtain a 'new' decision in a dispute that has already been adjudicated. They provide for the possibility of having a judgment amended or annulled.

334. The Judicial Code distinguishes between ordinary and extraordinary appellate remedies.[445] The ordinary remedies are opposition (*opposition – verzet*) and (ordinary) appeal (*appel – hoger beroep*). The extraordinary remedies comprise the petition for cassation (*pourvoi en cassation – cassatieberoep*), third-party opposition (*tiers opposition – derdenverzet*), revocation of res judicata (*requête civile – herroeping van het gewijsde*), redress against the judge (*prise à partie – verhaal op de rechter*) and repeal (*rétractation – herziening*).[446] The essential distinguishing feature is that, in principle, all decisions are susceptible to the application of ordinary appellate remedies,[447] whereas extraordinary remedies are only available if they are expressly provided for by statute.

335. In principle, the procedural rules governing the first instance proceedings also apply at the appellate level, without prejudice, however, to any special rules that derogate from the general procedural rules.[448]

336. Review proceedings are conducted in the language of the contested judgment.[449]

§2. Ordinary Appellate Remedies

I. Opposition

A. *Admissibility*

337. Opposition is only available to persons who were summoned to appear as a party in the proceedings but defaulted and are aggrieved by the default judgment[450].

445. Article 21 Judicial Code.
446. The extraordinary remedy of repeal is not regulated in the Judicial Code, so it is not included in the list of said Article 21 of the Judicial Code. It is governed by Article 16 of the Special Act of 6 January 1989 on the Constitutional Court (*Belgian Official Gazette*, 7 January 1989).
447. The right to appeal is, however, not constitutionally guaranteed, nor does it amount to a general principle of due process in civil matters (*see supra* , para. 64).
448. Article 1042 Judicial Code.
449. Articles 24–29 Language Act of 15 June 1935.
450. Articles 1047–1049 Judicial Code.

Opposition is not possible by third parties, but an extraordinary appellate remedy, third party opposition, is available to them (*see infra*, paragraphs 379–384).

338. As a general rule, a judgment rendered *in absentia* can be opposed by the party who defaulted, provided that this judgment is rendered at final instance and thus not susceptible to an (ordinary) appeal.[451] Although the underlying philosophy of the availability of an extra legal remedy for a defaulting person is that this person is assumed to have been unable to organise his defence in due course and must be given the opportunity to submit the case again to the court before which he was summoned to appear, the defaulting person is not required to give any reason or explanation for his absence. The possibility to lodge opposition against a non-appealable default judgment is a right of the defaulting party, irrespective of the reason of the default (and without prior leave by a court or other authority being required).

339. A statutory provision can provide that opposition is not possible against a certain decision, such as decisions which are deemed to have been rendered after a trial.[452] Some decisions are not susceptible to the application of any ordinary appellate remedies, such as decisions regarding the administration of the trial, for instance, decisions fixing the procedural calendar and trial date,[453] or decisions ordering certain investigation measures, such as decisions ordering a judicial site inspection[454] or appearance of the parties before the judge in person.[455]

340. Unlike the (ordinary) appeal, no statutory threshold must be met in order to lodge opposition. Opposition is available to the defaulting party who is aggrieved by the default judgment, regardless of the monetary value of the claim. The notice of the opposition must, however, on pain of nullity, indicate the reasons for the lodging of the opposition, meaning that the opposing party must explain why and to what extent he feels aggrieved by the default judgment.[456] This statement of the grounds of the opposition may be brief.[457]

341. Opposition can be lodged as soon as the default judgment has been rendered, even if it has not yet been served on the defaulting party.[458] The term for lodging opposition is generally one month from the date the judgment is served by a bailiff (or notified by the court registry by judicial letter). This is a peremptory time limit that

451. Article 1047 Judicial Code, as amended by the aforementioned so-called Potpourri V Act of 6 July 2017. This rule is also applicable when the judgment *in absentia* was rendered at second instance, closing appellate proceedings (Article 1067 Judicial Code).
452. Articles 747, §2, para. 6, 748, §2, para. 6, 804, para. 2, and 1113, para. 1, Judicial Code.
453. Articles 747, §2, para. 4, and 748, §2, para. 5, *juncto* Article 1046 Judicial Code.
454. Articles 1007–1008 Judicial Code.
455. Articles 992 and 996 Judicial Code.
456. Article 1047, para. 4, Judicial Code.
457. Court of Cassation 13 January 2011, C.10.0053.F.
458. As pointed out above under para. 315, before 1 November 2015, the default judgment had to be served on the defaulting party within a time limit of one year, in the absence of which the default judgment would be considered 'non-existent'. This implied that the defaulting party could enter a plea in the event that the other party wanted to enforce the judgment after the one-year time limit. The defaulting party could also oppose the judgment in court. However, the procedure prior to the default judgment was preserved, meaning that the party who obtained the 'defunct' judgment, could simply request a new hearing and judgment.

is provided for by statute under penalty of inadmissibility, which must be pronounced by the court *sua sponte*.[459]

342. If the party who did not enter an appearance failed to lodge opposition within the statutory time limit, for whatever reason, a petition for cassation may be filed (provided that the conditions of this extraordinary legal remedy are fulfilled).[460]

343. For the calculation, extension and suspension of the time limit, please refer to what is set out below in relation to the (ordinary) appeal (paragraph 352).

344. Opposition must be lodged before the same court that delivered the default judgment by service of a writ of summons upon the other party.[461] This formality may be abolished if all parties agree to appear voluntarily before the court.[462] In some cases, opposition can be lodged by means of a petition, i.e., a written request directly addressed to the court registry by the opposing party or his counsel.[463] The notice of opposition must be drawn up in the same language as the default judgment.[464]

345. If the party who has lodged opposition defaults again, no opposition is allowed against the second default judgment ('*opposition sur opposition ne vaut*').[465]

B. Scope of Review

346. Opposition allows the defaulting party to re-submit the case in its entirety to the scrutiny of the same court that delivered the default judgment. The court that has to decide upon the opposition can review and re-litigate upon both facts and legal assessments. The scope of the court's review is defined by the litigating parties, meaning that the court cannot re-litigate on points at issue that are not challenged in the notice of opposition.

347. Opposition has a relative effect, meaning that it cannot have adverse effects for the party that lodges the opposition. This relative effect does not prevent, however, the extension or amendment of the original claim under Articles 807 et seq. of the Judicial Code (*see supra*, paragraphs 209–211).

C. Consequences for (Provisional) Enforcement

348. As a general rule, the lodging of opposition entails a stay of the enforcement of the final decisions[466] contained in the default judgment, unless the court has, upon request of a party or on its own motion, authorised the (provisional) enforcement thereof in a well-reasoned decision,[467] or if a statutory provision expressly provides

459. Article 860, para. 2, *juncto* Article 865 Judicial. *See supra* para. 229.
460. Article 1076 Judicial Code.
461. Article 1047, para. 2, Judicial Code.
462. Article 1047, para. 3, *juncto* Article 706 Judicial Code.
463. For example, Article 1253*quater*(c) Judicial Code.
464. Article 24 Language Act of 15 June 1935.
465. Article 1049 Judicial Code.
466. *See supra* paras 283–285.
467. Article 1397, para. 2, Judicial Code.

for an exception to this rule.[468] Decisions before adjudicating contained in the default judgment are, by force of law, always open to provisional enforcement[469] on the sole risk of the party ordering such an enforcement.[470]

349. With regard to default judgments concerning the conviction of the defaulting party to pay a sum of money by a final decision, both the effective lodging of opposition, as well as the fact that the time limit to lodge opposition has not yet expired suspend the ability to enforce this order, unless the court has authorised the provisional enforcement thereof.[471] When the default judgment contains a final decision convicting the defaulting party to another obligation than paying a sum of money (i.e., to perform or refrain from a certain action), only the effective lodging of opposition has a suspending effect on this order.[472]

II. Appeal

A. Admissibility

350. As a general rule, each judgment rendered in first instance (whether it is an interlocutory judgment, a judgment before adjudicating, a standard final adversarial judgment or a default judgment which is not open to review by opposition (*see supra* paragraph 338)) may be subject to appeal, without prior leave by a court or other authority being required.[473,474] However, a statutory provision can provide that a certain decision is not appealable, such as decisions concerning the administration of the trial (for instance, administrative measures ordered by the court with respect to the progress of the proceedings)[475] or judgments rendered by the District Court.[476]

351. A statutory provision can also determine that a court decision is not appealable because judgment is delivered 'at first and final instance' (*en premier et dernier resort – in eerste en laatste aanleg*). In this type of cases, only extraordinary appellate remedies, such as a procedure before the Court of Cassation, are as a rule[477] available. This is the case if the amount in dispute does not exceed the threshold laid down in Article 617 of the Judicial Code: EUR 2,500 for judgments of the Courts of First Instance and the Commercial Courts; EUR 1,860.00 for judgments of the Justice of the Peace Courts and the Police Courts (in civil disputes). The judgments of the

468. For example, in summary or ex parte proceedings (*see* respectively Articles 1039 and 1029 Judicial Code), and for all decisions before adjudicating (Article 1397, para. 3, Judicial Code).
469. Article 1397, para. 3, Judicial Code (as amended by the so-called Potpourri V Act).
470. Article 1397 Judicial Code.
471. Article 1495, para. 2, Judicial Code.
472. Article 1397, para. 2, Judicial Code.
473. Articles 1050–1072 Judicial Code.
474. Article 616 Judicial Code.
475. For instance, decisions fixing the terms to file pleadings and the trial date (Articles 747, §2, para. 4 and 748, §2, para. 5, *juncto* Article 1046 Judicial Code).
476. Article 642 Judicial Code.
477. Article 1047 of the Judicial Code provides for an exception to this rule (*see supra*, para. 338).

Labour Courts, however, are always open to appeal, regardless of the monetary value of the claim.[478]

The monetary value of the claim is determined in accordance with Articles 557–562 of the Judicial Code (*see supra*, paragraph 148). The Court of Cassation ruled that the court may decide that the appeal is not admissible, even though the statutory threshold is met, if the appellant maliciously raised or exaggerated the monetary value of the (counter)claim with a view to circumvent the statutory threshold.[479] If the value of the claim is modified in the course of the proceedings, the amount of money claimed in the final pleadings will be considered.[480] If the claim cannot be expressed in terms of money, the judgment is presumed to be rendered in first instance.[481] Interlocutory judgments and judgments ordering an investigation measure are appealable if the value of the main claim exceeds the abovementioned amounts.[482] However, in case of a counterclaim for vexatious litigation, a counterclaim or an action to intervene seeking the conviction of a third party resulting from the same disputed contract or fact founding the main claim, the appealability of the judgment is determined on the basis of the added value of the main claim and the counterclaim, c.q., action to intervene.[483]

352. In principle, an appeal can be filed as soon as the judgment has been rendered, even if it has not yet been served or notified.[484] In some cases, a certain waiting period has to be observed before a judgment can be appealed. Appeal against an interlocutory judgment deciding upon the competence of the court is not immediately possible, and can only be lodged together with the appeal against a final decision on the admissibility or on the merits of the case.[485] As part of a recent reform of the Judicial Code by the aforementioned Potpouri I Act, decisions before adjudicating (such as decisions ordering investigation measures or measures aimed at the provisional settlement of the parties' dispute) rendered after 1 November 2015 are subject to the same rule, unless the court decides otherwise.[486]

The term for lodging an appeal is generally one month from the date of service or notification of the judgment.[487] The term is calculated starting from the day after the *dies a quo* (being the day of the act or event that triggers the time limit) until and inclusive the *dies ad quem* (being the last day, i.e., the day on which the time limit elapses).[488] For the calculation of the term of one month, one must count from the day

478. Article 617, para. 2, Judicial Code.
479. Court of Cassation 8 January 2004, C.01.0453.N.
480. Article 618, para. 2, Judicial Code.
481. Article 619 Judicial Code.
482. Article 621 Judicial Code.
483. Article 620 Judicial Code. Note that the Constitutional Court ruled that the limitation of the scope of Article 620 Judicial Code to 'actions to intervene seeking the conviction of a third party' – which do not cover all kinds of incidental claims possibly resulting from the same disputed contract or fact founding the other claims – is unconstitutional (Constitutional Court No. 79/2001 of 7 June 2001), precluding the application of this provision by the courts (Court of Cassation 5 February 2016, C.15.0011.F).
484. Article 1050, para. 1, Judicial Code.
485. Articles 1050, para. 2, *juncto* Article 19, para. 1, Judicial Code.
486. Articles 1050, para. 2, Judicial Code.
487. Article 1051, para. 1, Judicial Code.
488. Articles 52–53 Judicial Code.

after the *dies a quo* until the day before such day in the next month (*see also supra*, paragraph 225).[489] When the term expires on a Saturday, a Sunday or a public holiday, it will be prolonged until the next working day.[490]

The term of appeal is a peremptory time-limit and is provided for by statute under penalty of inadmissibility, which must be pronounced by the court *sua sponte*.[491] The term cannot be extended (or shortened) by the court, even with the agreement of the parties.[492] There are, however, a few exceptional circumstances that may result in an extension or suspension of the time limit:

- When a party has no (elected) domicile or place of residence in Belgium, the time limit is extended by fifteen days if this party resides in France, Luxembourg, the Netherlands, Germany or the United Kingdom; by thirty days if he resides in another state of Europe and by eighty days if he resides in another part of the world.[493] The same applies if the judgment is notified by judicial letter to a party who has no (elected) domicile or place of residence in Belgium.[494] Also, when the term of appeal begins and ends during the judicial holidays (from 1 July to, and including, 31 August),[495] it is (automatically) extended until the fifteenth day of the new judicial year (15 September).[496]
- The death of a party suspends the time limit imposed on that party to file an appeal. The term of appeal commences again only after the judgment has been served again at the place of residence of the deceased party. If the judgment is served before the expiry of the time limits to draw up an estate inventory and reflect hereupon, the term of appeal commences again after the expiry of those time limits. The judgment can be served jointly on the heirs, without stating their name and title. Any interested party can nevertheless be exempted from the expiry of the time limit if he was not informed of the service of the judgment.[497]
- The term of appeal can be suspended due to force majeure (for as long as the force majeure lasts), being an insurmountable impediment to lodge an appeal, which has to be proved by the party lodging the appeal after the expiration of the time limit. Only exceptional circumstances which happen in spite of human will and which cannot be foreseen or prevented are accepted as force majeure. The non- or malfunctioning of the mail delivery service is not considered force majeure since the documents could have been delivered in another way. Mistakes or negligence of an authorised representative (attorney, bailiff, etc.), which took place within the limits of the representation, are generally considered to be the

489. Article 54 Judicial Code.
490. Article 53, para. 2, Judicial Code.
491. Article 860, para. 2, *juncto* Article 865 Judicial Code. *See supra* para. 229.
492. Article 50, para. 1, Judicial Code.
493. Article 1051, para. 3, *juncto* Article 55 Judicial Code.
494. Article 1051, para. 4, *juncto* Article 55 Judicial Code.
495. Article 340 Judicial Code.
496. Article 50, para. 2, Judicial Code.
497. Article 56 Judicial Code.

mistakes or negligence of the person represented, and cannot give rise to force majeure.[498]

- The fact that the service or notification of the judgment does not contain any information regarding the available appellate remedies is generally not perceived as a circumstance which allows the addressee (whether he is domiciled in Belgium or abroad) to introduce his recourse after the expiry of the statutory time limit. Unless the judgment is notified in accordance with Article 792, paragraphs 2–3, of the Judicial Code (*see supra*, paragraph 299), the service or notification of a judgment is not required to contain any information regarding the appellate remedies, their time limit or the competent court. Such duty to inform was provided for in a new Article 46*bis* of the Judicial Code,[499] but until today this article did not enter into force. Nevertheless, one must take into account the judgment of the European Court of Human Rights in the case of *Faniel v. Belgium*.[500] In this case, Belgium was held in violation of Article 6.1 of the ECHR because Mr Faniel, a Belgian national who was sentenced in his absence to six months of imprisonment, had not been informed of the relevant formalities and time limits in order to lodge an appellate remedy against the judgment rendered in his absence. The European Court of Human Rights took into account that Mr Faniel did not have any legal assistance at the time of the lodging of the appellate remedy (which was declared inadmissible by the Belgian courts because of an alleged violation of the time limit). Legal doctrine is, however, divided as to whether the Faniel case entails a general duty to include information on the available appellate remedies in the act of service or notification of a judgment. In its judgment of 15 May 2015 (in a civil case), the (Dutch-speaking section of the) Court of Cassation ruled that Article 6.1 of the ECHR does not entail an obligation to provide information on the available legal remedies in case of the service of a judgment at the request of one of the parties to the other party.[501] On the other hand, in its judgment of 29 January 2016, the (French-speaking section of the) Court of Cassation ruled that the notification of the judgment by the court's registry will only trigger the running of the statutory time limit for lodging an appellate remedy if such effect is expressly provided for by statute and the notification contains information regarding the available appellate remedies and their statutory time limit. The Court referred to Article 6.1 of the ECHR.[502]
- For now, the conclusion seems to be that, although Article 6.1 of the ECHR must be taken into account with regard to the foreseeability, transparency and

498. Court of Cassation 3 May 2011, P.10.1865.N; Court of Cassation 27 April 2010, P.10.0512.N; compare with Court of Cassation 9 November 2011, P.11.1027.F.
499. Article 46*bis* of the Judicial Code would have stipulated that the act of service or notification of the judgment must contain information regarding the time limit to appeal the judgment by means of opposition, ordinary appeal or appeal to the Court of Cassation, as well as the way in which these appellate remedies are to be lodged.
500. *Faniel/Belgium*, ECtHR No. 11892/08 of 1 March 2011. *See* also *Assunção Chaves/Portugal,* ECtHR No. 61226/08 of 31 January 2012.
501. Court of Cassation 15 May 2015, C.12.0568.N. *See* also *Avotiņš/Letland*, ECtHR No. 17502/07 of 23 May 2016.
502. Court of Cassation 29 January 2016, C.14.00006.F.

recognisability of the procedural rules, the exact scope of the associated procedural guarantees is highly dependent on the precise circumstances of the case.

- The Court of Cassation ruled on many occasions that disloyal procedural behaviour cannot be tolerated. Pursuant to this case law, it is clear that the service of a judgment in a way that constitutes a violation of the addressee's rights of defence or a misuse or abuse of right on the side of the party who ordered the service cannot trigger the running of the time limit to lodge a legal remedy against this judgment.[503]

Cross appeals (*appel incident – incidenteel beroep*) can be lodged 'at all times', meaning until the hearings are closed, provided that the principal appeal was filed in time.[504]

353. Appeal is only available to persons who were a party (or represented by a party) in the first instance proceedings. Appeal is not possible by third parties, not even if they are aggrieved by the judgment; only third-party opposition is available to them (*see infra*, paragraphs 379–384). The respondent on appeal must also have been a party in the first instance proceedings and must have been the opponent of the appellant. The latter condition is fulfilled when the first instance judgment creates an obligation for the appellant towards that party. In principle, the appellant can freely choose against whom, among the parties to the case, he will lodge an appeal. This is only different in the case of an 'indivisible dispute' (*indivisibilité – onsplitsbaarheid*).[505] A cross appeal can only be filed by a party against whom a (principal or other cross) appeal is already pending. A cross appeal can be filed against all parties involved in the case before the appellate judge.[506]

354. Appeal is only available to parties in the first instance proceedings who are aggrieved by the first instance judgment. This means that the applicant must have a legitimate interest in bringing the case before the appellate court. For example, since the appeal aims at reversing the first instance judgment, no appeal can be filed on behalf of the party whose claim has been fully granted, but who is not satisfied with the judgment's reasoning.[507]

355. The notice of appeal can take on various forms. Appeal can be lodged (1) by service of a writ of summons upon the party against whom appeal is sought;[508] (2) by petition to be filed with the court registry of the competent appellate court, the date of arrival of the petition being the date of the appeal[509] (the court registry shall notify a copy thereof to the party against whom appeal is sought and its counsel, if any); (3)

503. Court of Cassation 27 September 2013, C.12.0627.F-C.12.0629.F; Court of Cassation 25 April 2014, C.13.0204.F; Court of Cassation 10 March 2008, C.06.0610.N; Court of Cassation 25 May 2007, F.05.0057.N; Court of Cassation 8 March 2002, C.01.0113.F; Court of Cassation 29 March 2001, C.00.0190.F.
504. Article 1054 Judicial Code.
505. Article 1053 *juncto* Article 31 Judicial Code. A dispute is indivisible if the joint enforcement of the first instance judgment and the (hypothetical conflicting) judgment to be rendered upon appeal would be impossible.
506. Article 1054, para. 1, Judicial Code.
507. Court of Cassation 19 February 1979, *Arresten van het Hof van Cassatie* 1978–1979, 725.
508. The date of the writ being the date of appeal.
509. Court of Cassation 27 November 1997, C.97.0213.N.

by registered letter where specifically provided by statute and (4) by written pleadings for lodging a cross appeal.[510]

356. The notice of appeal must mention, *inter alia*, the grounds for the appeal, on pain of nullity.[511] The grounds of the appeal are the grievances, complaints and reproaches of the appellant with respect to the contested judgment. The statement of the grounds of appeal may be brief, but a simple referral to the pleadings of the appellant filed during the proceedings in first instance is not sufficient.[512] The notice of appeal must be drawn up in the same language as the contested judgment.[513]

357. The waiting period between the notice of the appeal and the preliminary hearing before the appellate court is at least fifteen days.[514] This period can be extended if the respondent resides abroad (*see supra*, paragraph 255).

B. Scope of Review

358. Ordinary appeal submits the case to the scrutiny of a higher court, which can review and re-litigate upon both the facts and the legal assessments. The appellate court cannot restrict its review to questions of law, but must itself (re-)decide the case on the merits, including finding the facts in dispute (even if those facts only occurred after the decision of the first judge).[515]

359. In principle, the appeal brings the whole case before the appellate court for a new and independent adjudication. Even if the appellate court annuls the first judgment for purely procedural reasons (for instance, an irregular composition of the first instance court), it has to render judgment on the entire dispute.[516] Moreover, all (factual and legal) issues that have not yet been decided by the first instance court are transferred to the appellate court. The case is not remanded to the first instance court.[517] The appeal is thus said to have a 'devolutive effect'.[518] Even the appeal against a mere interlocutory judgment brings the entire dispute before the appellate court. There is only one exception to this rule: when the first judge has ordered an investigation measure, such as a witness examination or expert investigation, and this decision is – even partially – affirmed, the appellate court must remand the case to the first instance

510. Article 1056 Judicial Code.
511. Article 1057 Judicial Code.
512. Court of Cassation 14 December 2000, C.99.0359.F; Court of Cassation 9 October 1980, *Arresten van het Hof van Cassatie* 1980–1981, 138. There is no obligation to mention the legal grounds supporting the grievances (Court of Cassation 22 October 2012, S.12.0024.F), and the grievances may be completed during the appellate proceedings (Court of Cassation 1 June 2007, *Rechtspraak Antwerpen Brussel Gent* 2008, 666, note S. Berneman).
513. Article 24 Language Act of 15 June 1935.
514. Article 1062 Judicial Code.
515. Court of Cassation 16 November 1989, *Arresten van het Hof van Cassatie* 1989–1990, 369.
516. Court of Cassation 2 November 1989, *Arresten van het Hof van Cassatie* 1989–1990, 298.
517. Court of Cassation 29 May 2015, C.13.0615.N; Court of Cassation 19 December 1991, *Arresten van het Hof van Cassatie* 1991–1992.
518. Article 1068, para. 1, Judicial Code.

judge. If the appellate court reverses the decision ordering the investigation measure, it will deliver judgment with regard to the entire case.[519]

360. The 'devolutive effect' of the appeal is, however, without prejudice to the fact that the parties can restrict the scope of the appeal to designated issues (which is expressed by the Latin phrase '*tantum devolutum, quantum appellatum*').[520,521]

361. The appeal also has a relative effect, meaning that it cannot have adverse effects for the party who lodges the appeal. The position of such party may only become worse at the appellate level if the other party has lodged a cross appeal.

362. The scope of the case can be extended on appeal, meaning that the parties can modify their claims and submit new claims that have not been submitted in first instance, provided that such modified or new claims fulfil the requirements set forth in Articles 807–808 of the Judicial Code (*see supra*, paragraphs 209–211). Claims in intervention aimed at obtaining an order against the intervening party may, however, not occur in appeal for the first time.[522]

C. *Consequences for (Provisional) Enforcement*

363. Until recently, the general rule was that lodging an appeal imposed a complete stay of execution of the final decisions[523] contained in the first instance judgment, unless the first instance court authorised the (provisional) enforcement of these decisions notwithstanding an appeal. This feature of appeal proceedings was often perceived as frustrating, leading to abusive appeals only aimed at delaying the execution of the judgment. Therefore, the rule has recently been reversed. Lodging an appeal, as well as the fact that the time limit to lodge an appeal has not yet expired, no longer stays the (provisional) execution of the final decision contained in the judgment (under appeal). This is only different if the first instance court expressly ordered, at the request of a party or on its own motion, a deviation from this rule in a well-reasoned decision or if a statute expressly provides for an exception to this rule.[524]

---

519. Article 1068, para. 2, Judicial Code. If the judgment under appeal contains an investigation measure as well as decisions on other issues, the appellate court that (partially) affirms the investigation measure shall render judgment on the in appeal contested issues that have already been decided by the first instance court and shall remand the case with respect to the issues that have not yet been adjudicated in first instance (Court of Cassation 28 April 1980, *Arresten van het Hof van Cassatie* 1979–1980, 1070). The appellate court shall, however, not remand the case with respect to the latter issues, insofar as it can adjudicate those issues without having to rely on the results of the investigation measure (Court of Cassation 20 October 2000, C.99.0440.N; Court of Cassation 11 January 1990, *Arresten van het Hof van Cassatie* 1989–1990, 629).
520. Free translation: 'as much is brought up on appeal as has been appealed from'.
521. Court of Cassation 6 May 1993, *Pasicrisie belge* 1993, I, 449; Court of Cassation 21 November 1991, *Arresten van het Hof van Cassatie* 1991–1992, 255.
522. Article 812, para. 2, Judicial Code. *See* Court of Cassation 24 November 1972, *Arresten van het Hof van Cassatie* 1973, 298; compare with Court of Cassation 26 October 1987, *Arresten van het Hof van Cassatie* 1987–1988, 234.
523. *See supra* paras 283–285.
524. Article 1397, para. 1, Judicial Code.

Decisions before adjudicating contained in the first instance judgment are, by force of law, always open to provisional enforcement.[525]

364. The provisional enforcement of decisions contained in the judgment under appeal or before the expiry of the time limit for such a remedy is at the prevailing party's sole risk.[526] If the judgment is later on annulled or amended, such party has an obligation to return anything that he may have received out of the provisional enforcement (or e.g., bear the costs of the investigation measure ordered by the judge in a decision before adjudicating). Moreover, he must compensate the other party for any damages suffered in this respect.[527]

§3. Extraordinary Appellate Remedies

I. Appeal to the Court of Cassation

A. Admissibility

365. The Belgian judicial system provides for a further 'ultimate' recourse against judgments rendered in last instance, i.e., the petition for cassation, which is to be filed before the Court of Cassation.[528]

366. The petition for cassation can be filed only against judgments delivered in last instance, being judgments against which it is no longer (or has never been) possible to lodge an (ordinary) appeal on points of fact and law.[529] The petitioner is not required to obtain prior leave by a court or other authority.

367. The petition for cassation can be filed against both final decisions (for instance, decisions on the admissibility or the merits of the case) and decisions before adjudicating (for instance, decisions ordering an investigation measure). The petition against a decision before adjudicating, however, can only be lodged after the final judgment (i.e., the judgment in which the court has exhausted its power with regard to the entire dispute) has been rendered.[530]

368. The petition may be filed only on the grounds of violation of the law or violation of substantial procedural formalities or guarantees (such as the rights of defence). The petition must specify in which way and to what extent the judgment against which it is filed is not in accordance with the law. It must also precisely indicate the allegedly violated statutory provisions or general principles of law or due process.[531] The European Court of Human Rights has ruled that, even if imposing on the applicant

525. Article 1397, para. 3, Judicial Code (as amended by the so-called Potpourri V Act).
526. Article 1398 Judicial Code.
527. Court of Cassation 7 April 1995, *Arresten van het Hof van Cassatie* 1995, 383.
528. Articles 1073–1121 Judicial Code.
529. Article 608 Judicial Code.
530. Article 1077 Judicial Code.
531. Article 1080 Judicial Code.

the specification of the reasons of his application to the Court of Cassation is aimed at securing a legitimate goal, such rule must not be applied in a formalistic way.[532]

369. In civil cases, the petition must be signed by an attorney admitted to practice before the Court of Cassation (*see supra*, paragraph 130). A petition that is not signed by such specialised attorney will be declared inadmissible.[533] It is usual, before initiating cassation proceedings, to consult an attorney admitted to practice before the Court of Cassation about the chances for success of the remedy. In case of a negative advice, the intention to lodge an appeal before the Court of Cassation is mostly abandoned. However, in case a party persists in its intention, he can order an attorney who is admitted to practice before the Court of Cassation to initiate proceedings.

370. The petition for cassation must be served to the defendant by a bailiff and must subsequently be filed with the court registry of the Court of Cassation.[534] The petition has to be filed within three months from the date of service or notification of the contested judgment.[535] This term is a peremptory time limit and is provided for by statute under penalty of inadmissibility. If during this time limit the party against whom the petition for cassation must be filed dies, the term is extended with two months.[536] For other aspects of the calculation, extension and suspension of the time limit, please refer to the text above on the (ordinary) appeal (paragraph 352).

371. The defendant may file a response to the petition within three months of the service of the petition. The response equally has to be signed by an attorney admitted to practice before the Court of Cassation.[537] Normally, the petitioner does not have the possibility to file a reply, unless the defendant enters a plea of inadmissibility. In this case, the petitioner has one month to file his reply.[538]

372. If none of the parties has filed a petition for cassation within the statutory time limit, the public prosecutor at the Court of Cassation can do so in the interest of the law. The parties, however, will not benefit from this cassation appeal.

373. As with the ordinary appeal, the petition for cassation can only be filed by a legal subject who was a party (or represented by a party) in the previous (appellate) proceedings, provided that such party has an interest in bringing the case before the Court of Cassation. The latter means for example that a party cannot file a petition for cassation against a decision concerning the course and the administration of the proceedings that was rendered in accordance with this party's pleas, even though this decision constitutes a violation of the law.[539]

---

532. *Dattel/Luxemburg*, ECtHR No. 18522/06 of 30 July 2009; *RTBF/Belgium*, ECtHR No. 50084/06 of 29 March 2011.
533. Article 1080 Judicial Code.
534. Article 1079 Judicial Code.
535. Article 1073 Judicial Code.
536. Aticle 1074 Judicial Code.
537. Article 1092 Judicial Code.
538. Article 1094 Judicial Code.
539. Court of Cassation 29 January 2015, F.14.0007.F; Court of Cassation 7 February 2014, C.12.0571.F; Court of Cassation 15 November 2013, C.11.0656.F; Court of Cassation 3 May 2013, C.12.0350.N; Court of Cassation 16 March 2012, C.08.0323.F-C.09.0590.F; Court of Cassation 1 March 2012, C.10.0425.N).

374. The petition for cassation must be drafted in the same language as the contested judgment.[540] If the contested judgment is in German, the petition may be drawn up in Dutch, French or German, to the petitioner's choice.[541]

B. Scope of Review

375. The petition for cassation is not a second appeal or third instance procedure, but a review procedure that aims at reviewing only whether the judgment against which the petition for cassation is made is rendered in accordance with the law and the applicable formal requirements.[542] In other words, the Court of Cassation does not rule on the facts but only on questions of law. Hence, a petition for cassation may be lodged on points of law only, i.e., on the grounds that there has been a breach of the law or a general principle of law or due process.

376. The scope of review by the Court of Cassation in civil cases is set by the petitioner only.[543] The Court has no jurisdiction regarding points of law which are not included in the petition for cassation, not even if it is apparent that the judgment against which the petition is filed contains (other) violations of the law or general principles of law.[544]

377. When the petition for cassation is dismissed, the judgment against which the petition was made (including its res judicata) is preserved. If the petition is granted, the Court of Cassation quashes the judgment, in whole or in part. If the substance of the case has to be reconsidered, the case is referred to a court of the same level as the one that rendered the quashed judgment, or to the court that has rendered the quashed judgment. In the latter case, the court's composition has to be altered for this reconsideration.[545] The procedure before this court will be commenced by the service of a writ of summons accompanied by a copy of the judgment of the Court of Cassation.[546] In re-deciding the case, the court is bound by the decision of the Court of Cassation.[547] This recently introduced new rule confirms the decisive influence of the decisions of the Court of Cassation on the creation of case law.[548] Formerly, the lower courts usually followed precedents set by the Court of Cassation. The Court of Cassation only exceptionally overrules its own precedents.

540. Article 27 Language Act of 15 June 1935.
541. Article 27*bis* Language Act of 15 June 1935.
542. Article 147 Constitution; Article 608 Judicial Code.
543. In criminal cases, the Court of Cassation examines on its own initiative any (other) violations of the law or fundamental procedural requirements.
544. Article 1080 *juncto* Article 1095 Judicial Code.
545. Article 1110, para. 1, Judicial Code (as amended by the so-called Potpourri V Act).
546. Article 1110 *juncto* Article 1115 Judicial Code.
547. Article 1110, para. 4, Judicial Code (as amended by the so-called Potpourri V Act).
548. The advice of the prosecutor at the Court of Cassation, which is mandatory in all cases (Article 1107, para. 1, Judicial Code), is very useful to understand and establish the precise content and scope of the Court's decisions, as the motivation of the Court's decisions is usually rather brief.

C. *Consequences for Enforcement*

378. In civil cases, the filing of a petition for cassation does not entail a stay of the enforcement of the contested judgment, unless a statutory provision expressly provides otherwise.[549] In other words, the contested judgment is fully enforceable (i.e., has the force of res judicata – *see supra*, paragraph 295), notwithstanding the cassation appeal.

II. Third-Party Opposition

379. Third-party opposition is only available to persons whose rights are adversely affected by a judgment rendered pursuant to proceedings to which they were not a party.[550,551]

380. All judgments may be subject to third party opposition, except for decisions of the Court of Cassation.[552]

381. Third-party opposition has to be brought before the judge who rendered the contested judgment[553] within three months from the date of service of the judgment on the third party.[554] If the judgment is not served on the third party, a time limit of thirty years applies. Third-party opposition can, however, no longer be lodged after the expiry of the limitation period to enforce the judgment ('*actio judicati*'), which is set at ten years after the judgment has been rendered, albeit that this limitation period may be subject to suspension and interruption.[555]

382. If the remedy is successful, the judge shall annul the judgment, but only *vis-à-vis* the third party. In principle, the annulment does not affect the (res judicata[556] of the) judgment between the original parties to the case.[557] This is only different if the dispute is 'indivisible', i.e., if the joint enforcement of the contested judgment and the (conflicting) judgment rendered upon third-party opposition would be impossible.[558]

383. Third-party opposition does not stay the enforcement of the contested judgment, unless the court before which the remedy is brought (or the judge of attachments) decides otherwise.[559]

384. A decision rendered on third-party opposition may be subject to ordinary appeal, unless the contested judgment itself was rendered on appeal.[560]

---

549. Article 1118 Judicial Code.
550. Articles 1122–1131 Judicial Code.
551. Article 1122 Judicial Code.
552. Article 1123 Judicial Code.
553. By serving a writ of summons upon all the parties in the original action (Article 1125, para. 1, Judicial Code).
554. Article 1129 Judicial Code.
555. Article 1128 Judicial Code *juncto* Article 2262*bis*, §1, Civil Code.
556. Here to be understood as the binding force of the judgment.
557. Article 1130, para. 1, Judicial Code.
558. Article 1130, para. 2, *juncto* Article 31 Judicial Code.
559. Article 1127 Judicial Code.
560. Article 1131 Judicial Code.

III. Revocation of Res Judicata

385. This extraordinary legal remedy is subject to very strict conditions[561]. The grounds on the basis of which a party may request the revocation of a judgment's res judicata are listed exhaustively in Article 1133 of the Judicial Code: (1) the judgment is vitiated by fraud; (2) the withholding of evidence by one of the parties; (3) false testimonies of witnesses or court-appointed experts; (4) the judgment is based on a criminal judgment that later has been annulled; (5) the judgment is based on procedural acts performed on behalf of a party who did not authorise such acts (*see also infra*, paragraphs 415–418); (6) irreconcilable judgments rendered between the same parties regarding the same object and the same cause of action.

386. The request is introduced by means of a petition, which must be signed by three attorneys, two of whom must be members of the bar for at least twenty years.[562] The petition is served with a writ of summons to appear before the court that rendered the judgment. It must be brought within six months after discovery of the facts on which the request for revocation is based.[563]

IV. Redress Against the Judge

387. In a limited number of cases, a party may file a direct civil liability claim against the judge (or the public prosecution service)[564]. Article 1140 of the Judicial Code provides for an exhaustive list of circumstances where such action against the judge can be undertaken: (1) the judge committed fraud; (2) the judge refused to render judgment; (3) action against the judge is explicitly provided for by a statutory provision; (4) the judge is held responsible for possible damages by a statutory provision.

388. The claim has to be brought before the Court of Cassation within thirty days after the facts on which the claim is based or within thirty days after the fraud has been discovered.[565] If the claim is found to be grounded, the Court of Cassation can either annul the judgment (if any) or order the judge to pay damages.[566]

V. Repeal

389. The repeal is a legal remedy that can be applied against judgments that are based on a statutory or regulatory provision which has subsequently been nullified by the Constitutional Court (*see supra*, paragraphs 96-99).[567] The action is brought before

561. Articles 1132–1139 Judicial Code.
562. Article 1134 Judicial Code.
563. Article 1136 Judicial Code.
564. Articles 1140–1147 Judicial Code.
565. Article 1142–1143 Judicial Code.
566. Article 1147 Judicial Code.
567. The rules regarding the repeal are laid down in Article 16 of the Special Act of 6 January 1989 on the Constitutional Court.

the court that rendered the judgment. This court may, within the limits of the repeal, pronounce a new judgment based on a different legal ground.

Part VI. Incidents

390. Incidents (*incident – tussengeschil*) is a generic term that refers to all procedural events that may occur in the course of the proceedings, and that may lead to a suspension or interruption of the proceedings. In other words, it concerns all procedural matters or questions to be dealt with by the court before a final judgment on the merits can be rendered. The Judicial Code deals with a variety of incidental issues, some of which have been discussed above, such as the ancillary claims and the pleas of nullity, some of which will be discussed later on, such as the discovery procedures. This section deals with five other types of incidents:

(1) The resumption of the proceedings after a suspension thereof (*reprise d'instance – hervatting van het geding*).
(2) The withdrawal by the applicant of the proceedings (*désistement d'instance – afstand van geding*), the withdrawal by the applicant of the action (*désistement d'action – afstand van rechtsvordering*) and the withdrawal by the applicant of a procedural act (*désistement d'un acte de procedure – afstand van proceshandeling*).
(3) The challenge of judges (*récusation – wraking*).
(4) The removal of the case from the court (*dessaisissement – onttrekking*).
(5) The repudiation (or rejection) of procedural acts performed without lawful representation (*désaveu – ontkentenis van proceshandelingen*).

Chapter 1. Resumption of the Proceedings

391. Article 815 of the Judicial Code provides for three situations in which the proceedings are suspended: (1) the death of a party; (2) the change of a party's legal status (the exact scope of this incident is unclear; it is clear, however, that the transition of minority to majority of a party does not suspend the proceedings[568]); and (3) the change of a party's legal standing with respect to the object of the claim (for instance, in case of a transfer of ownership with respect to the object of the claim to a third party in the course of the proceedings).[569] The proceedings will, however, be suspended only if one of these situations arises before the closing of the hearings, and provided that the court and the other parties are notified thereof.

392. If all of the abovementioned conditions are fulfilled, the proceedings are suspended, and any procedural acts performed after such suspension are to be considered null and void. Articles 816–819 of the Judicial Code explain how to resume the proceedings. This resumption can be voluntary, i.e., at the initiative of the party that caused the suspension, by the filing of a document with the court's registry explaining the reason for the resumption of the proceedings. This document must also contain the identity of the person who resumes the proceedings. If the resumption does not happen voluntarily, it can be enforced by the other parties by the service of a writ of summons upon the person who now has the required legal capacity and legal standing to continue the proceedings (for instance, the heir(s) of the deceased party).

393. After the resumption, the proceedings are continued on the basis of the last pleadings, unless the act of resumption itself contains new pleadings.

568. *See* S. Dufrene, 'La determination des parties en litige et le lien d'instance (spécialement en cas de reprise d'instance)', in J. Linsmeau & M. Storme (eds.), *De respectievelijke rol van de rechter en partijen in het burgerlijk geding*, Diegem, Kluwer, 1992, 34–36.

569. Court of Cassation 31 May 2012, C.11.0343.N; Court of Cassation 1 March 1984, *Arresten van het Hof van Cassatie* 1983–1984, 742.

Chapter 2. Withdrawal of the Proceedings, Withdrawal of the Action and Withdrawal of a Procedural Act

394. The Judicial Code provides for three types of withdrawal: (1) withdrawal of the proceedings; (2) withdrawal of the action; and (3) withdrawal of a procedural act.

395. Withdrawal of the proceedings means that the claimant simply renounces the proceedings, without waiving his right to (re-)introduce the claim.[570] This type of withdrawal is allowed in all circumstances.[571]

396. Withdrawal of the action, on the other hand, implies that the claimant does not only renounce the proceedings, but also the legal action as such.[572] Hence, no new claim can be introduced on the same basis. Withdrawal of the action is only possible with respect to substantive rights that can be freely disposed of.[573]

397. Withdrawal of a procedural act means that a party waives the legal effects of a procedural act on his behalf.[574]

398. Withdrawal of the proceedings may be express or implicit in the behaviour of the party concerned. Express withdrawal is done by means of a document signed by the party that wishes to withdraw the proceedings or its legal representative with special power of attorney. Implicit withdrawal may only be derived from certain documents or facts indicating a clear and unambiguous intention to withdraw the proceedings.[575]

399. To be valid, withdrawal of the proceedings requires the consent of the other party, unless it is done prior to this party filing its first written pleadings. In case of dispute, the court will rule on the matter.[576]

400. Withdrawal of the proceedings restores the parties' situation as it existed prior to the initiation of the proceedings.[577]

401. The party that withdraws the proceedings or the action is liable for the expenses incurred by the other party.[578]

570. Article 820 Judicial Code.
571. Article 823, para. 2, Judicial Code.
572. Article 821 Judicial Code.
573. Article 823, para. 1, Judicial Code.
574. Article 822 Judicial Code.
575. Article 824 Judicial Code.
576. Article 825 Judicial Code.
577. Article 826 Judicial Code.
578. Article 827 Judicial Code.

Chapter 3. Challenge of Judges

402. Despite the guarantees provided for in the ECHR, the Constitution and the Judicial Code with regard to the independence and impartiality of judges (*see supra*, paragraphs 55–58), it might occur in a particular case that there are reasons to remove the judge from that case. The Judicial Code provides for a special procedure that enables a party to prevent a judge from dealing with the case at hand, if there is reasonable doubt about that judge's independence or impartiality.

403. The grounds for challenging a judge are listed exhaustively in Articles 828 and 829 of the Judicial Code.

404. Article 828, 2°-12° of the Judicial Code lists certain specific grounds for challenging a judge (such as the fact that the judge or his spouse have a personal interest in the outcome of the dispute; the fact that the judge is a close relative of one of the parties; the fact that the judge is an associate of an institution or firm that is a party in the dispute; the fact that the judge has taken part in the deliberation of the case in first instance and subsequently must adjudicate the case on appeal; or the fact that the relationship between the judge and one of the parties is clearly characterised by tension, annoyance and animosity). In addition, the ground of Article 828, 1° of the Judicial Code – 'legal (i.e., justified) suspicion' – is considered as a residual category that includes all circumstances in which there might be reasonable doubt about the judge's independence or impartiality.

405. Article 829 of the Judicial Code adds two grounds which apply only to judges in the Labour Courts, the Labour Courts of Appeal and the Commercial Courts. These judges can also be challenged on the ground that they have previously been the employer or employee of one of the parties to the dispute or when they have previously been a member of the staff or board of directors of the company that has employed one of the parties to the dispute.

406. The grounds for challenging a judge are also applicable to lay judges, members of the public prosecutor's office (except when they act as a party to the proceedings),[579] and court-appointed experts.[580]

407. The party who wants to challenge a judge must do so before the start of the pleadings, unless the grounds of objection only arise later in the procedure.[581]

408. The challenge is initiated by the filing of a petition with the court's registry, which must be signed by an attorney who has been a member of the bar for at least ten years.[582] The petition must contain the grounds of objection.[583]

579. Article 832 Judicial Code.
580. Article 966 Judicial Code.
581. Article 833 Judicial Code.
582. This requirement is designed to prevent abuses and to ensure that the procedure to challenge a judge is used with caution.
583. Article 835 Judicial Code.

409. The judge in question is notified of the petition by the court's registry within twenty-four hours.[584] The judge has two days to decide whether he will refrain from dealing with the case.[585]

410. The challenge is assessed by a higher court than the one of which the challenged judge is a member.[586] The decision of this court can only be challenged through a cassation appeal. If the challenge is accepted, the costs of the procedure are borne by the judge who has refused to excuse himself from the case. If the challenge is rejected, the judge who has excused himself from the case can claim damages from the petitioner.[587] Moreover, a fine may be imposed on the petitioner, if the challenge is apparently unfounded.[588]

---

584. Article 836, para. 1, Judicial Code.
585. Article 836, para. 2, Judicial Code.
586. Article 838 Judicial Code.
587. Articles 840–841 Judicial Code.
588. Article 838, paras 3–4, Judicial Code.

Chapter 4. Removal of the Case from the Court

411. The court may be removed from the case on a limited number of grounds that are specified in Articles 648–652 of the Judicial Code. These grounds include, *inter alia*, the lack of independence or impartiality of the court as a whole (a presumption with regard to one of the judges is not sufficient) or the fact that the court has failed to render judgment within six months after the closing of the hearings.

412. The removal of the case from the court differs from the challenge of judges because it concerns the court as a whole, and not just an individual judge. Hence, if the request for removal is granted, the case is removed from the court in question and subsequently referred to another court (at the same level).

413. The request for removal is initiated by means of a petition, which is to be signed by an attorney.

414. The Court of Cassation is competent to decide on the request.

Chapter 5. Repudiation of an Act of Procedure

415. Procedural acts performed on behalf of a party in the absence of any lawful representation can be rejected by this party. This special procedure is used mainly to rebut the presumption of lawful representation by an attorney (*see supra*, paragraph 129).

416. The request for repudiation can be filed by the party on whose behalf the act was performed or by the other parties to the proceedings, unless the first party confirms or ratifies the act in due time.[589] If the case is still pending, the request for repudiation is initiated by means of a claim in intervention, directed against the person who performed the procedural act in question.[590] If the judgment has already been rendered, the request for repudiation is introduced together with the appeal (or the request for revocation of the judgment's res judicata if the judgment is not susceptible to appeal).[591]

417. If the request for repudiation is granted, the procedural act in question is annulled, as well as any decisions that were rendered following the repudiated act.

418. The person who performed the rejected procedural act may be ordered to pay damages.[592]

589. Article 848 Judicial Code.
590. Article 849, para. 1, Judicial Code.
591. Article 849, paras 2–3, Judicial Code.
592. Article 849, para. 5, Judicial Code.

Part VII. Legal Aid and Legal Costs

Chapter 1. Legal Aid and Legal Assistance

419. Article 10 of the Constitution states that all people are equal before the law, whereas Article 23 of the Constitution recognises the right to lead a life in keeping with human dignity. These fundamental rights entail the right to have equal access to justice and the right to legal aid. In order to prevent that people with insufficient or limited means would be de facto deprived of their right of access to justice, the Belgian justice system provides for several mechanisms available to people who do not have the resources needed to cover the costs of litigation. These mechanisms are available to both claimants and defendants.

420. A distinction must be made between legal aid (assistance judiciaire – rechtsbijstand) and legal assistance (aide juridique– juridische bijstand).

§1. Legal Aid

421. Legal aid means that a person with limited resources is (entirely or partially) exempt from the payment of certain litigation costs (with the exception of attorney's fees), such as the various court fees, costs for the intervention of public officials, such as bailiffs, and expenses concerning investigation measures.[593]

422. The request for legal aid has to be made to the court that is competent to rule on the merits of the case.[594] Within every court there is a bureau for legal aid (*bureau d'aide juridique – bureau voor rechtsbijstand*), i.e., a special chamber presided by a single judge that decides on the requests for legal aid. In the Justice of the Peace Court and the Police Court, however, where there is no such bureau, it is the judge himself who decides whether or not to grant the request.

423. The request for legal aid can be made in writing or orally before the court registry that shall take note of the request.[595] In any case, the request has to be documented.

593. Article 664 Judicial Code.
594. Article 670 Judicial Code.
595. Article 675 Judicial Code.

424. Applicants must have the Belgian nationality. They must demonstrate that their resources are insufficient to cover the costs of litigation[596] and that their claim has merit.[597] In practice, the request will be granted if the applicant's claim is not prima facie inadmissible or unfounded. The bureau decides on the basis of the petition and accompanying documents. The applicant may be heard, but this rarely happens in practice. In any event, the opposite party (if any) is not involved in the procedure and is not even informed thereof.

425. Persons who are not Belgian nationals can enjoy legal aid under the same conditions provided that they are EU nationals or non-EU nationals legally residing in the EU.[598] Legal aid may also be granted to foreigners who are involved in proceedings against the Belgian State with regard to a matter relating to the access to, or the residence in, or the removal from the Belgian territory, and even to foreign nationals residing illegally in Belgium, if they have tried to legalise their stay in Belgium, and provided that their claim is urgent and relates to a 'fundamental right'.[599]

426. The bureau takes its decision within eight days after the filing of the petition. The decision is notified to the applicant within three days.[600] In case of a negative decision, the applicant can appeal the decision within one month after its notification.[601] If the applicant does not understand the language used in the bureau, he has the right to an interpreter, whose fees are at the expense of the Belgian State.[602]

427. If the request for legal aid is granted, the costs and fees are paid for by the Belgian State. They can, however, be recovered from the opposite party if the applicant wins the case. Under certain conditions, the costs can also be recovered from the applicant, for instance, if he comes to better fortune.

428. The benefit of legal aid is only valid for one stage of the proceedings. If the decision rendered in first instance is appealed, a new request for legal aid is required if one wishes to obtain legal aid for the appeal proceedings.[603]

§2. Legal Assistance

429. The Judicial Code distinguishes between primary legal assistance and second line legal assistance.

430. Primary legal assistance is organised by the commissions for legal assistance, which are established in every judicial district.[604] The availability of primary legal

596. The decision of the bureau for legal assistance appointing a (partially) free of charge attorney serves as an irrefutable presumption that the applicant does not dispose of sufficient resources (Article 667, para. 2, Judicial Code).
597. Article 667, para. 1, Judicial Code.
598. The difference in living expenses between the Member State of which the applicant is a national and Belgium can serve as a ground for the granting of legal aid (Article 699*ter* Judicial Code).
599. Article 668 Judicial Code.
600. Article 678 Judicial Code.
601. Article 689 Judicial Code.
602. Article 691 Judicial Code.
603. Article 671 Judicial Code.
604. Articles 508/2–3 Judicial Code. In the judicial district of Brussels, there is a Dutch-speaking and a French-speaking commission for legal assistance.

assistance is not dependent upon a person's financial situation. It is available to all persons seeking justice. The scope of primary legal assistance is, however, limited to the provision of practical and judicial information, basic legal advice and the referral to specialised institutions.[605]

431. Second line legal assistance means that a person with limited resources and in need for legal counsel is appointed an attorney whose services are paid (in full or in part)[606] by the Belgian State.[607] The application for legal assistance has to be made (in writing or orally) to one of the bureaus for legal assistance, which are established within every local bar under the auspices of the respective bar councils.[608] Except in urgent cases, the bureau decides within fifteen days after the application.[609] If the applicant does not understand the language to be used in the proceedings, the bureau shall appoint an attorney who speaks the applicant's language. If this is not possible, the bureau will appoint an interpreter, whose fees are at the expense of the Belgian State.[610] In case of a negative decision (e.g., because the applicant's resources exceed the statutory threshold or the applicant's claim is clearly inadmissible or unfounded[611]), the applicant can appeal the decision before the Labour Court within one month after its notification.[612] The compensation of *pro bono* attorneys is calculated using a points system. Each type of legal service corresponds with a number of points and each point equals a certain amount of money, which varies yearly.

432. In principle, all Belgian attorneys have an ethical duty to volunteer for one of these organisations. For trainee attorneys, it is mandatory as part of their training to take on some *pro bono* cases.

605. Article 508/1, 1°, Judicial Code.
606. People whose resources are above a certain threshold are asked to pay a small non-refundable contribution.
607. Article 508/1, 2°, Judicial Code.
608. Articles 508/7–9 Judicial Code.
609. Article 508/15 Judicial Code.
610. Article 508/10 Judicial Code.
611. Article 508/14, para. 6, Judicial Code.
612. Article 508/17 Judicial Code.

Chapter 2. Legal Costs

433. With the exception of parties who enjoy the benefit of legal aid and/or legal assistance, each party has to advance its own litigation costs, including the fees and expenses of its legal counsel.

434. The court determines in every final judgment the (total) litigation costs as well as the party who has to bear them. To this end, parties are required to give a clear estimate of their costs in their pleadings.[613]

435. In principle (and unless parties have concluded an agreement with respect to the litigation costs), the losing party has to pay or reimburse the costs of the litigation to the winning party.[614] Exceptions to the 'loser pays'-principle are, *inter alia*, cases relating to social security law (the costs are always borne by the social security institution, even if it wins the case) or where a party has made useless or vexatious costs (such costs will remain fully at the expense of the party who has made them, even if this party wins the case). If the claim is only partially granted, or when the parties are spouses or close relatives, the court may apportion (divide) the costs.[615] The apportionment of the costs is optional, not mandatory. In practice, the apportionment of the costs often implies that the court will order each party to bear its own costs and expenses.

436. Article 1018 of the Judicial Code provides for a (non-exhaustive) list of litigation costs. Special attention should be paid to the compensation for attorneys' fees and expenses, which is a fixed lump sum allowance awarded by the court to the winning party[616] who was represented by an attorney during the proceedings.[617] The amount of the compensation depends on the monetary value of the claim. The amounts are determined in a Royal Decree of 26 October 2007.[618] The Decree provides for a basic amount, maximum amount and minimum amount. In principle, the basic amount is awarded, but the court can increase or reduce the basic amount (without exceeding the fixed minimum and maximum amounts) at the request of one of the parties, thereby taking into account (one or more of) the following criteria: the financial capacity of the losing party (in order to lower the amount of compensation), the complexity of the litigation, the contractually agreed compensation for the winning party and the manifestly unreasonable nature of the situation. No party can be obliged to pay additional compensation for the attorney's intervention of the opposite party above the lump sum allowance awarded by the court.

437. The costs of the enforcement of the judgment must be paid by the party against whom the judgment is enforced.[619]

613. Article 1021 Judicial Code.
614. Article 1017, para. 1, Judicial Code.
615. Article 1017, para. 4, Judicial Code.
616. Not to his attorney (Court of Cassation 20 October 2014, C.13.526.F).
617. Article 1022 Judicial Code. *See* for a recent analysis: B. Van den Bergh & S. Sobrie, *De rechtsplegingsvergoeding in al zijn facetten*, Mechelen, Kluwer, 2016.
618. *Belgian Official Gazette*, 9 November 2007.
619. Article 1024 Judicial Code.

Part VIII. Evidence

Chapter 1. Burden of Proof

438. The basic (procedural) rule regarding the burden of proof in civil cases is laid down in Article 870 of the Judicial Code: every party has the burden to adduce evidence for his allegations. In other words, each party has to prove his claim, c.q., defence, i.e., the facts it adduces.[620] Contrary to for example American law, where there are different standards of proof in different circumstances (e.g., 'preponderance of the evidence' and 'clear and convincing evidence'), Belgian law does not provide for different standards of proof.

439. Only facts in dispute need to be proved. Facts of general knowledge must not be proved. Foreign law is regarded as a question of law, not as a matter of fact to be proven. In the Babcock-Smulders case,[621] the Court of Cassation ruled that, if the Belgian rule of reference declares foreign law to be applicable, the court is obliged to apply foreign law by virtue of his office. It is up to the court to gather the necessary information in order to determine the scope and content of the applicable foreign law, with due respect however for the rights of defence.[622] The latter implies that the court that invokes ex officio the applicability of foreign law has to invite the parties to debate thereon.

440. The court has to decide the case on the basis of the rules of evidence applicable to the type of action concerned.[623] The action will either be civil or commercial. The law of evidence in civil matters is described in Articles 1315 et seq. of the Civil Code. It is a closed system with tightly regulated forms of evidence ruled by a strict

620. Court of Cassation 21 January 2016, C.14.0470.N; Court of Cassation 7 May 2015, C.14.0011.F; Court of Cassation 26 December 2014, C.12.0488.N; Court of Cassation 25 June 2004, C. 03.0326.F.

621. Court of Cassation 9 October 1980, AR 6142, *Arresten van het Hof van Cassatie* 1980–1981, 142 and *Pasicrisie belge* 1981, 159; Court of Cassation 18 June 1993, *Revue générale des assurances et des responsabilités* 1994, para. 12.366, note M. Fallon. *See* also Article 15 Code of Private International Law.

622. Court of Cassation 12 December 1985, AR 7444, *Arresten van het Hof van Cassatie* 1985, 550: When the case urges an immediate decision of the judge hindering him to do the necessary research, he may provisionally apply Belgian law to render his judgment.

623. Article 876 Judicial Code.

hierarchy.[624] The law of evidence in commercial matters is described in Article 25 of the Commercial Code. It is an open system with open forms of evidence.[625]

441. The rules regarding the burden of proof and the admissibility of evidence are in principle supplementary rules, meaning that the parties may validly derogate from those rules by mutual agreement.[626]

624. Note, however, that the rules are only applicable to the proof of legal acts between the parties (e.g., the existence and content of a sales contract). The proof of legal facts, on the other hand, such as the gross negligence of a person, may be delivered by all types of evidence, and such evidence is freely evaluated by the court.
625. The same is true in criminal cases.
626. Court of Cassation 20 April 1978, *Arresten van het Hof van Cassatie* 1978, 958.

Chapter 2. Admissibility of Evidence

442. In civil matters, the rules on evidence have been strictly regulated in the Civil Code. The Code provides for five means of evidence in civil cases, described as follows.

443. Written evidence[627]

As in most civil law countries, written evidence is the most important type and primary source of evidence. A claim with an economic value of more than EUR 375 must in principle be proven by means of a written document.[628] The Civil Code distinguishes between public and private deeds. Public deeds (*acte authentique – authentieke akte*) are drafted by a public officer, such as a notary public, judge or bailiff. Private deeds (*acte sous seing privé – onderhandse akte*) are written documents prepared by the parties themselves without the intervention of a public officer. A public deed has a particular legal probative value as to the public officer's authentic notes (i.e., the information that was verified by the public officer with his own senses, such as the date of signature and the identity of the signatories). Public and private deeds have the same probative value as to their content: the content is deemed to be true and does not have to be proved unless it is contested.

In this context, the 'attorney's deed' (*acte d'avocat – advocatenakte*) is also worth mentioning. The attorney's deed is a fairly new instrument which allows the parties' attorneys to countersign a private deed, which 'upgrades' its probative value.[629] In practice, it is rather seldom used.

444. Witnesses[630]

Oral evidence is not admissible in claims exceeding EUR 375, unless prima facie written evidence is presented or when it is (materially or morally) impossible to produce written evidence. For claims below EUR 375, oral evidence may be permitted, but does not override documentary evidence. The probative value of witness evidence is freely assessed by the judge.

445. Presumptions[631]

Presumptions are conclusions deduced by a statutory provision or by the court from a known fact in order to decide an unknown fact. They are subject to the same admissibility conditions as oral evidence (*see supra*, paragraph 444).

446. Admission[632]

Admission is a unilateral legal act whereby a party acknowledges a certain fact. It delivers conclusive evidence against the person who made the admission. Admissions may be made both in and out of court.

447. Oath[633]

627. Articles 1317–1340 Civil Code.
628. Article 1341 Civil Code.
629. The attorney's deed was introduced by the Act of 29 April 2013 (*Belgian Official Gazette*, 3 July 2013).
630. Articles 1341–1348 Civil Code.
631. Articles 1349–1353 Civil Code.
632. Articles 1354–1356 Civil Code.
633. Articles 1357–1369 Civil Code.

The oath is a sworn statement made by a party in order to have the case decided on that basis (similar to affidavits in common law). The oath is seldom used as a way of adducing evidence.

448. Electronic evidence?

Over the last decade, the use of electronic evidence has increased significantly. The legal framework, however, has not kept up with this evolution. The Act of 20 October 2000[634] introduced the use of telecommunication as well as the electronic signature in judicial and extra-judicial procedures. A signature created by an electronic device to identify the signatory of a legal act may not be denied legal effectiveness and admissibility as evidence in legal proceedings. It is, however, only acknowledged as equivalent to a hand-written signature if it satisfies a number of technical security criteria.[635] As of today, there are no specific rules regarding the collection, preservation and presentation of electronic evidence in court. Nonetheless, the general rules and procedures for traditional evidence are applied by analogy.[636]

449. The abovementioned rules do not apply in commercial cases. All types of evidence are declared admissible in commercial matters, irrespective of the economic value of the dispute. The judge freely evaluates the evidence presented by the parties. There is, however, a specific type of evidence which has a particular legal probative value, namely the receipted invoice in case of a contract of sale: provided that the debtor has not protested the invoice within a short, reasonable period of time, the invoice will constitute conclusive evidence.

634. *Belgian Official Gazette*, 22 December 2000.

635. *See* also the Act of 9 July 2001 regarding the legal framework for electronic signatures and certification-service-providers (*Belgian Official Gazette*, 9 September 2001).

636. Court of Cassation 22 April 2015, P.14.1462.F.

Chapter 3. Discovery and Disclosure

450. Since Belgium has a civil law tradition, rules regarding evidence are not as elabourate as in most common law countries. There is no formal pre-trial discovery in civil proceedings, nor does the Judicial Code contain any specific rules as to the preservation of evidence. If urgency or the necessity of a 'surprise' effect[637] can be demonstrated, one may seek an injunction to preserve evidence before the president of the court, if necessary via ex parte proceedings (*see supra*, paragraphs 316–321 and paragraph 323).

451. With respect to disclosure, each party must disclose and allow inspection of all documents on which they wish to rely. Failure to disclose will result in a stay of the proceedings.[638] Despite the fact that there is no obligation to submit evidence which might adversely affect one's case (or support the opponent's case), the fair-play principle requires parties to collaborate in good faith in the delivery and gathering of evidence. Therefore, when a party is shown to hold a piece of evidence which could prove or disprove a fact that is relevant to the case, the judge may order that party to submit that evidence (*see also infra*, paragraphs 454–455).

637. For instance, in order to prevent the destruction, spoliation or alteration of evidence.
638. Article 736 Judicial Code.

Chapter 4. Administration of Evidence

§1. Domestic Rules

452. As far as the administration of evidence goes, the judge is the master of the proceedings. If the parties fail to produce (sufficient) evidence allowing to grant or reject the claim, the judge may order any additional investigation measure which may provide him with more certainty as to the substance of the claim.[639] When doing so, the judge must have due regard for the principle of subsidiarity, meaning that he must choose the quickest, cheapest and most simple method of inquiry, taking into account the economic value of the claim.[640]

453. The Judicial Code contains a variety of techniques on the delivery and gathering of evidence. The most important ones are discussed below.

I. Forced Production of Documents

454. In principle, the parties can freely decide on which documents they wish to rely to make their case, and only such documents that are referred to in the pleadings must be submitted.[641] There is no general obligation to submit documents which are harmful to a party's case or support the opponent's case.

455. The court can, however, order a party, or even a third party, to submit certain documents (or certified copies thereof) which could constitute proof of certain facts relevant to the outcome of the case. The forced production of documentary evidence may only be ordered if there are serious, precise and concurring reasons to believe that the person concerned is in possession thereof.[642] Failure to comply with the court's order to produce certain documents may result in the payment of damages.[643] The court can also impose a non-compliance penalty to be paid in the event that the order is not voluntarily complied with (*see supra*, paragraphs 306–308). Furthermore, criminal sanctions can be imposed if the document concerned has been fraudulently destroyed, altered or hidden.[644]

639. In accordance with Article 875*bis*, para. 1, of the Judicial Code, the judge may order an investigation measure only after having considered the claim to be admissible, unless the investigation measure aims at determining whether or not the claim is admissible.
640. Article 875*bis*, para. 2, Judicial Code.
641. Articles 877–882 Judicial Code.
642. Article 877 Judicial Code. *See* also Court of Cassation 16 October 2015, C.14.0512.F.
643. Article 882 Judicial Code.
644. Article 495*bis* Criminal Code.

II. Testimony of Witnesses

456. The court can order a witness testimony if a party proposes to establish certain specific[645,646] and relevant[647] facts by means of a witness.[648] The court may also order a witness testimony ex officio. If a party's request for a witness deposition has been granted, the opposite party has the right to summon his own witness for questioning, provided that he files a request thereto within thirty days after the communication of the minutes of the witness examination.[649]

457. Witnesses are obliged to testify, unless they have a justified reason (e.g., professional secrecy) not to do so. The witness examination is conducted under oath; false testimony constitutes a punishable offence.[650] Contrary to for example the English system of trial, the witness is interrogated by the judge. There is no cross-examination by the parties (or their counsel). Nevertheless, parties can request the judge to ask certain questions to the witness that may clarify or complete the latter's testimony.[651]

458. Witness examinations before the court can be very time-consuming and burdensome. With this in mind, the Act of 16 July 2012[652] introduced the submission of written testimonies as a means of evidence. Witnesses may now submit their testimonies in writing to the court, provided that a number of formal conditions are met.[653]

III. Testimony by the Parties Themselves

459. Usually, parties do not appear in person at court hearings, but are mostly represented by their counsel.[654] The judge can, however, even on his own initiative, order the parties (or one of them) to appear in court with a view to an oral examination. Said examination is not conducted under oath, so prosecution for perjury is not possible. The procedure is almost identical to the witness examination.

460. The court does not frequently resort to this type of investigation measure, although it could be useful to discover the truth or provoke confessions. In certain disputes, such as certain family-related matters, the parties have a legal obligation to appear in person at court hearings.[655] The parties' personal appearance must allow the

645. Articles 915–961 Judicial Code.
646. Witnesses are allowed to testify about events they were not personally involved in (Court of Cassation 25 February 1980, *Arresten van het Hof van Cassatie* 1979–1980, 769).
647. *See* Court of Cassation 7 January 1983, *Arresten van het Hof van Cassatie* 1982–1983, 600.
648. The court can deny the request for a witness testimony if the (opposite of the) facts to be established by such testimony is already proven through other types of evidence (Court of Cassation 18 May 1981, *Arresten van het Hof van Cassatie* 1980–1981, 1075).
649. Article 921 Judicial Code.
650. Article 220 Criminal Code.
651. Articles 936–938 Judicial Code.
652. *Belgian Official Gazette*, 3 August 2012.
653. The rules regarding written testimonies are laid down in Articles 961/1–3 Judicial Code.
654. Articles 992–1004 Judicial Code. Special rules apply regarding the hearing of minors (Articles 1004/1–2 Judicial Code).
655. Articles 1253*ter*/2 and 1253*ter*/4 Judicial Code.

judge to attain a clear understanding of the situation and to explore whether, and to what extent, the parties would be able to come to an agreement. Furthermore, the legislature wanted parents to take responsibility in procedures concerning their children. Where appropriate, the case may be referred to the chambers for amicable settlement (*see supra*, paragraph 261).

IV. Expert Evidence

461. Contrary to other (such as common law) systems, Belgian courts mostly rely on court-appointed experts[656]. Parties can present their own expert evidence, but this is not considered to be objective.[657] Therefore, in most cases where there is a technical dispute, the court will appoint an expert.

462. The expert's mission is limited to the delivery of an independent and impartial advice on technical issues. The judge is not allowed to request an expert to render legal advice as to the merits of the case.[658] Accordingly, the judge is not bound by the expert findings,[659] which may be contested by the parties (although, in practice, the court will mostly attach great importance to the expert report provided that it has been drafted regularly).

463. Experts have a legal duty trying to reconcile the parties.[660]

464. Experts are usually appointed in the context of pending proceedings. The appointment of an expert can, however, also be the object of an independent action, in anticipation of a future dispute.[661] If urgency can be demonstrated, one may seek the appointment of an expert before the president of the court (*see supra*, paragraphs 316–320), if necessary via ex parte proceedings (*see supra*, paragraph 323).

465. An important feature of the expert investigation is its adversarial nature. This means, *inter alia*, that the expert must give the parties the opportunity to present their arguments[662] before the filing of the expert report with the judge.[663]

466. The parties have a duty to cooperate in good faith in the expert investigation, for instance, by communicating to the expert all useful documentation and providing

656. Articles 962–991*bis* Judicial Code.

657. This does not, however, prevent the court from taking the parties' expert evidence into account as a presumption, the probative value of which is freely evaluated by the court (Court of Cassation 14 September 1984, *Arresten van het Hof van Cassatie* 1984–1985, 88; Court of Cassation 22 December 1983, *Arresten van het Hof van Cassatie* 1983–1984, 473). The same rule applies when a court-appointed expert neglects the limits of his assignment and, e.g., gives advice on legal matters (Court of Cassation 6 March 2014, C.12.0615.N).

658. Article 11, para. 1, and Article 962, para 1, Judicial Code. *See* also Court of Cassation 19 February 2010, C.08.0127.F; Court of Cassation 3 June 2004, C.03.0111.N.

juni 200414 September 1992, *Arresten van het Hof van Cassatie* 1991–1992, 1099.

659. Article 962, para. 4, Judicial Code.

660. Article 977, §1, Judicial Code.

661. Article 962, para. 1, Judicial Code.

662. Article 976 Judicial Code.

663. Article 978 Judicial Code.

him with the necessary explanation. If they fail to do so, the court shall draw the appropriate conclusions.[664]

467. Experts can be challenged for the same reasons as judges (*see supra*, paragraphs 403–404).[665] Experts can also be replaced by the court if they do not perform their duties properly.[666]

468. The cost of the expert investigation is part of the litigation costs, which will in the end have to be paid by the party losing the case.

V. Affidavit

469. The affidavit is a sworn statement made by a party in order to have the case decided on that basis[667]. The affidavit has become very unusual in Belgian procedural law as a means of evidence.

VI. On-Site Inspection by the Judge

470. The judge can order an official visit to the scene and thereby perform certain fact finding operations.[668] The Justice of the Peace, for instance, frequently resorts to this measure in rental damage cases. Usually, the parties are required to be present on the scene.[669] The minutes of the on-site inspection are drawn up by the court registrar and subsequently notified to the parties.

§2. International Rules

471. As far as EU regulations are concerned, there is the EU Regulation (EC) No. 1206/2001 of 28 May 2001 on Cooperation between the Courts of the Member States in the Taking of Evidence in Civil or Commercial Matters.[670] The aim of this Regulation is to improve, simplify and accelerate cooperation between the Member States as regards the taking of evidence in legal proceedings in civil and commercial matters.[671]

The Evidence Regulation is applicable in civil and commercial matters where the court of a Member State, in accordance with the provisions of the law of the State,

664. Article 972*bis*, §1, Judicial Code. *See* also Court of Cassation 2 November 2012, C.11.0018.N.
665. Article 966 Judicial Code.
666. Article 979 Judicial Code.
667. Articles 1005–1006 Judicial Code.
668. Articles 1007–1016 Judicial Code.
669. Article 1012 Judicial Code.
670. *Official Journal* L174/1 of 2001. *See* for a more detailed account: B. Allemeersch & A.-S. Houtmeyers, 'De bewijsverordening' in B. Allemeersch & T. Kruger, *Handboek Europees Burgerlijk Procesrecht*, Antwerp-Cambridge, Intersentia, 2015, 253–274.
671. Denmark is not participating in the Regulation and is therefore not bound by it nor subject to its application.

requests (1) the competent court of another Member State to take evidence or (2) permission to take evidence directly in another Member State.

The Regulation applies as a general rule only if the court of a Member State decides to take evidence according to one of the two methods provided for by the Regulation, in which case it is required to follow the procedures relating to those methods. The Regulation is not to be interpreted, however, as meaning that the competent court of a Member State, which wishes to hear as a witness a party residing in another Member State, must, in order to have such a hearing, always use the means of taking evidence laid down by the Regulation. To the contrary, that court has the possibility to summon that party to appear before it and hear him in accordance with the law of its Member State.[672]

472. At the international level, there is the Hague Convention of 18 March 1970 on the Taking of Evidence Abroad in Civil or Commercial Matters.[673]

The Hague Evidence Convention provides for the taking of evidence (1) by means of 'letters of request' from one Signatory State (where the evidence is sought) to another Signatory State (where the evidence is located) and (2) by diplomatic or consular agents and commissioners.

As of 2017, sixty-one States are parties to the Hague Evidence Convention. Between States of the European Union, the Hague Evidence Convention has largely been supplanted by the aforementioned EU Evidence Regulation.

672. *Lippens et al./Kortekaas et al.*, ECOJ No. C-170/11 of 6 September 2012, ECLI:EU:C:2012:540. Compare with Prorail/Xpedys et al., ECOJ No. C-332/11 of 21 February 2013, ECLI:EU:C:2013:87, regarding the taking of evidence entrusted to an expert to be carried out in another Member State.

673. *See* for more information: https://www.hcch.net/en/instruments/conventions/full-text/?cid=82 (accessed September 2017).

Part IX. Seizure for Security and Enforcement of Judgments

Chapter 1. Seizure for Security

§1. In General

473. Similar to freezing injunctions in common law, the seizure for security or the preliminary seizure (*saisie conservatoire – bewarend beslag*) could be described as the blocking of a debtor's assets without prior notice. This protective measure allows creditors to secure their claim without already having an enforceable title in their possession. It prevents the debtor, over a given period, from disposing freely over his assets. In other words, a measure of this kind ensures that the debtor's assets are maintained in their present condition.[674] The debtor, however, remains the owner of the seized goods and is in principle entitled to continue to use and enjoy them, in compliance with the standard of a 'prudent man', i.e., duly responsible person.[675]

474. The seizure can be executed on all goods that belong to the debtor's property: movable goods[676] (saisie mobilière conservatoire – bewarend beslag op roerend goed), immovable goods[677] (saisie immobilière conservatoire – bewarend beslag op onroerend goed) and goods owed by a third person (for instance the debtor's employer) to the debtor[678] (*saisie-arrêt conservatoire – bewarend beslag onder derden*).

674. Providing for such a legal remedy makes ex parte proceedings compatible with the requirements of Article 6 ECHR (Court of Cassation 14 January 2005, C.02.0221.N).

675. Cf. Articles 1443–1444 Judicial Code. If, however, perishable goods, such as food, are seized, the goods will be sold, provided that the creditor obtains the prior authorisation from the judge of attachments, and with the understanding that the proceeds of the sale will be deposited at the Deposit and Consignation Office (Article 1421 Judicial Code).

676. Articles 1422–1428 Judicial Code.

677. Articles 1429–1444 Judicial Code.

678. Articles 1445–1460 Judicial Code.

§2. Statutory Prerequisites

475. Precautionary attachment of the debtor's assets is only possible with respect to claims that are certain, of a fixed amount and due.[679] A claim is certain if it prima facie appears to be sufficiently well-founded. A conditional or possible claim shall therefore not constitute a valid ground for a preliminary attachment. A disputed claim, however, may serve as a basis, provided that the dispute does not appear to be sufficiently serious. A claim is said to be liquid, or of a fixed amount, when that amount is or can be (provisionally) determined. A claim is considered to be due and payable from the date that the creditor can demand immediate payment.

476. Furthermore, the creditor may only proceed to the preliminary attachment of his debtor's assets in case of urgency.[680] This means that the creditor must demonstrate that the debtor's solvency is being or may be jeopardised.[681] In other words, it must be shown that the debtor's attitude or the situation of his assets might give reasonable cause to believe that, if no such protection measure were taken, future recovery of the debt would be at risk.[682] This may, for instance, be the case if the debtor is facing major cash flow problems or possibly bankruptcy or if the creditor has reasonable grounds for believing that the debtor is deliberately making himself insolvent by making all of his valuable assets disappear. The creditor must show that his fears are justified; vague rumours and hearsay do not suffice to authorise a preliminary seizure. In any event, there is no urgency if the sole ground for the precautionary seizure is that the creditor is in need of money.

§3. Proceedings

I. In General

477. In principle, the preliminary seizure requires the prior authorisation of the judge of attachments,[683] which is requested by means of a unilateral petition (*see also infra*, paragraphs 323–324).[684] Where appropriate, the judge shall determine the amount for which the seizure is permitted.[685] If the request is denied, the creditor can lodge an appeal.[686] The creditor can also file a new request when the circumstances of the case have changed (e.g., when it is now clear, unlike before, that the debtor's solvability is being jeopardised), as the judgment denying the request only has a limited authority of res judicata.

679. Article 1415 Judicial Code.
680. Article 1413 Judicial Code.
681. Article 1413 Judicial Code.
682. Court of Cassation 18 February 2016, C.15.0168.N; Court of Cassation 23 December 2010, C.09.0441.F.
683. Article 1413 Judicial Code.
684. Article 1417 *juncto* Articles 1025–1034 Judicial Code.
685. Article 1418, para. 2, Judicial Code.
686. Article 1419, para. 1, *juncto* Articles 1031–1034 Judicial Code.

478. The debtor or any person having a legitimate interest may lodge an extraordinary appellate remedy against the judgment authorising the preliminary seizure, i.e., third-party opposition (*see also supra*, paragraphs 379–384). This remedy has to be brought before the judge who authorised the seizure within one month from the date of service of the judgment. Third-party opposition does not stay the enforcement of the contested judgment, unless the judge decides otherwise.[687] If the time limit has elapsed or if the third-party opposition has been rejected, the debtor can still try to have the judgment revoked, provided that he can prove that the circumstances of the case have changed.[688]

479. A judgment on the merits of the case, rejecting the claim of the creditor, does not automatically result in the lifting of the preliminary seizure. The debtor has to make a request thereto before the judge deciding on the merits or before the judge of attachments (in the context of a third-party opposition or request for revocation of the judgment authorising the preliminary seizure).

480. There are a few exceptional circumstances in which no prior authorisation from the judge of attachments is required. In this event, the creditor may directly instruct the bailiff to carry out the preliminary attachment. This is particularly the case if the creditor is acting on the basis of an existing judgment or other enforceable title.[689] Even if the judgment is subject to appeal, it remains valid as a base for a preliminary seizure, unless this has been precluded in the judgment.[690] The same goes for foreign judgments, even if no prior exequatur has been obtained. In the case of third-party attachment, even a simple private deed, such as a contract or invoice, may serve as a valid legal basis for the attachment.[691] The judgment (or other title) must, however, clearly specify the debtor's obligation to pay a debt of an amount that has been (provisionally) determined. Furthermore, the requirement of urgency must be fulfilled (*see supra*, paragraphs 475–476). If the preliminary seizure is executed without prior authorisation from the judge of attachments, the debtor can, at any time, summon the creditor before this judge in order to have the seizure lifted.[692]

II. Preliminary Seizure of Movable Property

481. The preliminary seizure of movables, i.e., tangible assets owned by the debtor, is subject to essentially the same procedural rules as those in respect of the attachment for sale of movables (*see infra*, paragraphs 516–529).[693]

482. The preliminary seizure of movable property is effected by the service of a writ of seizure upon the debtor. This writ must contain, on pain of nullity, a copy of the petition and of the court order authorising the preliminary seizure, or a copy of the

687. Article 1127 Judicial Code.
688. Article 1419, para. 2, Judicial Code.
689. For instance, a notarial deed.
690. Article 1414 Judicial Code.
691. Article 1445 Judicial Code.
692. Article 1420 Judicial Code.
693. Article 1424 Judicial Code.

judgment or other enforceable title that qualifies as a valid legal basis for the preliminary seizure.[694]

483. The seizure is carried out by a bailiff, who is to be assisted by an adult witness not being blood or otherwise related to the bailiff or either of the parties.[695] Accompanied by his witness, the bailiff goes to the place where the goods that are to be seized are located. The creditor is prohibited from being present at the time of the seizure.[696]

484. If the seizure involves goods located outside of the debtor's domicile and held by a third party, the creditor must obtain prior authorisation from the judge of attachments.[697]

485. If the doors are locked and one refuses to open them, the bailiff can appoint a gatekeeper, designated by the local police force, or the mayor or the Justice of the Peace if there is no local police department.[698]

486. The bailiff shall draw up an official report of the seizure, containing an extensive and detailed description of the seized goods.[699]

487. The preliminary seizure of movable property is valid for a period of three years from the date of the judgment authorising the seizure or, if the seizure is executed without prior judicial authorisation, from the date of service of the writ of seizure on the debtor.[700] After the three-year period, the seizure shall cease automatically, unless it has been renewed at the creditor's request.[701] The creditor who wishes the renewal of the seizure must file a petition before the judge of attachments, and must demonstrate that the renewal is justified under the circumstances.[702] The decision granting the renewal must be served on the debtor before the expiry of the first seizure.[703]

III. Preliminary Seizure of Immovable Property

488. The preliminary seizure of immovables owned by the debtor, is subject to essentially the same procedural rules as those in respect of the attachment for sale of immovable goods (*see infra*, paragraphs 530–539).[704]

489. The preliminary seizure of immovable property is effected by the service of a writ of seizure upon the debtor containing, on pain of nullity, a copy of the petition and of the court order authorising the preliminary seizure,[705] or a copy of the judgment

694. Article 1424, 2°, Judicial Code.
695. Article 1501, para. 1, Judicial Code.
696. Article 1501, para. 3, Judicial Code.
697. Article 1503 Judicial Code.
698. Article 1504 Judicial Code.
699. Article 1506 Judicial Code.
700. This term can be shortened by the judge of attachments.
701. Article 1425 Judicial Code.
702. Article 1426 Judicial Code.
703. Article 1427 Judicial Code.
704. Article 1424 Judicial Code.
705. This court order must be followed by a writ of seizure within one month after it has been rendered, in absence of which the court order shall be considered 'non-existent' (Article 1433 Judicial Code).

or other enforceable title that qualifies as a valid legal basis for the seizure. The writ must also contain a detailed description of the goods to be seized, as well as an excerpt from the Land Register (*cadastre – kadaster*).[706]

490. The writ of seizure must be presented at the Mortgage Register (*bureau des hypothèques – hypotheekkantoor*), with a view to its publicity (the content of the writ is transferred on the property deed, which is kept at the Mortgage Register), in order to properly inform third parties of the seizure and make it opposable to them.[707]

491. The preliminary seizure of immovable property is valid for a period of three years from the date of transfer of the writ of seizure on the property deed. After the three-year period, the seizure shall cease automatically, unless it has been renewed at the creditor's request.[708] The creditor who wishes the renewal of the seizure must file a petition before the judge of attachments, at least fifteen days before the expiry of the first seizure. The creditor must demonstrate that the renewal is justified under the circumstances.[709]

IV. Preliminary Third-Party Attachment

492. Third-party attachment, also referred to as 'garnishment', is the procedure whereby a creditor attaches money or other movables that belong to the debtor, but are (still) in the hands of a third party. This type of seizure differs from the previous two in the sense that there are not just two parties involved (the creditor and the debtor) but three: the creditor, the debtor and the third-party garnishee. This type of protective measure is typically used to attach bank accounts (banking seizure), or for the direct attachment of the debtor's earnings in the hands of his employer (attachment on wages).

493. Any creditor in possession of an enforceable title – a judgment or other authentic instrument – or even a simple private agreement – i.e., a written document in due and proper form, effective against the debtor and testifying to the existence of a claim that is certain, payable and of a fixed amount (such as a contract, invoice, cheque, insurance policy) – can proceed to preliminary third-party attachment by the service of a writ of seizure upon the third-party garnishee.[710] In this event, no prior authorisation from the judge of attachments is required.

494. Even if the creditor does not hold an authentic or private deed, he may request the court to authorise preliminary third-party attachment[711] In this event, a copy of the petition and of the court order authorising third-party attachment is sent

706. Article 1432 Judicial Code.
707. Article 1433 Judicial Code.
708. Article 1436 Judicial Code.
709. Article 1437 Judicial Code.
710. Article 1445, para. 1, Judicial Code.
711. Article 1447 Judicial Code.

by the court registry to the creditor and the third-party garnishee by judicial mail (*see supra*, paragraph 296).[712] Hence, no intervention of the bailiff at that stage is required.[713]

495. From the date of receipt of the judicial mail or the writ of seizure, the third party may no longer dispose of the seized goods (by giving them to the debtor), under penalty of being held personally liable for the debt, and without prejudice to the creditor's right to full compensation.[714] Within eight days after the date of receipt of the judicial mail or the writ of seizure by the third party, the creditor has to give notice of the seizure to the debtor by registered mail with acknowledgement of receipt or by writ served by a bailiff.[715]

496. Within fifteen days after receipt of the writ of seizure, the third party must provide a written statement regarding the seized goods. This statement must be sent to the bailiff or the creditor (with copy to the debtor)[716] and must mention, *inter alia*, the cause and amount of the debt and its due date, as well as any other third-party attachments previously notified to the third party.[717] If the third party fails to comply with these requirements, he can be held personally liable for the debt and the costs of seizure.[718]

497. The precautionary third-party attachment is valid for a period of three years from the date of service of the court order or, if the attachment is carried out without prior judicial authorisation, from the date of service of the writ of seizure on the third party. After the three-year period, the seizure shall cease automatically, unless it has been renewed at the creditor's request.[719] The creditor who wishes the renewal of the seizure must file a petition before the judge of attachments, and must demonstrate that the renewal is justified under the circumstances.[720] The decision granting the renewal must be served on the third party and the debtor before the expiry of the first seizure.[721]

§4. Consignment

498. The debtor has the right to prevent or release the preliminary seizure of his assets by depositing an amount sufficient to cover the debt in principal, interest and charges, at the Deposit and Consignation Office (*Caisse des dépôts et consignations – Deposito- en Consignatiekas*), or with a sequestrator appointed for this purpose.[722]

712. Article 1449 Judicial Code.
713. If, however, the creditor wishes to speed up the procedure, he can request a copy of the petition and of the court order and commission a bailiff to serve those documents on the third party immediately after the court order has been rendered (Article 1450 Judicial Code).
714. Article 1451 Judicial Code.
715. Article 1457 Judicial Code.
716. Article 1453 Judicial Code.
717. Article 1452 Judicial Code.
718. Article 1456 Judicial Code.
719. Article 1458 Judicial Code.
720. Article 1459 Judicial Code.
721. Article 1460 Judicial Code.
722. Article 1403, para. 1, Judicial Code.

To this end, the debtor must summon the creditor before the judge of attachments, who shall determine the amount and other conditions of the consignment.[723]

499. Consignment is also possible through the depositing of an amount sufficient to cover the debt in principal, interest and charges, with the bailiff acting on behalf of the creditor. Within three days, the bailiff must transfer the amount to the Deposit and Consignation Office.[724] Creditor and debtor may also agree between them on the amount and other conditions of the consignment, which results in a so-called out of court consignment or consignment by agreement.[725]

500. In case of precautionary third-party attachment, all parties involved can request the judge of attachments to order consignment of the seized goods.[726]

501. Consignment in the context of preliminary seizure is not to be considered as a conditional payment of the debt. Hence, in case of bankruptcy of the debtor, the creditor for whose benefit the consignment was done, will not have priority over the other creditors. The debtor's bankruptcy declaration will lead to a so-called *concursus creditorum*, meaning that all (unsecured) creditors of the debtor will be entitled to a share of the deposited amount on a *pari passu* basis.

723. Article 1403, para. 3, Judicial Code.

724. Article 1405 Judicial Code.

725. Court of Cassation 2 February 2007, C.05.0367.N; Court of Cassation AR 6657 9 November 1990, *Rechtskundig Weekblad* 1991–1992, 535, note E. Dirix.

726. Article 1407 Judicial Code.

Chapter 2. Enforcement of Judgments

§1. Enforcement of Domestic Judgments

I. In General

502. The losing party is expected to satisfy or comply voluntarily with a judgment that is (provisionally) enforceable, but if he fails to do so, the prevailing party may have it enforced on him.

503. If the obligation of the losing party relates to the delivery of a good or the payment of a sum of money, the prevailing party may proceed to the attachment for sale of the losing party's movable property[727] (*saisie-exécution mobilière – uitvoerend beslag op roerend goed*) and/or immovable property[728] (*saisie-exécution immobilière – uitvoerend beslag op onroerend goed*). The attachment for sale may also relate to amounts or goods owed by a third party to the debtor (*saisie-arrêt-exécution – uitvoerend beslag onder derden*).[729]

504. The obligation of the losing party that consists of the duty to perform or refrain from a certain action, however, cannot be enforced by institutionalised force (*manu militari*). To solve this problem, the creditor could request the court for authorisation for having the action performed by a third party at the expense of the debtor, but this does not often happen in practice.[730] It is more common that the creditor requests the court to impose a non-compliance penalty to be paid in the event that the debtor does not voluntarily comply with the judgment (*see supra*, paragraphs 306–308).

II. Statutory Prerequisites

505. The right of access to justice would prove to be very illusory if there would be no guarantee that the judgment in question will in fact bring about the anticipated effects. Hence, the right to enforcement is a natural extension of the right to bring a dispute before court. Nonetheless, recourse to enforcement measures is only possible if a number of statutory conditions are fulfilled, which are laid down in the Judicial Code.[731]

506. First, the creditor must be in possession of a judgment that is (provisionally) enforceable or another enforceable title. If the enforceable title takes the form of a court decision, its enforcement is provisional for as long as the decision is not definite yet but still susceptible to an ordinary appellate remedy, i.e., opposition and/or appeal,

727. Articles 1499–1538 Judicial Code.
728. Articles 1560–1626 Judicial Code.
729. Articles 1539–1544 Judicial Code.
730. Articles 1143–1144 Civil Code.
731. Articles 1494–1495 Judicial Code.

or if such a remedy is pending. Such provisional enforcement is at the creditor's sole risk.[732] If the judgment is later on annulled or amended, the creditor has an obligation to return anything that he may have received out of the provisional enforcement. Moreover, he must compensate the debtor for any damages suffered in this respect. Note that, in principle, only the lodging of opposition entails a stay of the enforcement of the (default) judgment, unless the judge has authorised the provisional enforcement thereof. With regard to default judgments concerning the conviction of the defaulting party to pay a sum of money, both the effective lodging of opposition as well as the fact that the time limit to lodge opposition has not yet expired suspends the ability to enforce the judgment, unless the judge has authorised the provisional enforcement thereof (*see supra*, paragraphs 348–349).[733] The lodging of other appellate remedies, in principle, does not suspend the ability for the creditor to proceed with the (provisional) enforcement of the judgment (*see supra*, paragraphs 363–364). The statute of limitations to enforce the judgment ('*actio judicati*') is set at ten years after the judgment has been rendered.[734] This limitation period may be subject to suspension and interruption.

507. Second, the claim established by this title must be certain, of a fixed amount and due (*see supra*, paragraph 475).

508. Third, the judgment, as well as a formal order of payment, must be served on the debtor. A court decision ruling against a party can only be enforced after it has been served on that party by a bailiff.[735] This is to ensure that the debtor is fully aware of the judgment and the fact that the opposite party pursues its enforcement. Further on, the seizure must be preceded by a formal order of payment (*commandement de payer – bevel tot betaling*) served on the debtor by a bailiff (the judgment and the payment order are usually served together at the same time).[736] This order is intended as a last warning and last opportunity for the debtor to comply with the judgment voluntarily. If the debtor fails to do so, the bailiff will proceed with the seizure and subsequent (public) sale of the goods of the debtor.

509. In principle, enforcement measures in execution of a judgment (or other enforceable title) do not require the prior authorisation or intervention of the judge of attachments (or any other judge). However, any party may bring an action before this specialised judge if a dispute arises in relation to the execution.[737]

---

732. Article 1398 Judicial Code.
733. Article 1495, para. 2, Judicial Code. The fact that the enforceability of the judgment is suspended, does not prevent the creditor from taking recourse to the precautionary attachment of the debtor's assets.
734. Article 2262*bis*, §1, Civil Code. *See supra*, para. 381.
735. Article 1495, para. 1, Judicial Code.
736. Articles 1499 and 1564 Judicial Code. The service of a formal order of payment is, however, not required in case of third-party attachment.
737. Article 1395 *juncto* Article 1498 Judicial Code.

III. Unseizable Amounts and Property

510. In principle, all assets owned by a debtor can be subjected to execution by his creditors.[738] Article 1408 of the Judicial Code, however, contains a list of goods which cannot be seized from the debtor. In essence, they are goods and utensils necessary for everyday life and employment. Due to evolving social and economic circumstances, however, the list – which was thoroughly adapted for the last time in 1993 – has become rather outdated. Pursuant to Article 1409, §1, of the Judicial Code, the amount of income from employment which may be seized is subject to certain limitations (which are indexed annually).[739] These limitations do not apply, however, to maintenance creditors, who are said to have a 'super-privilege' in respect of maintenance claims.[740]

511. The State, the regions, the communities, the provinces, the municipalities and certain state-owned entities benefit from enforcement immunity. These entities may, however, draw up a list of goods which are susceptible to seizure. If no such list has been made up or if the goods listed thereon are insufficient to cover the creditor's claim, the creditor may seize property which is clearly not useful for the realisation of the entity's mission or the continuity of public service.[741] In addition, there exists a particular immunity in favour of cultural goods which are situated on Belgian territory in the framework of a public and temporary exhibition, but belong to a foreign state.[742]

IV. Consignment

512. The debtor who has lodged an appeal or opposition against the judgment of which the (provisional) enforcement is sought, has the right to prevent or release the seizure of his assets by depositing an amount sufficient to cover the debt in principal, interest and charges, at the Deposit and Consignation Office (or with a sequestrator appointed for this purpose or with the bailiff acting on behalf of the creditor or at a common bank account of creditor and debtor (or their legal representatives) via an out of court consignment),[743] unless this right has been explicitly excluded in the judgment.[744]

---

738. Articles 7–8 Mortgage Act.
739. These limitations also apply when the employer transfers the debtor's wages to his bank account (Articles 1411*ter-quatur* Judicial Code). The seizure of income from self-employment may be limited in a similar way by the judge of attachments (Article 1409*bis* Judicial Code). The seizure of others sources of income (e.g., out of rental, capital) is also subject to certain limitations, which are indexed annually (Article 1409, §1*bis*, Judicial Code).
740. Article 1412 Judicial Code.
741. Article 1412*bis* Judicial Code.
742. Article 1412*ter* Judicial Code. The fairly new Article 1412*quinquies* of the Judicial Code also provides for a particular immunity in favour of a foreign state's property that is situated on Belgian territory, including bank account balances.
743. Articles 1404 and 1405 Judicial Code.
744. Article 1406 Judicial Code. The right to consignment can also be excluded by a statutory provision, for instance, with regard to maintenance claims.

513. In case of third-party attachment, all parties involved can request the judge of attachments to order consignment of the seized goods.[745]

514. Contrary to consignment in the context of a preliminary seizure, this consignment is to be considered as a conditional payment of the debt. Hence, if the debtor goes bankrupt, only the creditor for whose benefit the consignment was done, will be entitled to the amount deposited.

V. Proceedings

A. *In General*

515. The bailiff plays a central and leading role in the enforcement proceedings. First of all, a judgment can only be enforced after it has been served on the debtor by a bailiff (*see supra*, paragraph 508). Further on, the seizure itself is also performed by a bailiff at the request of the creditor.

B. *Attachment for Sale of Movable Property*

516. The attachment for sale of movables is an attachment of the tangible assets owned by the debtor (such as furniture, vehicles, etc.).

517. The attachment must be preceded by a formal order of payment to be served on the debtor, at the latest one day before the attachment.[746] The debtor can challenge the payment order before the judge of attachments, but this does not have a suspensive effect.[747] The attachment can be executed from the day following the day on which the payment order was served on the debtor onward.

518. The seizure is carried out by a bailiff, who is to be assisted by an adult witness not being blood or otherwise related to the bailiff or either of the parties.[748] Accompanied by his witness, the bailiff goes to the place where the goods that are to be seized are located. The creditor is prohibited from being present at the time of the seizure.[749]

519. If the seizure involves goods located outside of the debtor's domicile and held by a third party, the creditor must obtain prior authorisation from the judge of attachments.[750]

520. If the doors are locked and one refuses to open them, the bailiff can appoint a gatekeeper, designated by the local police force, or the mayor or the Justice of the Peace if there is no local police department.[751]

745. Article 1407 Judicial Code.
746. Article 1499 Judicial Code.
747. Article 1498 *juncto* Article 1513 Judicial Code.
748. Article 1501, para. 1, Judicial Code.
749. Article 1501, para. 3, Judicial Code.
750. Article 1503 Judicial Code.
751. Article 1504 Judicial Code.

521. The bailiff shall draw up an official report of the seizure, containing an extensive and detailed description of the seized goods.[752] The seizure report shall indicate the date, time and place of sale of the seized goods.[753] A copy of the report is notified to the debtor.[754]

522. A waiting period of at least one month must be observed between the notice of the seizure report to the debtor and the sale of the seized goods.[755]

523. The sale of the seized goods takes place at the bailiff's auction gallery or at a local public market.[756] The sale must be advertised at the place of the sale, at least three working days prior to the sale. The sale must also be published in the local newspaper.[757]

524. The seized goods are sold by public auction,[758] until the proceeds of the sale equal the amount of the debt as well as the costs of enforcement. The remaining assets are returned to the debtor.[759]

525. The goods are sold to the highest bidder against immediate payment of the sales price. In the absence of immediate payment, the goods are immediately resold, and the original buyer is responsible for any difference in the sales price.[760]

526. Other creditors of the debtor do not need to take separate action against the debtor whose property has already been seized. They can participate in the seizure, and share in its proceeds, by opposing the seizure in the hands of the acting bailiff[761] or by filing a notice of opposition with the Central Database of Reports concerning Attachments[762] (*see infra*, paragraph 547).

527. After having deducted his expenses, the bailiff distributes the sales price among the creditors whose identity is known to the bailiff via the mandatory reference to the Central Database of Reports concerning Attachments[763] or who have informed him of their claims, taking into account any priority rights they might have. Creditors of the same rank are entitled to a share of the proceeds on a *pari passu* basis. The judge of attachments shall resolve any issue that might arise in respect of the distribution of the proceeds proposed by the bailiff.[764]

528. The debtor can oppose the sale by demonstrating that the creditor's claim does not meet the statutory quality requirements (*see supra*, paragraph 507) or on the

752. Article 1506 Judicial Code.
753. Article 1511 Judicial Code.
754. Article 1512 Judicial Code.
755. Article 1520 Judicial Code.
756. Article 1522 Judicial Code. Special rules apply to the sale of works of art (Article 1519 Judicial Code), stock options and foreign currencies (Article 1523 Judicial Code).
757. Article 1516 Judicial Code.
758. At the request of the debtor, the goods can also be sold by private agreement. The debtor must submit the proposals made thereto within ten days after receipt of the seizure report from the bailiff (Article 1526*bis* Judicial Code).
759. Article 1527 Judicial Code.
760. Article 1526 Judicial Code.
761. Article 1515 Judicial Code.
762. Article 1390, §2, Judicial Code.
763. Article 1391, §2, para. 1, *juncto* Article 1627 Judicial Code.
764. Articles 1627–1638 Judicial Code.

ground that a procedural irregularity has been committed.[765] To this end, the debtor must summon the creditor before the judge of attachments.

529. The property right of movables is governed by the statutory presumption that all tangible movable goods in possession of a person are presumed to be his property (‘*possession vaut titre*’).[766] Third parties, however, who claim to be the true owner of the seized goods can oppose the sale by summoning both the debtor and the creditor before the judge of attachments.[767]

C. Attachment for Sale of Immovable Property

530. The attachment for sale of immovable property is equally to be preceded by a formal order of payment that is served on the debtor, at the latest fifteen days before the attachment.[768] The attachment can be executed at the earliest after fifteen days following the day on which the payment order was served on the debtor.[769]

531. The payment order can be transcribed at the Mortgage Register, the result being that any subsequent property transfer by the debtor shall not be opposable to the creditor, meaning that the latter does not have to accept the existence and effects of such property transfer.[770]

532. The payment order is valid for a period of six months. If the seizure has not been carried out within the six-month period, or if the writ of seizure has not been transcribed at the Mortgage Register within this period, the payment order shall automatically lose its effects.[771]

533. The writ of seizure must be transcribed at the Mortgage Register within a period of fifteen days following the service of the writ upon the debtor, on pain of nullity.[772]

534. Within one month after the transcription of the seizure, the creditor must file a petition with the judge of attachments, requesting the appointment of a notary public who shall be charged with the public auction (or private sale) of the seized goods, as well as the distribution of the sale proceeds.[773]

535. The appointed notary public has a right of access to the property, with a view to visits by interested parties.[774]

536. The judge of attachments may order the private sale of the property if this appears to be in the best interests of the parties,[775] or at the request of the creditor.[776] Furthermore, the judge may stipulate that the property has to be sold to the buyer who

765. Article 1498 Judicial Code.
766. Article 2279 Civil Code.
767. Article 1514 Judicial Code.
768. Article 1564 Judicial Code.
769. Article 1566 Judicial Code, on pain of nullity ex Article 1622 Judicial Code.
770. Article 1565 Judicial Code.
771. Article 1567 Judicial Code.
772. Article 1569 Judicial Code.
773. Article 1580, paras 1 and 2, Judicial Code.
774. Article 1580, para. 3, Judicial Code.
775. Article 1580*bis* Judicial Code.
776. Article 1580*ter* Judicial Code.

leaves the use of the property in the hands of the debtor in case the property is the debtor's main residence.[777]

537. In case of a public sale, the seized goods are auctioned and sold to the highest bidder.[778] Within fifteen days following the public auction, any prospective buyer is entitled to submit a higher bid.[779]

538. The notary public shall distribute the sales price among the creditors whose identity is known to him via the mandatory reference to the Central Database of Reports concerning Attachments[780] or who have informed him of their claims, according to the distribution ratio that applies to the attachment for sale of movables (*see supra*, paragraph 527).[781]

539. The debtor can oppose the sale on procedural grounds or by demonstrating that the creditor's claim does not meet the statutory quality requirements (*see supra*, paragraph 507).[782] To this end, the debtor must summon the creditor before the judge of attachments.

D. Third-Party Attachment

540. Third-party attachment is an attachment whereby the creditor seizes movables (such as money, shares, securities, etc.) that belong to the debtor, but are (still) in the hands of a third party.

541. Third-party attachment is executed by the service of a writ of seizure by the bailiff on the third party. The debtor is notified of the attachment by the bailiff within eight days following the service of the writ of seizure on the third party.[783] Unlike the attachment for sale of movables and immovables, third-party attachment does not need to be preceded by a formal order of payment, nor does a waiting period need to be observed.

542. From the date of receipt of the writ of seizure, the third-party garnishee may no longer dispose of the seized goods (by giving them to the debtor), under penalty of being held personally liable for the debt, and without prejudice to the creditor's right to full compensation.[784]

543. Within fifteen days after receipt of the writ of seizure, the third-party garnishee must provide a written statement regarding the seized goods. This statement must be sent to the acting bailiff or the creditor (with copy to the debtor) and must mention, *inter alia*, the cause and amount of the debt and its due date, as well as any other third-party attachments previously notified to the third party. If the third-party garnishee fails to comply with these requirements, he can be held personally liable for the debt, as well as the costs of seizure.[785]

777. Article 1580*bis* Judicial Code.
778. Article 1587 Judicial Code.
779. Article 1592 Judicial Code.
780. Article 1391, §2, para. 1, *juncto* Article 1627 Judicial Code.
781. Articles 1639–1654 Judicial Code.
782. Article 1498 Judicial Code.
783. Article 1539 Judicial Code.
784. Article 1540 Judicial Code.
785. Article 1542 *juncto* Article 1452 Judicial Code.

544. The debtor can oppose the third-party attachment by summoning the creditor before the judge of attachments within fifteen days following the notification of the attachment. The opposition, as well as the decision thereon, is notified to the third-party garnishee.[786]

545. The third-party garnishee shall hand over the seized goods to the bailiff at the earliest two days after expiry of the fifteen-day period following the notification of the third-party attachment to the debtor. In case of opposition by the debtor, the handing over of the seized goods shall not take place until after notification of the decision of the judge of attachments to the third-party.[787]

546. If the third-party attachment was not notified to the debtor in person, nor at his (elected) domicile, the third-party garnishee can require the creditor to obtain the prior approval from the judge of attachments before handing over the seized goods.[788]

VI. Publicity

547. As of 31 January 2011, all reports in respect of seizure are centralised in a digital database, the so-called Central Database of Reports concerning Attachments (*Fichier central des avis de saisie, de délégation, de cession, de règlement collectif de dettes et de protêt – Centraal bestand van berichten van beslag, delegatie, overdracht, collectieve schuldenregeling en protest*).[789] Up until then, seizure reports were only collected and retained in hard copy at the court registries. Hence, a trip to the court was required in order to have access to seizure information. Moreover, as seizure reports were held per local court, a change of the debtor's address was sufficient to enable him to 'start over' with a spotless seizure record. The Central Database responds to these deficiencies. Further on, it allows preventing attachment against debtors whose property has already been seized, with all the unnecessary expenses that incurs (*see supra*, paragraph 526). A consultation of this database, prior to any form of attachment for sale or distribution of the sale proceeds, is mandatory for the official (bailiff, notary public) in charge of this task.[790]

§2. Recognition and Enforcement of Foreign Judgments

548. A distinction is made between the 'recognition' and the 'enforcement' of a foreign court decision. Recognition means that a foreign judgment has the same legal effects in Belgium as in the state where it was rendered. This implies that the Belgian courts may need to respect the foreign judgment's res judicata. Further on, the foreign judgment constitutes a valid legal base for a preliminary seizure, without the need for prior authorisation by the judge of attachments. Enforcement means that a foreign

786. Article 1541 Judicial Code.
787. Article 1543 Judicial Code.
788. Article 1544 Judicial Code.
789. Articles 1389*bis*/1–18 and 1390–1391 Judicial Code.
790. Article 1391, §2, Judicial Code.

judgment permits the creditor to have his claim against the debtor collected by means of forced execution in Belgium.

549. Roughly speaking, the recognition and enforcement of a foreign court's decision may be governed by: (1) EU Regulations, of which the most important one in this area is the Brussels I-Regulation No. 44/2011 of 22 December 2000,[791] which was recast by the Brussels I*bis*-Regulation No. 1215/2012 of 12 December 2012;[792] (2) international and bilateral treaties; or (3) the Belgian Code of Private International Law of 2004, applicable in cases for which there is no regulation or treaty between Belgium and the state where the judgment was given.[793]

550. The abovementioned instruments generally provide for an automatic (*de plano*) recognition of foreign judgments without there being a need for a special (preliminary) procedure before the Belgian courts. On the other hand, the enforcement of a foreign judgment generally requires the assistance of the Belgian courts, to which an application must be made for the granting of a declaration of enforceability (the so-called exequatur).

551. It should be noted that decisions rendered by an international jurisdiction are considered to be foreign judgments and therefore require an exequatur to be enforceable in Belgium. The decisions rendered by the European Court of Justice, however, enjoy automatic or de jure full enforceability in Belgium.

I. Rules Applicable in the Absence of a Treaty

552. Belgian domestic law on the recognition and the enforcement of foreign court decisions is elabourated in Articles 22–29 of the Belgian Code of Private International Law.

553. Foreign court decisions, whether in private or professional matters, shall be recognised automatically without prior approval by the Belgian courts (or any other authority in Belgium), and without distinction as regards the foreign state in which the decision was rendered.[794] If, however, a dispute would arise regarding the *de plano* recognition, any person who has an interest in the foreign judgment may initiate a legal claim for recognition or for denial of recognition before the Court of First Instance, according to the same rules as those applying to the exequatur procedure (*see infra*, paragraph 554).[795] Recognition shall be refused if the foreign judgment infringes upon one or more of the grounds for refusal, as listed exhaustively in Article 25 of the Code of Private International Law (for instance, if the result of such recognition is manifestly incompatible with Belgian (international) public policy, or if the Belgian courts have exclusive jurisdiction over the dispute).[796] In addition, any Belgian court that is faced

791. *Official Journal* L12/1 of 2001.
792. *Official Journal* L351/1 of 2012.
793. For example, decisions rendered by US courts.
794. Article 22, §1, para. 2, Code of Private International Law.
795. Article 22, §2, Code of Private International Law.
796. Article 22, §1, para. 4, Code of Private International Law.

with a (preliminary or interlocutory) recognition issue, has jurisdiction to resolve this issue.[797]

554. If enforcement of a foreign judgment would be needed in Belgium, prior court approval and attachment of the declaration of enforceability is required. Article 23 of the Code of Private International Law provides for an ex parte exequatur procedure, which is to be initiated before the competent Court of First Instance.[798] Article 24 of the Code contains a list of documents to be supplied by the petitioner. The review by the Court of First Instance does not imply under any circumstance a review of the merits of the foreign judgment. A retrial of the substance of the matter before the Belgian courts is therefore excluded.[799] The Court of First Instance must, however, check whether the enforcement does not infringe upon one or more of the grounds for refusal as listed in Article 25 of the Code.

II. International Treaties

555. The rules of the Code of Private International Law apply only for cases that do not fall within the scope of one of the EU Regulations, or a bilateral or international treaty. As to the latter, Belgium is a party to a few treaties containing rules regarding the recognition and enforcement of foreign judgments. The Lugano Convention of 30 October 2007,[800] for instance, contains rules regarding issues of recognition and forced execution of court decisions in civil and commercial matters rendered in Iceland, Norway and Switzerland, in terms copied from the 2000 version of the Brussels I-Regulation. Another treaty obligation that holds rules of recognition and enforcement is the Hague Convention of 23 November 2007 on the International Recovery of Child Support and Other Forms of Family Maintenance, applicable since 1 August 2014.[801]

556. As far as European law of recognition and enforcement is concerned, the most important instrument is the Regulation No. 1215/2012 of 12 December 2012 on Jurisdiction and the Recognition and Enforcement of Judgments in Civil and Commercial Matters. This is the so-called Brussels I*bis*-Regulation, already mentioned above as the most important source of jurisdictional criteria inside the European Union (*see supra*, paragraphs 191–192). In addition, the Brussels I*bis*-Regulation contains rules to facilitate the flow of court decisions (in civil and commercial matters) across the borders of the Member States. The Brussels I*bis*-Regulation is a recast of the Brussels I-Regulation. The recast I*bis*-version is applicable to court decisions rendered on or after 10 January 2015. Both regulations provide for the automatic recognition of Member States' judgments, without there being a need for a special (preliminary)

797. Article 22, §1, para. 3, Code of Private International Law.
798. Article 570 Judicial Code. The Court of First Instance has exclusive jurisdiction over claims regarding the recognition and enforcement of foreign judgments. The local jurisdiction of the court is determined by reference to the place of domicile of the party against whom enforcement is sought or the place of enforcement (Article 23, para. 2, Code of International Private Law).
799. Court of Cassation 9 February 2015, *Tijdschrift@ipr.be* 2016, Vol. 2, 17.
800. *Official Journal* L339/3 of 2007.
801. *See* for more information: www.hcch.net (accessed September 2017).

procedure before the Belgian courts. The grounds for refusal of recognition are limited. Article 45 of the Brussels I*bis*-Regulation[802] provides for five possible grounds on the basis of which the recognition of a judgment can be refused, on the application of any interested party (for instance, if the judgment is irreconcilable with an earlier judgment given in another Member State or in a third State involving the same cause of action and between the same parties, provided that the earlier judgment fulfils the conditions necessary for its recognition in the Member State addressed). With respect to the forced execution of judgments rendered in another Member State, the Brussels I-Regulation provides for an ex parte exequatur procedure, similar to the procedure applicable to non-EU judgments (*see supra*, paragraph 554), but the formalities are simplified, thus allowing the swift enforcement of Member States' judgments. The Brussels I*bis*-Regulation has even abolished the need for an exequatur. This implies that a judgment given in a Member State shall be enforceable in another Member State without any special procedure or declaration of enforceability being required. The creditor only needs to obtain a 'certificate' in the Member State in which the judgment is rendered (certifying that the judgment is enforceable in that Member State), which is to be served on the debtor, together with the judgment. The grounds for rejection are limited; no retrial of the merits is allowed, and the jurisdiction of the court of origin is not to be reviewed (except for the mandatory jurisdiction criteria listed in Article 26 of the Brussels I*bis*-Regulation). Articles 46–51 *juncto* Article 45 of the Regulation, however, provide, for an important safeguard: the courts of the Member State in which the enforcement is sought may refuse such enforcement on the application of the party against whom the enforcement is sought, provided that one of the grounds for refusal as referred to in Article 45 is found to exist.

557. For some areas, specific EU regulations have been issued, which contain similar recognition rules resulting in mutual 'full faith and credit' of EU decisions throughout the territory, as well as enforcement without there being a need for a prior exequatur procedure. To name but a few: Regulation No. 2015/848 of 20 May 2015 on Insolvency Proceedings;[803] Regulation No. 4/2009 of 18 December 2008 on Jurisdiction, Applicable Law, Recognition and Enforcement of Decisions and Cooperation in Matters Relating to Maintenance Obligations;[804] and Regulation No. 2201/2003 of 27 November 2003 Concerning Jurisdiction and the Recognition and Enforcement of Judgments in Matrimonial Matters and the Matters of Parental Responsibility.[805]

558. Other European instruments which provide for enforcement without exequatur are the European Enforcement Order for Uncontested Claims,[806] the European Small Claims Procedure[807] and the European Order for Payment Procedure (*see supra*, paragraph 326).[808] These instruments, however, have not enjoyed great success in Belgium.

802. Compare with Article 34 Brussels I-Regulation.
803. *Official Journal* L141/19 of 2015.
804. *Official Journal* L7/1 of 2009.
805. *Official Journal* L338/1 of 2003.
806. *Official Journal* L143/15 of 2004.
807. *Official Journal* L199/1 of 2007.
808. *Official Journal* L399/1 of 2006.

Chapter 3. The Collective Debt Settlement Procedure

559. The Judicial Code provides for a specific type of insolvency proceedings, namely the collective debt settlement procedure (*règlement collectif de dettes – collectieve schuldenregeling*).[809] This procedure gives over-indebted private individuals the opportunity to reorganise their finances and re-establish their economic capability under the supervision of a court-appointed debt mediator.

560. The collective debt settlement procedure is only available to physical persons who are not engaged in commercial activities,[810] provided that they are chronically unable to honour their debs. Temporary financial problems are not considered to be sufficient. Further on, the applicant must be unfortunate, meaning that he may not be to blame for his over-indebtedness.

561. The procedure is initiated by means of a unilateral petition, which is to be filed before the Labour Court. If the court finds the applicant's petition to be admissible, it will appoint a debt mediator (*médiateur des dettes – schuldbemiddelaar*). This decision leads to a so-called *concursus creditorum*, meaning that all claims against the debtor must be halted, execution suspended, and interest calculation stopped.

562. The debt mediator will try to reach an amicable settlement with the creditors. If no amicable settlement can be reached, the court shall impose a recovery plan. This plan may provide for, *inter alia*, a debt rescheduling, deferral of payment, partial reduction of debts, and even a total debt cancellation.

563. If the debtor wrongfully sustains or increases his financial difficulties, the court may revoke the recovery plan, as a result of which the creditors will regain the possibility to launch execution measures on the debtor's assets.

809. *See* Articles 1675/2–1675/19 Judicial Code.

810. Merchants that are chronically unable to honour their debts can file for bankruptcy or apply for reorganisation measures, aimed at rescuing their business by means of a recovery plan drawn up under court supervision.

Part X. Arbitration

Chapter 1. Introduction

564. Parties may grant the power of adjudication to an arbitral tribunal, provided that the dispute is susceptible to settlement.

565. On 1 September 2013, a new Arbitration Act[811] came into effect in Belgium, which aims to promote Belgium as an even more attractive place for arbitration.[812] The Act, which is incorporated in the Judicial Code,[813] is largely inspired on the UNCITRAL Model Law. Nevertheless, the legislature has chosen to retain a number of divergent rules in cases where Belgian legal practice and doctrine have proven these to be better suited for Belgium. The scope of application of the arbitration rules, for instance, is not limited to commercial disputes.[814]

566. The rules on arbitration apply equally to both national and international arbitration.[815] They acknowledge the particularities of international arbitration in the context of private international law.

567. As far as the relationship between the arbitral tribunals and the state courts is concerned, it is clear that parties who agree to grant the power of adjudication to an arbitral tribunal, waive their right to submit their dispute to the state courts. Nevertheless, those courts can play a meaningful role at the start (regarding the jurisdiction and composition of the arbitral tribunal – *see infra*, paragraph 573), during (regarding interim and conservatory measures – *see infra*, paragraphs 575–577), and after the

---

811. Act of 24 June 2013 (*Belgian Official Gazette*, 28 June 2013 (ed. 2)). An (unofficial) English version of the Belgian Arbitration Act is available at www.cepani.be/en/arbitration/belgian-judicial-code-provisions (accessed September 2017). This Act has been slightly amended by the so-called Potpourri III Act of 25 December 2016 (*Belgian Official Gazette*, 30 December 2016 (ed. 1)).

812. The former Belgian Arbitration Act, which dates back to 1972, was based on the European Convention providing a Uniform Law on Arbitration (Strasbourg, 20 January 1966). Austria and Belgium were the only Member States to sign the European Convention and Belgium was the only country that ratified and implemented the Convention. The proposed aim of unification could thus not be achieved at that time.

813. *See* Part VI ('Arbitration') of the Judicial Code (Articles 1676–1723).

814. *See* for a more detailed account: M. Piers & D. De Meulemeester, *The Adoption of the UNCITRAL Model Law Encourages Arbitration in Belgium*, 2 b-Arbitra 369, (2013), para. 2; M. Piers & D. De Meulemeester, *A New Arbitration Law in Belgium: UNCITRAL Enters the Scene*, 25 The Am. Rev. Int'l Arb. 63–83 (2014).

815. The Act only makes a minor distinction between national and international arbitration with respect to the annulment procedure (Article 1718 Judicial Code).

completion (regarding the recognition and enforcement of arbitral awards (*see infra*, paragraphs 598–602), as well as the annulment thereof (*see infra*, paragraph 597) of the arbitration proceedings.[816] The Judicial Code also provides for specific rules to identify the competent state court and the applicable procedural law in case of international, cross-border disputes.[817]

816. *See* M. Piers & D. De Meulemeester, *The Adoption of the UNCITRAL Model Law Encourages Arbitration in Belgium*, 2 b-Arbitra 392–400 (2013) paras 58–71.

817. *See* , for instance, Article 1676, §§6–8, Judicial Code.

Chapter 2. Arbitrability

568. An essential element of a valid arbitration agreement is the arbitrability of the dispute, which refers to the autonomy of the parties to submit a dispute to arbitration.[818] Article 1676 of the Judicial Code provides for two types of claims that may be submitted to arbitration: any 'pecuniary claim' and 'non-pecuniary claims with regard to which a settlement agreement may be made'.[819] The latter confirms that public legal entities may conclude an arbitration agreement regarding all contractual disputes, other than regulatory disputes arising from sovereign (rather than commercial) acts of the State.

818. W. Craig, W. Park & J. Paulsson, *International Chamber of Commerce Arbitration* 37 (Oceana Publications 2000).

819. A statutory provision may provide for exceptions to this general rule. For example, Article 1676, §5, of the Judicial Code states that an arbitration agreement concerning a dispute that belongs to the jurisdiction of the Labour Courts may only be concluded after the dispute has arisen.

Chapter 3. Arbitration Agreement and Party Autonomy

569. An arbitral tribunal derives its jurisdiction from the explicit consent of all parties involved. This consent can either be expressed in an arbitration clause in an existing contract, or the parties may enter into a specific arbitration agreement once the dispute has arisen.

570. In accordance with the UNCITRAL Model Law, the Belgian legislature has opted for a modern definition of what constitutes an 'arbitration agreement' by no longer requiring it to be made in writing, which promotes the *favor arbitrandum* trend strived for in Belgian arbitration.[820] The burden of proof of the existence of the arbitration agreement, however, lies with the party who wants to rely on it.[821] The validity of the arbitration agreement is subject to the normal rules of contract law.[822]

571. The decision to submit the dispute to arbitration is not the only aspect of arbitration that is governed by the principle of party autonomy. Most of the statutory rules on arbitration are of a supplementary nature, meaning that parties are free to deviate from them in the arbitration agreement.

820. M. Piers & D. De Meulemeester, *The Adoption of the UNCITRAL Model Law Encourages Arbitration in Belgium*, 2 b-Arbitra 373–374 (2013), para. 12.
821. Article 1681 Judicial Code.
822. Articles 1108 et seq. Judicial Code.

Chapter 4. Arbitral Tribunal

572. Both the criteria that the arbitrator(s) should meet and the appointment procedure are governed by the principle of party autonomy. The only statutory requirement is that the arbitral tribunal must be composed of an odd number of arbitrators.[823] The parties' freedom to agree upon the procedure for appointing the arbitrator(s) is furthermore restricted by the fundamental requirements of impartiality and independence of the arbitrator(s).[824] Anyone who is approached in connection with his possible appointment as an arbitrator shall disclose any circumstances likely to give rise to justifiable doubts as to his independence or impartiality.[825] Like judges, an arbitrator may be challenged if there is reasonable doubt about his independence or impartiality.[826]

573. If the parties fail to establish an arbitral tribunal within a reasonable time, the president of the Court of First Instance may be requested to appoint the arbitrator(s). The president rules 'as in summary proceedings' (*see supra*, paragraph 322), upon the unilateral request of the diligent party.[827]

574. If a dispute that is subject to a valid arbitration agreement is brought before a state court, the latter shall declare itself without jurisdiction at the request of a party, provided that the *exceptio arbitri* is raised in the asserting party's first pleadings.[828] The state court can rule on its own jurisdiction, without prejudice however to the right of the arbitral tribunal to rule on its jurisdiction, including any objections with respect to the existence or validity of the arbitration agreement.[829] The arbitral tribunal's decision establishing its jurisdiction may only be contested together with the award on the merits and in the course of the same procedure. At the request of a party, the Court of First Instance may also rule on the merits of the arbitral tribunal's decision that it lacks jurisdiction.[830]

---

823. A sole arbitrator is allowed (Article 1684, §1, Judicial Code).
824. Article 1685 Judicial Code. Compare with Article 11 UNCITRAL Model Law.
825. Article 1686, §1, Judicial Code.
826. The procedure for challenging the arbitrator can be freely agreed upon by the parties (Article 1687, §1, Judicial Code).
827. Article 1680, §1, *juncto* Article 1685, §§3–4, Judicial Code.
828. Article 1682, §1, Judicial Code.
829. For that purpose, an arbitration clause in a contract shall be treated as an agreement independent of the other terms of the contract. A decision by the arbitral tribunal that the contract is null and void shall not entail *ipso jure* the invalidity of the arbitration clause (Article 1690, paras 1–3, Judicial Code).
830. Article 1690, para. 4, Judicial Code.

Chapter 5. Interim Measures and Preliminary Awards

575. The Judicial Code provides for a system of parallel powers in which both the state courts (ruling in summary proceedings) and the arbitral tribunal have the power to issue interim or conservatory measures in relation to the arbitration proceedings. A request to a state court to grant such measure, shall not imply a waiver of the arbitration agreement.[831]

576. The state court shall exercise such power in accordance with its own procedures, thereby taking into account the specific features of arbitration.[832] In addition, a party may apply to the president of the Court of First Instance, ruling as in summary proceedings, to order all necessary measures for the taking of evidence.[833]

577. Without prejudice to the powers accorded to the state courts, and unless otherwise agreed by the parties, the arbitral tribunal may order any interim or protective measures it deems necessary (with the exception of attachment orders).[834] Such measures, however, can only be enforced after having been given executive power (exequatur) by the Court of First Instance.[835]

831. Article 1683 Judicial Code.
832. Article 1698 Judicial Code.
833. Articles 1680, §4, and 1708 Judicial Code.
834. Article 1691 Judicial Code.
835. Articles 1696–1697 Judicial Code.

Chapter 6. Conduct of Arbitral Proceedings

578. The parties may freely agree upon the procedural rules to be followed by the arbitral tribunal, with the understanding that the guarantee of due process may not be compromised.[836] Great attention is paid to the observance of the principles of equality and the rights of defence throughout the entire arbitral proceedings.[837] These requirements of due process and equality are of public policy and limit the parties' freedom to choose arbitration rules that go against these principles.[838]

579. In practice, many arbitration agreements are conducted in the framework of a professional arbitration organisation,[839] in which case parties often refer to a fixed set of rules laid down in the regulation of this organisation. They may also charge a third party with the organisation of the arbitration proceedings.[840] In the absence of such agreement, the arbitral tribunal may, subject to the rules on arbitration in the Judicial Code, determine the rules of procedure applicable to the arbitration as it considers appropriate.[841]

580. The place of arbitration may also be freely agreed upon by the parties. Failing such agreement, the place of arbitration shall be determined by the arbitral tribunal having regard to the circumstances of the case, including the convenience of the parties. Failing determination of the place of arbitration by the parties or the arbitral tribunal, the place where the arbitral award is rendered, will be considered to be the place of arbitration.[842] The place of arbitration is important as it determines which local state courts will have jurisdiction to solve certain disputes that might arise at the start and during the course of the arbitral proceedings.

581. Furthermore, the parties freely determine the language(s) to be used in the arbitral proceedings, in the absence of which the arbitral tribunal shall do so. This agreement or decision, unless otherwise specified therein, shall apply to any communication between the parties, any hearing and any award, decision or other communication by the arbitral tribunal.[843] The arbitral tribunal may order that any written evidence shall be accompanied by a translation into the language(s) agreed upon by the parties or determined by the arbitral tribunal.[844]

582. Unless otherwise agreed by the parties, the arbitral proceedings start on the date on which an arbitration application is received by the respondent, in accordance with the communication provided for in Article 1678, §1, of the Judicial Code.[845]

836. Article 1700 Judicial Code. Compare with Article 19 UNCITRAL Model Law.
837. For example, Article 1699 Judicial Code.
838. M. Piers & D. De Meulemeester, *The Adoption of the UNCITRAL Model Law Encourages Arbitration in Belgium*, 2 b-Arbitra 383–384 (2013), para. 33.
839. For example, CEPANI (*see* www.cepani.be (accessed September 2017)).
840. Article 1677, §2, Judicial Code.
841. Article 1700, §2, Judicial Code.
842. Article 1701, §1, para. 2, Judicial Code.
843. Article 1703, §1, Judicial Code.
844. Article 1703, §2, Judicial Code.
845. Article 1702 Judicial Code.

583. As to the course of the arbitral proceedings, Article 1704, §1, of the Judicial Code[846] provides that within the timeframe as agreed by the parties or determined by the arbitral tribunal, the parties shall develop all the pleas and arguments supporting their claim or defence, as well as all facts in support thereof. Practical arrangements for exchanging pleadings shall be laid down in a binding but, if so agreed by the parties, flexible procedural calendar, which is issued by the arbitral tribunal. Unless otherwise agreed, parties are allowed to amend or supplement their original claim or defence during the course of the proceedings, unless the arbitral tribunal considers the amendment or supplement to be inappropriate, notably having regard to the delay in submitting such modified claims.[847] Article 1706 of the Judicial Code allows for the arbitration to proceed without losing sight of the fundamental guarantees of due process, even though one of the parties fails to cooperate or acts in bad faith.

584. Unless otherwise agreed by the parties, the arbitral tribunal may order any investigation measure, including the appointment of one or more experts.[848] If a party is shown to hold a piece of evidence, the tribunal may order this party to submit such evidence. The tribunal can also impose a non-compliance penalty to be paid in the event that the order is not voluntarily complied with.[849] With the approval of the arbitral tribunal, a party may also apply to the president of the Court of First Instance, ruling as in summary proceedings, to order all necessary measures for the taking of evidence.[850]

585. Unless the parties have agreed that no oral hearings shall be held, the arbitral tribunal shall hold such hearings at an appropriate stage of the proceedings, if so requested by a party.[851]

586. The arbitral tribunal decides the dispute in accordance with the rules of law[852] chosen by the parties.[853] Failing any designation by the parties, the tribunal shall apply the law determined by the rules of private international law that it considers applicable.[854] The arbitral tribunal may also decide the case using standards of reasonableness and fairness ('*ex aequo et bono*'), but only if the parties have expressly authorised it to do so.[855]

587. If parties settle the dispute during arbitral proceedings, the arbitral tribunal shall terminate the proceedings and, if requested by the parties, record the settlement in an award on agreed terms. Such an award may not be contrary to public policy and must be in accordance with the rules that apply to 'regular' arbitral awards. The

846. Inspired by Article 23 UNCITRAL Model Law.
847. Article 1704, §2, Judicial Code.
848. Article 1700, §4, para. 1, *juncto* Article 1707 Judicial Code.
849. Article 1700, §4, para. 3, Judicial Code.
850. Article 1708 Judicial Code.
851. Article 1705 Judicial Code.
852. The reference to 'rules of law' permits the arbitral tribunal to base its award on instruments such as the Unidroit Principles of International Commercial Contracts (M. Piers & J. Erauw, *Application of the Unidroit Principles of International Commercial Contracts in Arbitration*, 8 JPIL 451 (2012).
853. Any designation of the law of a given State shall be construed, unless otherwise expressed, as directly referring to the substantive law of that State and not to its rules of private international law (Article 1710, §1, Judicial Code).
854. Article 1710, §2, Judicial Code.
855. Article 1710, §3, Judicial Code.

settlement award has the same status and effect as any other award on the merits of the case.[856]

856. Article 1712 Judicial Code.

Chapter 7. Arbitral Award

588. Unless otherwise agreed by the parties, any decisions of the arbitral tribunal (which is made up of more than one arbitrator) shall be taken by a majority of its members. Decisions on procedural matters, however, may be taken by the presiding arbitrator alone if so authorised by the parties.[857] The parties are also free to decide that the presiding arbitrator's vote shall be decisive where no majority can be obtained.[858] When an arbitrator refuses to participate in the deliberations or in the voting on the arbitral award, the other arbitrators are free to decide without him, unless otherwise agreed by the parties. In order to guarantee a maximum protection of the parties' due process rights, the parties must be given advance notice of the intention to deliberate or decide as a 'truncated arbitral tribunal'. This should leave the parties the option to challenge the obstructing arbitrator.[859]

589. The arbitral tribunal can make a final decision or render interlocutory decisions by way of one or several awards.[860] Parties may determine the time limit within which the arbitral tribunal must render its award, or the terms for setting such a time limit. If no such agreement exists and the arbitral tribunal failed to render an award within a period of six months after the date on which the last arbitrator has accepted his assignment, the tribunal is considered late in rendering its award and the parties may request the president of the Court of First Instance to impose a time limit. The assignment of the arbitrators ends automatically if the award has not been rendered at the expiry of this time limit.[861]

590. An arbitral award must be made in writing and must be signed by the sole arbitrator. In arbitral proceedings with more than one arbitrator, the signatures of the majority of all members of the arbitral tribunal shall suffice, provided that the reason for any omitted signature is communicated.[862] In order to ensure recognition and avoid annulment, the arbitral award must state the reasons upon which it is based[863] and should meet certain formal requirements.[864] The arbitral tribunal may impose a non-compliance penalty to be paid in the event that a party does not voluntarily comply with the arbitral award. Articles 1385*bis* et seq. of the Judicial Code shall apply accordingly (*see supra*, paragraphs 306–308).[865]

591. The costs of the arbitration, as well as the party who has to bear them, are fixed in the final award. Unless otherwise agreed by the parties, these costs shall include the fees and expenses of the arbitrators, the fees and expenses of the parties' counsel

857. Article 1711, §2, Judicial Code.
858. Article 1711, §3, Judicial Code.
859. Article 1711, §4, Judicial Code.
860. Article 1713, §1, Judicial Code.
861. Article 1713, §2, Judicial Code.
862. Article 1713, §3, Judicial Code.
863. Article 1713, §4, Judicial Code.
864. Article 1713, §5, Judicial Code.
865. Article 1713, §7, Judicial Code.

and representatives, the costs of services rendered by the instances in charge of the administration of the arbitration and any other expenses arising from the arbitration.[866]

592. Once the arbitral award has been rendered, an original thereof shall be notified by the sole arbiter or by the presiding arbitrator to each party.[867]

593. Within one month of receipt of the award, a party may request the arbitral tribunal to correct any clerical errors in the award, such as calculation or typographical errors.[868] If so agreed by the parties, the arbitral tribunal may also give an interpretation of a specific point or part of the award.[869] Unless otherwise agreed by the parties, a party may even request the arbitral tribunal to render an additional award as to claims submitted in the original proceedings, but omitted in the award.[870] In the event that the same arbitrators can no longer be reunited, the request for interpretation, correction or additional award shall be submitted to the Court of First Instance.[871]

866. Article 1713, §6, Judicial Code.
867. Articles 1713, §8, *juncto* 1678 Judicial Code.
868. Article 1715, §1, a), Judicial Code.
869. Article 1715, §1, b), Judicial Code.
870. Article 1715, §3, Judicial Code.
871. Article 1715, §6, Judicial Code.

Chapter 8. Recourse Against Arbitral Award

594. Parties have only limited means of challenging the arbitral award.

595. Appeal against an arbitral award is only possible if the parties have provided for that possibility in the arbitration agreement. Unless otherwise agreed, the time limit for such an appeal is one month as of the notification of the arbitral award.[872]

596. Parties may also, in a limited number of cases, challenge the arbitral award through an annulment procedure before the Court of First Instance, provided that the award can no longer be challenged before the arbitrators. The award may be set aside solely for a cause mentioned in Article 1717 of the Judicial Code, such as the lack of reasoning in the award and fraud. In the event that a procedural rule concerning due process is violated, the award may not be set aside if it is established that the irregularity had no effect on the arbitral award.[873] Moreover, several grounds for annulment can no longer be raised if the party that wishes to invoke them became aware of such grounds in the course of the arbitration proceedings but failed to invoke them at that time.[874]

597. The state court that has jurisdiction to rule on a request for annulment is the Court of First Instance of the seat of the Court of Appeal in the jurisdiction of which the place of arbitration is fixed.[875] Review of the decision on annulment has to be brought directly before the Court of Cassation.

---

872. Article 1716 Judicial Code.
873. Article 1717, §3, ii) and v), Judicial Code.
874. Article 1679 *juncto* Article 1717, §5, Judicial Code.
875. Article 1717, §2, Judicial Code.

Chapter 9. Recognition and Enforcement of Awards

598. An arbitral award is binding upon the parties and can serve as the basis for a preliminary attachment,[876] but it is not an enforceable instrument in itself. The award can only be enforced after it has been given executive force (exequatur) by the Court of First Instance.[877] The state court with territorial jurisdiction is the Court of First Instance of the seat of the Court of Appeal in the jurisdiction of which the person against whom the enforcement is sought has his domicile or, in the absence of a domicile, his usual place of residence or, where applicable, its registered office or, failing this, its place of business or branch office. If that person is neither domiciled in, or a resident of, Belgium, nor has its registered office, place of business or branch office in Belgium, the application is made to the Court of First Instance of the seat of the Court of Appeal in the jurisdiction of which the award is to be enforced.[878]

599. The Court of First Instance can render the award enforceable only if it can no longer be contested before the arbitrators, or if the award has been declared to be provisionally enforceable notwithstanding an appeal.[879]

600. The exequatur is requested by means of a unilateral petition, which is to be accompanied by the original copy or a certified copy of the arbitral award and of the arbitration agreement.[880]

601. The Court of First Instance may only refuse to recognise or enforce an arbitral award, irrespective of the country in which it was made, if the award infringes upon one or more of the grounds for refusal, listed in Article 1721, §1, of the Judicial Code. For instance, if the result of such recognition or enforcement would be contrary to public policy, or if the award deals with a dispute not contemplated by, or not falling within the scope of the arbitration agreement, or if the subject matter of the dispute is not susceptible to arbitration.

602. The enforcement of the arbitral award shall be time barred ten years after the date on which the arbitral award has been communicated to the parties.[881]

---

876. *See* Article 1713, §9, Judicial Code: 'The award shall have the same effect as a state court decision in the relationship between the parties.'
877. Article 1719, §1, Judicial Code.
878. Article 1720, §2, Judicial Code.
879. Article 1719, §2, Judicial Code.
880. Article 1720, §§1/1–2, Judicial Code.
881. Article 1722 Judicial Code.

Part XI. Mediation

Chapter 1. Introduction

603. Mediation could be defined as a process of voluntary consultation between conflicting parties that is conducted by an independent person who facilitates the parties' communication and assists them in finding a solution by themselves.[882] The most essential feature of mediation is that a mediator does not impose a solution. Contrary to a judge (or arbitrator), a mediator does not decide the dispute, but assists the parties in communicating with each other so they can try to settle the dispute themselves. Mediation leaves the control of the outcome of the dispute with the parties.

604. Since the entry into force of the Mediation Act of 21 February 2005,[883] the rules on mediation form an integral part of the Judicial Code.[884] As such, the legislator sends out a clear signal that the different dispute resolution mechanisms are on an equal footing.

605. In 2008, the European Parliament and the Council adopted the Mediation Directive 2008/52/EC.[885] The Belgian legislature considered that no formal implementation of this European legal instrument was required as the 2005 Mediation Act already

---

882. Note that the concept of 'mediation' is not defined in Belgian law, although some insisted on developing such definition in order to avoid any confusion with other types of alternative dispute resolution (*see,* for instance, H. Verbist, 'Analyse van de Belgische bemiddelingswet in het licht van de Europese richtlijn inzake bemiddeling', *Tijdschrift voor Mediation en conflictmanagement* 2010, Vol. 14, 33–49, who expressed the view that it would be useful to incorporate the definition of mediation stated in Article 3, (a), of the Mediation Directive into Belgian law). Nevertheless, as mediation is essentially an informal way of solving disputes, it is of great importance to consider carefully why and to what extent it needs to be regulated.

883. *Belgian Official Gazette*, 22 March 2005. An (unofficial) English version of the Belgian Mediation Act is available at http://www.cepani.be/en/mediation/belgian-legislation (accessed September 2017). *See* for an in-depth analysis of the Belgian Mediation Act: M. Traest, *Belgium*, in *Civil and Commercial Mediation in Europe* 45–68 (C. Esplugues, J.-L. Iglesias & G. Palao eds, Vol. I, *National Mediation Rules and Procedures*, Intersentia 2012); I. Verougstraete, *Regulation of Dispute Resolution in Belgium: Workable Solutions?*, in *Regulating Dispute Resolution. ADR and Access to Justice at the Crossroads* 93–113 (edited by F. Steffek & H. Unberath eds, Oxford, Hart Publishing 2013); P. Taelman & S. Voet, *Mediation in Belgium: A Long and Winding Road*, in *New Developments in Civil and Commercial Mediation* 89–112 (C. Esplugues & L. Marquis eds, Springer 2015).

884. *See* Part VII ('Mediation') of the Judicial Code (Articles 1724–1737).

885. Directive 2008/52/EC of the European Parliament and of the Council of 21 May 2008 on certain aspects of mediation in civil and commercial matters, *Official Journal* L136/3 of 2008.

implemented the spirit of it, a least to a very large extent. Whereas the Directive only applies to cross-border disputes, the Belgian Mediation Act does not make a distinction between national and international mediation.

Chapter 2. Rights That Can Be Subject to Mediation

606. The Mediation Act considerably broadened the scope of mediation from family matters to all types of civil, commercial and labour matters.

607. Pursuant to Article 1724 of the Judicial Code, mediation is not only possible in disputes that are susceptible to settlement, but also in disputes related to family matters, such as divorce, legal cohabitation, maintenance allowance, etc. Family matters are considered to implicate public policy, but this does not mean that mediation should be excluded for family disputes. To the contrary, mediation has proven to be particularly valuable in situations where, after the settlement of the dispute, the parties are, by necessity, still dependent on each other. Even disputes with public authorities can be addressed through mediation when it is permitted by a statutory provision.

Chapter 3. Mediation Agreement

608. Pursuant to Article 1725, §1, of the Judicial Code, any contract may contain a mediation clause. This is an agreement according to which parties commit themselves to first attempt to resolve any dispute that may arise regarding the validity, performance, interpretation, enforcement or termination of their contract through mediation before resorting to other forms of dispute resolution. Such a clause, which is binding upon the parties to the contract, does not prevent them from seeking provisional or conservatory measures before the state courts (for instance, the appointment of an expert or a standstill measure). The application for such measures does not imply that parties waive mediation.[886] As a matter of public policy, parties should always have their day in court to obtain provisional measures to protect interests that could be seriously imperiled if no judicial relief were available.

609. When a party initiates judicial (or arbitral) proceedings in a case where a mediation clause applies, its opponent can invoke the 'mediation exception' or 'mediation plea'.[887] If the clause is valid, the case will be suspended until the parties or one of them have informed the court registry (or the arbitrator) that the mediation has ended. If the clause appears to be invalid or the mediation has already been ended, the proceedings will not be suspended.[888]

610. Mediation remains by and large a voluntary affair. If one of the parties refuses to respect the mediation clause, the other party can, in principle, enforce it, but this will be pointless since the former will not be cooperative. It is considered to be a fundamental rule of mediation that parties are, in all circumstances, free to choose for mediation, as well as to end it, without prejudice.[889] Accordingly, no negative consequences are linked to the decision of a party to refuse or end the mediation.

886. Article 1725, §3, Judicial Code.
887. This must be done *in limine litis* (in the first pleadings).
888. Article 1725, §2, Judicial Code.
889. Article 1729 Judicial Code.

Chapter 4. Persons/Institutions That Can Act as Mediator

611. There is a Federal Mediation Commission (*commission fédérale de médiation – federale bemiddelingscommissie*), composed of a general commission (with decision authority) and three specialised commissions[890] (with advisory authority). The general commission's main mission is to supervise the development and quality of the mediation procedures and mediators. To this end, it is charged with, *inter alia*, the accreditation of mediators, as well as the accreditation of the providers of mediation training and the training they provide; the adoption of the criteria for the accreditation of mediators;[891] and the establishment of a code of conduct and the sanctions deriving therefrom.[892]

612. There is no legal obligation for a mediator to be accredited,[893] but a settlement agreement that is reached through the assistance of a non-accredited mediator is not eligible for 'homologation' (*see infra*, paragraphs 620–622), making it non-enforceable.

890. One for family matters, one for civil and commercial matters and one for labour matters.
891. The statutory minimum requirements for accreditation are listed in Article 1726, §1, Judicial Code.
892. Article 1727, §6, Judicial Code.
893. As a rule, in case of 'judicial' mediation, the mediator has to be accredited.

Chapter 5. Mediation Procedure

613. The Judicial Code distinguishes between 'voluntary' (out-of-court) mediation and 'judicial' (court-instigated) mediation, but the scope of both forms of mediation is identical. Voluntary mediation implies that the choice for mediation is made freely by the parties before, during or even after judicial or arbitral proceedings,[894] without prompting or other involvement by a judge. Judicial mediation is court-connected mediation, i.e., mediation ordered by the court in the framework of pending court proceedings, but always with the consent of the parties.[895] Taken into consideration the voluntary character of every mediation, including judicial mediation, the terms 'judicial' and 'voluntary' are poorly chosen, as they suggest that judicial mediation without the voluntary consent of the parties is possible, which is actually not the case. Under no circumstances, the court can force parties into mediation. Judicial mediation neither means that the court mediates. The court simply appoints a third person – in principle an accredited mediator – to conduct the mediation.

614. The decision ordering judicial mediation explicitly mentions the agreement of the parties to try mediation as well as the name, professional capacity and address of the mediator. The decision also states the lapse of time provided for the parties to reach a solution (which cannot be longer than six months) and the date on which a court hearing will be held.[896] At this hearing, the parties inform the court about the outcome of the mediation process. If they have not reached an agreement they can opt for a new term or ask the court to resume the court proceedings.[897] In case the parties want an extension of the mediation period, the court may limit this period in order to avoid an abuse of proceedings. The court's decision to order mediation or extend or end it, is not susceptible to any legal remedy.[898]

615. If parties agree to (out-of-court or court-instigated) mediation,[899] a mediation protocol must be drafted. It constitutes the framework in which the parties, with the assistance of the mediator, mutually determine the rules for the conduct of the mediation,

---

894. For example, in the course of review proceedings.
895. Judicial mediation may be ordered at every stage of the proceedings, even in summary proceedings, but not in proceedings before the Court of Cassation or before the District Court (Article 1734, §1, para. 1, Judicial Code).
896. Article 1734, §2, Judicial Code.
897. Article 1734, §3, Judicial Code.
898. Article 1737 Judicial Code.
899. If the proposal for voluntary mediation is sent by registered letter and if it contains a claim to a right, it is assimilated to a formal notice which shall suspend the statute of limitations regarding that claim for one month as of the presumed date of receipt of the letter (Article 1730, §§2–3, Judicial Code). In case of judicial mediation, the statute of limitations is automatically tolled because judicial mediation is considered to be part of the court proceedings (as the case is still pending before the court during the mediation process).

including its duration.[900] The mediation protocol is signed by the parties and the mediator and acts as a contract between them.[901]

616. The mediation protocol must set out the method by which the fees and expenses of the mediator are determined, his fee rate as well as the terms of payment. The mediation costs and fees are equally shared between the parties, unless they agree otherwise.[902] When the parties have limited means, they can apply for legal aid. The rules on legal aid (*see supra*, paragraphs 421–428) are applicable to (voluntary and judicial) mediation, provided that the mediator is accredited.[903]

617. An important aspect of the mediation procedure is its confidentiality. All documents, statements and communications made during and for the purpose of the mediation process are confidential.[904] They may not be used in any judicial, administrative or arbitral procedures or in any other dispute resolution procedure and they are not admissible as evidence, not even as an out-of-court confession.[905] The duty of confidentiality may only be lifted with the consent of the parties with a view to, *inter alia*, allowing a state court to homologate the settlement agreement (*see infra*, paragraphs 620–621). The court or arbitral tribunal is empowered to award damages if the duty of confidentiality is violated by one of the parties.[906]

618. The mediator is bound by a duty of professional secrecy.[907] He may not disclose the facts with which he becomes acquainted as a result of his function, nor may he be called upon by the parties as a witness in civil or administrative proceedings relating to the facts with which he has become acquainted in the course of the mediation.

---

900. Article 1731, §1, Judicial Code.
901. Some have argued that the draft of such protocol is burdensome and too formalistic, especially since mediation itself is meant to be an informal procedure. If the mediation protocol does not contain the legal requirements as prescribed by Article 1731, §2, Judicial Code, the parties' settlement agreement is not eligible for homologation by a judge.
902. Article 1731, §1, Judicial Code
903. Article 665, 5°, Judicial Code
904. Information available outside this framework is not covered by the duty of confidentiality and may be submitted in judicial, administrative or arbitral procedures.
905. Article 1728, §1, para. 1, Judicial Code.
906. Article 1728, §1, para. 2, Judicial Code.
907. Article 458 of the Penal Code regarding the violation of the duty of professional secrecy is applicable to the mediator (Article 1728, §1, para. 3, Judicial Code).

Chapter 6. Settlement Agreement

619. Successful (out-of-court or court-instigated) mediation results in a settlement agreement, which is laid down in a document dated and signed by parties and the mediator.[908] The agreement sets out the precise commitments of each party.

620. The parties (or one of them) may ask the competent state court to approve or homologate the settlement agreement, making it enforceable as a 'regular' (consent) judgment. The competent state court is the court that would have had jurisdiction if the dispute had been submitted to it without mediation taking place. The request for homologation is made by means of a unilateral petition, which is to be signed by an attorney. The petition can, however, be signed by the parties themselves, if it emanates from all the parties involved in the mediation.[909] In case of judicial mediation, the mediator informs the judge in writing at the end of his mission about the outcome of the mediation and whether or not the parties have reached a settlement agreement. If the mediation was successful, the parties (or one of them) may ask the court to homologate the agreement.[910]

621. Homologation can only be granted if parties have concluded a mediation protocol (which fulfils the statutory requirements) and if the mediation was conducted by an accredited mediator. This reflects the distrust of the Belgian legislator *vis-à-vis* (voluntary) agreements made without the assistance of an accredited mediator.

908. If the mediator is accredited, this is mentioned (Article 1732 Judicial Code).
909. Article 1733, para. 1, Judicial Code.
910. Article 1736, para. 3, *juncto* Article 1043 Judicial Code.

Chapter 7. Setting Aside a Settlement Agreement

622. If the settlement agreement has been homologated by the competent state court, it has the same effect as a consent judgment within the meaning of Article 1043 Judicial Code (*see supra*, paragraph 238). In principle, a consent judgment is not susceptible to any appellate means.

623. Homologation of the settlement agreement may be refused only in a limited number of cases. Homologation may be refused for formal reasons, for example, if the mediation agreement has not been made in writing or has not been signed. Substantive grounds for refusal of homologation may be that the settlement agreement is contrary to public policy or, in the case of a mediation in family matters, if the agreement is against the interests of underage children.[911] The grounds for refusal should be interpreted narrowly.

911. Articles 1733, para. 2, and 1736, para. 4, Judicial Code.

Selected Bibliography

B. Allemeersch, *Taakverdeling in het burgerlijk proces*, Antwerp, Intersentia, 2007.

B. Allemeersch & T. Kruger, *Handboek Europees Burgerlijk Procesrecht*, Antwerp-Cambridge, Intersentia, 2015.

B. Allemeersch, P. Taelman, P. Van Orshoven & B. Vanlerberghe (ed.), *Nieuwe Justitie*, Antwerp-Cambridge, Intersentia, 2014.

H. Boularbah & J.-F. Van Drooghenbroeck (ed.), *Pot-pourri I et autres actualités de droit judiciaire*, Brussels, Larcier, 2016.

K. Broeckx, *Het recht op hoger beroep en het beginsel van de dubbele aanleg in het civiele geding*, Antwerp, Maklu, 1995.

G. de Leval, *Eléments de procédure civile*, Brussels, Larcier, 2005.

G. de Leval (ed.), *Droit judiciaire*, Tome 2, *Manuel de procédure civile*, Brussels, Larcier, 2015.

G. de Leval & F. Georges (eds.), *Droit judiciaire*, Tome 1, *Institutions judiciaires et éléments de compétence*, Brussels, Larcier, 2014.

E. Dirix & K. Broeckx, *Beslag*, *Algemene Praktische Rechtsverzameling*, Mechelen, Kluwer, 2010.

A. Fettweis, *Manuel de procédure civile*, Liège, Fac. Droit Liège, 1987.

A. Fettweis, *Précis de droit judiciare*, II, *La compétence*, Brussels, Larcier, 1971.

J. Laenens, D. Scheers, P. Thiriar, S. Rutten & B. Vanlerberghe, *Handboek Gerechtelijk Recht*, Antwerp-Cambridge, Intersentia, 2016.

A. Le Paige, *Précis de droit judiciare*, IV, *Les voies de recours*, Antwerp, Standaard, 1973.

P. Taelman, *Het gezag van het rechterlijk gewijsde: Een begrippenstudie*, Diegem, Kluwer, 2001.

B. Allemeersch & P. Taelman (ed.), *De hervorming van de burgerlijke rechtspleging door Potpourri I*, Bruges, die Keure, 2016.

Index

The numbers here refer to paragraph numbers.

www.ingramcontent.com/pod-product-compliance
Ingram Content Group UK Ltd.
Pitfield, Milton Keynes, MK11 3LW, UK
UKHW020143290926
15471UKWH00004B/666

9 789041 195807